The Pilot's Guide to Affordable Classics

2nd Edition

Bill Clarke

TAB Books
Division of McGraw-Hill, Inc.
Blue Ridge Summit, PA 17294-0850

3893591

SECOND EDITION
FIRST PRINTING

Library of Congress Cataloging-in-Publication Data

Clarke, Bill (Charles W.)
   The pilot's guide to affordable classics / by Bill Clarke. — 2nd ed.
     p.   cm.
   Includes index.
   ISBN 0-8306-4106-8   ISBN 0-8306-4107-6 (pbk.)
   1. Used aircraft—Purchasing. 2. Airplanes—Conservation and restoration. I. Title.
TL685.1.C545 1993
629.133′34′0297—dc20   92-41242
                                       CIP

Acquisitions Editor: Jeff Worsinger
Editorial team: Charles Spence, Editor
               Susan Wahlman, Supervising Editor
               Joanne Slike, Executive Editor
               Jodi Tyler, Indexer
Production team: Katherine G. Brown, Director
               Ollie Harmon, Typesetting
               Susan Hansford, Typesetting
               Rhonda E. Baker, Layout
               Donna Harlacher, Layout
               Lorie L. White, Proofreading
               Kelly S. Christman, Proofreading
               N. Nadine McFarland, Quality Control
Design team: Jaclyn J. Boone, Designer
               Brian Allison, Associate Designer
Cover design: Carol Stickles
Cover photograph courtesy of Geza Szurovy, Sudbury, Ma.   AV1

Contents

4   Ercoupe   45

5   Luscombe   61

6   Piper   77

7 Stinson   111

8 Taylorcraft   121

9 Engines   133

10   Propellers   153

11   Avionics   163

12   Buying your classic   179

13   FARs you need to know   211

Acknowledgments

SO MANY years have passed since the classic airplanes were built that it has become difficult to obtain accurate information about them. A plethora of information relative to the classics exists. However, this information often is incomplete or nonfactual. My desire was to make this book as accurate as possible; therefore considerable research was done. I gratefully acknowledge the following for their assistance:

Michael Sellers, of UNIVAIR, for data, reprints, and illustrations.

Ray Stits for expert re-covering and refinishing instructions.

The men and women who operate the various owners clubs. They are experts on their planes and always stand ready to share their knowledge.

A special thanks to the research librarians at the Voorheesville Public Library, of Voorheesville, New York—the finest small-town library a writer could ask for.

Introduction

I THINK there is not a pilot anywhere who hasn't at least given passing thought to owning an airplane. But, like everything else, airplane ownership costs money, and, like everything else, these costs have elevated over the years.

New airplanes are expensive and complex. Their operational costs and mechanical upkeep are high. As examples of these high costs: In 1990 a new Piper 181 (4-place, 180-hp engine, all-metal plane) had a price tag in the vicinity of $120,000. At the same time, a well-equipped and very fast Mooney was selling for nearly $170,000 and a Beech A36 for well over $300,000. Of course you must keep in perspective that these planes are designed for transportation from point A to point B, not for fun flying. However, even an Aviat Husky, a two-place airplane of similar design and purpose to the Piper Super Cub, lists for well over $60,000.

Now, what happens to the pilot who wants to fly inexpensively, retain reliability and safety, yet have fun doing it? Can it be done without a second mortgage on the family castle? You bet it can!

The Pilot's Guide to Affordable Classics, 2nd Edition, brings alive a delightful alternative to the high prices and complexities of 1990's flying—an alternative that includes a little history, loads of fun, inexpensive flying time, and real pride of ownership. In this book you'll learn what classic flying means and discover what specific airplanes are considered classics. The history of these airplanes and their manufacturers is included, as are specifications, diagrams, and photographs of the popular makes and models.

This book discusses the engines powering these older airplanes, including current maintenance problems, how they cope with the new low-lead fuels, and methods for extending their useful lives. The new space-age avionics are approached from a no-nonsense angle, and cost-saving advice is given about their needs and purchase.

See how to save money and get to know these planes better by performing preventive maintenance on them. Learn what it means to re-cover a tube-and-fabric airplane and how to polish and paint a metal airplane.

Find out where to go for help, parts, and advice about specific makes and models of classic airplanes. A list of the many classic airplane organizations, parts suppliers, and the FAA offices is included.

The prospective purchaser will find where and how to locate a good used classic airplane, and more importantly, how to avoid getting stung in the process of purchase. Learn to decode those infamous abbreviations used in all the ads—the language of airplane buying and selling. A price guide, based upon the current market, is included.

Chapter 12 contains an easy-to-follow prepurchase inspection plan, followed by a walk-through of the necessary paperwork including examples of the typical FAA forms required.

In summary, *The Pilot's Guide to Affordable Classics, 2nd Edition*, was written to aid the potential classic aircraft buyer, by assisting in practical decision-making and sidestepping of the many pitfalls of buying and owning aircraft.

1

Classic, a definition

CLASSIC, as an aviation term, refers to a unique frame of mind, a style of flying, a specific time in our history, and certain well-defined airplanes—all combined with simplicity.

A UNIQUE FRAME OF MIND

Ah, to smell the old hangar on a hot West Texas afternoon when the smells of avgas, oil, dust, and hot fabric permeated the air and filled one's soul. To again hear the great south wind blowing past the hangar, making the timbers creak and the doors rattle. That surely would be heaven. A sense of the simplicity of the times may be felt in advertisements shown in Fig. 1-1A and B. But, the old times are gone forever, or are they?

A STYLE OF FLYING

As a teenager, I learned to fly in an Aeronca 7AC. It was a two-seat plane that sat on its tail like an airplane should. The good little bird had 65 horses up front that sipped about four gallons of fuel an hour. It had no electrical system and a panel so simple that I still chuckle when I think of it (Figs. 1-2 through 1-4).

I learned to fly when pilots navigated with a compass and looked for towns, rivers, railroads, mountains, highways, and other landmarks as their way points. It was called pilotage. My best navigation chart was an ESSO road map.

Of course, flying was low and slow by today's standards. I saw the world go by with my own eyes, not through the invisible eyes of some magical black box. Every time I climb into a late model airplane and see all the radios and gadgets (Fig. 1-5) it reminds me of fast traffic and car phones. But, the old times are gone forever, or are they?

Now don't go off and get me all wrong, there is a place for all the modernization found in today's flying. After all, isn't everyone going at a faster pace now than they were forty years ago? Maybe that is why today's pilots fly faster and need all those hi-tech gadgets in their complicated airplanes, which land only on paved runways and require expensive aircraft service centers to keep it all working (Fig. 1-6). After all, speed is the essence of today, isn't it?

Fig. 1-1A. Piper promoted safety in this 1946 advertisement.

Fig. 1-1B. In 1947 Piper heavily advertised a factory-installed two-way radio and an electric starter.

Fig. 1-2. New Aeronca 7AC and an 11AC as they appeared just after the war.

Fig. 1-3. This two-place tube-and-fabric airplane offers loads of flying at a minimal cost. Visibility is great, just perfect for sightseeing on a sunny afternoon.

Fig. 1-4. The simple panel of an Aeronca 7AC. It's really all you need for inexpensive flying enjoyment.

Fig. 1-5. This modern Cessna is loaded with black boxes and can go anywhere at nearly any-time. But, it misses a real touch with early aviation.

Fig. 1-6. The Piper Archer is a fine plane for going from one place to another, but its spamcan design lacks the classic appeal of tube and fabric.

To me, there is nothing like taking an old Cub up on a cool summer's evening to put a proper end to a busy day. Passing over the hills, through the valleys, maybe over a small lake, flying so close to the earth that I can smell the freshly cut grass in a farmer's field—that's flying.

A SPECIFIC TIME IN HISTORY

The planes and type of flying that I refer to are *classic* and represent the great airplane boom of the postwar (World War II) era until the end of 1955. The planes manufactured during that period are the substance of inexpensive flying. Built of practical and solid design, they provide a touch with flying that cannot be duplicated by today's airplanes.

CERTAIN WELL-DEFINED AIRPLANES

Most of the classic airplanes are still flying today and you can see them at rural airports all over the country. Many of these airports have grass strips instead of the paved runways generally associated with aviation. You're unlikely to see many classics at the typical suburban airport unless there happens to be an air show the day you go looking. City life just isn't their cup of tea.

Many of these planes are tube-and-fabric structures, (Fig. 1-7) have only two seats, and have conventional landing gear. These include the Aeronca Champs and Chiefs, Piper Cubs, and Taylorcrafts. There are metal covered planes such as the Cessna 120/140 series and the Luscombe 8s, and even the Ercoupe (Fig. 1-8) with its tricycle landing gear. For the family man there are the Cessna 170s, Luscombe Sedans, Piper Pacers/Tri-Pacers, and the Stinson 108 series (Fig. 1-9).

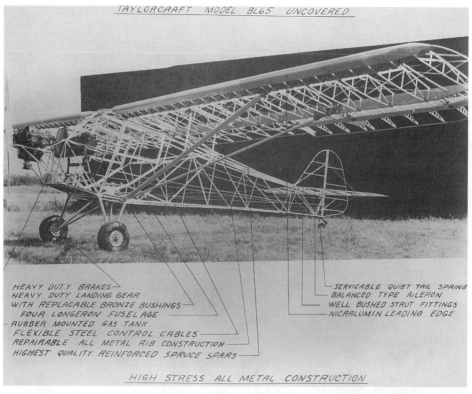

TAYLORCRAFT MODEL BL65 UNCOVERED

HEAVY DUTY BRAKES
HEAVY DUTY LANDING GEAR
WITH REPLACABLE BRONZE BUSHINGS
FOUR LONGERON FUSELAGE
RUBBER MOUNTED GAS TANK
FLEXIBLE STEEL CONTROL CABLES
REPAIRABLE ALL METAL RIB CONSTRUCTION
HIGHEST QUALITY REINFORCED SPRUCE SPARS

SERVICABLE QUIET TAIL SPRING
BALANCED TYPE AILERON
WELL BUSHED STRUT FITTINGS
NICRALUMIN LEADING EDGE

HIGH STRESS ALL METAL CONSTRUCTION

Fig. 1-7. Without its fabric cover, this is the tubular structure of a Taylorcraft. All tube-and-fabric planes are similar in design.

Fig. 1-8. Tricycle landing gear and metal construction make the Ercoupe appealing to many classic owners.

Fig. 1-9. Notice the tailwheel on this Stinson 108. With only a few exceptions, conventional gear is the rule on classics.

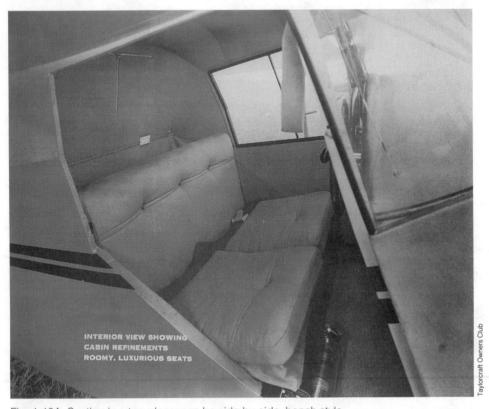

INTERIOR VIEW SHOWING
CABIN REFINEMENTS
ROOMY, LUXURIOUS SEATS

Fig. 1-10A. Seating in a two-placer can be side-by-side, bench style.

THE REASON WHY

Today classic airplanes represent a bit of history and a touch of nostalgia, but not to the extent that ownership becomes prohibitively expensive. In fact, it can be quite the contrary. Compared to today's airplanes, the classics are inexpensive to purchase, uncomplicated to fly, and easy to maintain. After all, they don't have retractable landing gear, autopilots, turbochargers, or, in some cases, any electrical system (Figs. 1-10A, B).

Classic airplanes may well be the last vestiges of affordable flying. They also provide a connection with our past; something many strive for.

SIMPLICITY

Classic airplanes do not have the complexities of modern airplanes with their long check lists and frequent operational changes. There is nothing elaborate or demanding to be found. They are simple and functional (Figs. 1-11 and 12A and B). Yes, life does not have to be complicated to be better (Fig. 1-13). Just efficient, safe, and satisfying. In a word—classic.

Smithsonian Institution Photo No. 92-8009

Fig. 1-10B. Or seating can be tandem in bucket seats.

Cockpit Checklist

Starting:

1. Check amount of gas and oil
2. Both fuel valves--On.
3. Mixture--Full Rich.
4. Carburetor Heat--Off.
5. Prime two to six strokes--Lock plunger.
6. Throttle--Crack one-eighth inch.
7. Ignition on--Pull starter.
8. Warm up--700 to 900 rpm.

Before Takeoff:

1. Carburetor Heat--Off.
2. Oil Temperature--90 degrees minimum.
3. Oil Pressure--35 lbs/sq in.
4. Full throttle--(2050 rpm).
5. Ignition check--Max 75 rpm drop.

Flight:

1. Oil Pressure--30 to 40 lb/sq in.
2. Oil Temperature--100 to 220 degrees.
3. Adjust mixture for best rpm.

Landing:

1. Mixture--Full rich.
2. Carburetor Heat--On.
3. Reduce Throttle--Idle.
4. Open throttle periodically during glide.

Fig. 1-11. Typical checklist for a classic airplane. Simple isn't it?

C.A.A. Approved
February 4, 1948

PIPER AIRCRAFT CORPORATION
Lock Haven, Pennsylvania

Piper PA-15
Normal Category

C.A.A.Identification No..

AIRPLANE FLIGHT MANUAL

1. Limitations

The following limitations must be observed in the operation of this airplane:

ENGINE	Lycoming O-145-B2.
ENGINE LIMITS	For All Operations—2550 RPM.
FUEL	80 Minimum Octane Aviation Fuel.
Propeller	Fixed Pitch Wood 70" Maximum Diameter.
	68.5" Minimum Diameter.

Static Limits: Maximum 2320 RPM.
 Minimum 2160 RPM.

POWER INSTRUMENTS Oil Temperature Unsafe if indicator exceeds **RED** line (220°F.).

Oil Pressure: Unsafe if indicator exceeds **RED** line (85 lbs. maximum) or below the **RED** line (25 lbs. minimum).

Normal flight operation GREEN arc (65 lbs.—85 lbs.).

Caution or idling YELLOW arc (25 lbs.—65 lbs.).

Tachometer: **RED** line at rated engine speed. **DO NOT EXCEED.**

AIRSPEED LIMITS
(True Indicated Airspeed)

	Normal Category
Never Exceed	126 MPH
Maximum Cruising Speed	100 MPH
Maneuvering Speed	**87 MPH**

FLIGHT LOAD FACTORS

Maximum Positive Load Factor	3.8
Maximum Negative Load Factor	
(No Inverted Maneuvers Approved)	

MAXIMUM WEIGHT 1100 lbs. Take-Off and Landing.
C. G. RANGE
 (Aft W.L.E.) 12.5" to 19.0"
 (% M.A.C.) 19.6% to 30.2%
MAXIMUM BAGGAGE
ALLOWED: 40 lbs.

NOTE: It is the responsibility of the airplane owner and the pilot to insure that the airplane is properly loaded.

LEVELING MEANS: Plumb from upper door channel to center punch mark on front seat cross tube.

AIRSPEED INSTRUMENT (a) Radial **RED** line (126) marks the never exceed speed which is the maximum safe airspeed.
MARKINGS AND THEIR
SIGNIFICANCE

(b) **YELLOW** arc (100-126) on indicator denotes range of speed in which operations should be

Fig. 1-12A. This is the first page of the flight manual for the Piper PA-15. UNIVAIR conducted with caution and only in smooth air.

(c)   **GREEN** arc (45-100) denotes normal operating speed range.

2. Procedures

(a)   Carburetor heat **shall** be used during all ground operations such as engine warm-up, taxiing, etc.

(b)   All other operations are normal.

3. Performance Information

The following performance figures were obtained during Civil Aeronautics Administration type tests and may be realized under conditions indicated with the airplane and engine in good condition and with average piloting technique.

All performance is given for the Lycoming 0-145-B2 engine installation, fixed-pitch propeller, 1100 pounds weight, with no wind and on level, paved runways.

In using the following data allowance for actual conditions must be made.

ITEM	ALT.	OUTSIDE AIR TEMPERATURE					
		0°F	20°F	40°F	60°F	80°F	100°F
Take-Off Distance (In Feet)	Sea Level	1273	1369	1470	1572	1680	1799
Distance to Take-Off	3000	1815	1964	2122	2302	2486	2699
and climb 50 ft. at	5000	2374	2599	2860	3130	3407	3755
full throttle MPH 63 T.I.A.S.	7000	3325	3695	4140	4675	5205	5855
Landing Distance (In Feet)	Sea Level	1224	1243	1261	1280	1297	1316
Distance required to land over	3000	1273	1293	1315	1335	1356	1378
50 ft. obstacle and stop	5000	1310	1332	1356	1376	1399	1422
Approach at 63 MPH T.I.A.S.	7000	1350	1373	1398	1425	1447	1471
	Sea Level	555	530	508	490	472	456
Normal Rate of Climb	3000	427	408	390	370	353	337
In feet per minute Airspeed	5000	345	325	305	290	272	255
MPH 65 T.I.A.S.	7000	260	245	225	208	190	175

UNIVAIR

Angle of Bank Stalling Speeds (MPH T.I.A.S.) Power Off	0	10	20	30	40	50	60
	48	49	50	52	55	60	69

Approved by: *Charles F. Dyerson*

Director, Aircraft and Components
Service, Civil Aero. Administration

Fig. 1-12B. The second, and last, page of the flight manual. Compare this two-page manual to the 50 or better pages found in the typical late-model Piper or Cessna.

Fig. 1-13. Piper promoted flying small planes as a family event.

2

Aeronca

THE AERONCA airplanes are among the most numerous of the classic planes, due to their popularity as trainers during the postwar period. Designed to meet the requirements of flight training, they were inexpensive to purchase and operate, required little maintenance, were easy to repair, and were ruggedly built to withstand the rigors of student pilots. These same requirements generally meet the needs of today's weekend aviators.

Aeronca airplanes are fun and easy to fly, yet are among the least expensive to operate. Although rather slow by today's standards, they allow you to see what you are flying over. Most Aeroncas have conventional landing gear, but don't let that scare you. They're honest little airplanes displaying few bad habits.

During the heyday of general aviation, Aeronca rolled out airplanes at the rate of 30 a day (Fig. 2-1). By early 1951, Aeronca had built its last airplane, a 7EC.

ABOUT AERONCA

Although no longer building airplanes, the original Aeronca Company is still in business in Middletown, Ohio. It makes subassemblies for the aerospace industry, thereby maintaining its ties with aviation.

THE CHAMPS

The 7 series Champs were a completely newly designed airplane, based on the WWII TA Defender and the L3 liaison military planes, specifically for the postwar period (Fig. 2-2). The airframes were welded tubing and the wing spars were built of wood with metal ribs and an aluminum leading edge. The structure was covered with fabric. Although originally covered with grade-A cotton, the examples you'll most likely find today are covered with one of the new synthetic products.

Champs offered excellent visibility through large side windows and over a low-slung engine to the front. An oleo-spring shock absorber landing gear system was used. Several planes were part of the 7 (Champ) series, most differing in engine horsepower or minor structural changes.

Aeronca Production Numbers

Model	Production total
7AC	7200
7ACA	71
7BCM/L–16A	509
7CCM/L–16B	100
7DC	184
7EC	773
7FC	472
11AC	1960
11BC	181
11CC	277
15AC	550

Fig. 2-1. Aeronca production numbers, indicating the model numbers, production total, and serial number series.

7AC. This model was powered by an A-65 Continental 65-hp engine. Although some were built with Franklin or Lycoming engines, most you see today have the Continental. Often referred to as *airknockers* as a play on the name Aeronca because of the engine sound, the 7ACs were produced from 1945 through 1948. All were painted yellow with red trim. According to historical

Fig. 2-2. Aeronca 7AC Champ.

records, Aeronca once produced 56 Champs in a single day. The usual time needed to build one was 291 man-hours, and the original price was $2999.

7BCM. The 7BCM (Fig. 2-3) was introduced in 1947 and powered with an 85-hp Continental engine. This plane was known as the L-16A in the military version.

Fig. 2-3. Aeronca 7BCM. The 7BCM was built in 1946 and is powered with a Continental C-85 engine.

7CCM. The 7CCM was introduced in 1948 with the 90-hp Continental. It had a slightly larger fin and other minor structural changes. The military configuration of this plane was the L-16B (Fig. 2-4).

Fig. 2-4. Aeronca L-16B. It is the wartime version of the 7 series. Notice the greenhouse that allowed plenty of visibility.

7DC. With the C-85-8F Continental 85-hp engine, the 7DC entered production in 1949 and sported a metal propeller, larger dorsal fin, and additional fuel capacity. (Fig. 2-5.)

7EC. This model was the last try for Aeronca. It was powered by a Continental C-90-12F engine and had an electrical system and a metal propeller. (Fig. 2-6.)

Fig. 2-5. This showstopping 7 series Aeronca has a custom paint job and wheel pants.

Fig. 2-6. The frontal appearances of all 7 series Aeroncas are similar.

THE CHIEFS

In addition to the Champ, Aeronca built the 11 series Chief. With a slightly wider body than the Champ, it seated two side-by-side. Although a few prewar Chiefs are still around, they are not to be confused with the postwar 11AC Chiefs (Fig. 2-7), which entered production in 1946.

Fig. 2-7. Aeronca 11AC Chief. Of similar power to the 7AC, it seats two side-by-side.

The wings, struts, engine, tail surfaces, and many other parts were interchangeable between 7AC and 11AC airplanes. The tube and fabric design was constant between the models. Overall performance of the Chief was quite similar to the Champ series.

The 11BC Chief was the same as the 11AC, except that it was powered with a Continental C-85 engine. An updated version, the 11CC Super Chief, was introduced in 1947. Like the 11BC, it was powered with a Continental C-85-8F engine. The Super Chief had dual control wheels, toe brakes, and a metal propeller.

THE SEDAN

Aeronca built a four-place airplane called the 15AC Aeronca Sedan (Fig. 2-8). Like other Aeronca airplanes of the period, the Sedan was built of tube and fabric design. It did, however, have all-metal wings.

Only 550 Sedans were built, all between 1948 and 1950. Today more than 250 remain in service, with many registered in Alaska. The large number in use in Alaska is a real testimonial to their worth and strength. Many Sedans are on floats (Fig. 2-9) and are regularly used for bush flying. 15AC Sedans are quite rare on the used market; however, from time to time you can see one or two listed for sale.

Fig. 2-8. Aeronca 15 Sedan.

Fig. 2-9. Typical of many Sedans, this plane has spent most of its life on floats. This fine example belongs to Dick Welch.

An interesting note: In 1950, an Aeronca Sedan set an in-the-air endurance record of 42 days. This feat required inflight refueling for both airplane and pilots.

THE NEW CHAMPS

A good design is hard to kill and the Aeronca, as so many other postwar-era planes, is no exception. In 1954, the Champion Aircraft Company of Osceola, Wisconsin, was formed and reintroduced the Aeronca 7 series airplanes. The new Aeronca 7EC Champion Traveler was upholstered, carpeted, and had a propeller spinner.

In 1957, a tricycle-gear version of the 7EC called the 7FC Tri-Traveler was introduced (Fig. 2-10). This model was built between 1957 and 1964. There is nothing unusual about this fine little plane, just an airknocker with a nosewheel. Unfortunately, its popularity was never that of the Piper or Cessna competition. I personally liked it and often flew one from an old hayfield.

Fig. 2-10. The Champion 7FC, which is actually a 7EC on trigear, never achieved the popularity of Cessna or Piper trigear trainers.

LATE ARRIVAL

I realize that this book is supposed to be about classics; however, I have made a few exceptions for modern airplanes with true classic family trees, built by classic methods. The last example of an Aeronca fitting this requirement is the 7ACA. It is properly called the Bellanca Champion Champ, because it was built after the 1970 Bellanca takeover of Champion Aircraft.

First appearing in 1971, the 7ACA was designed to be a cheap airplane. The base price was just $4995. It looked like a 7 series, but it was powered by a Franklin 60-hp two-cylinder engine. The Franklin engine proved unpopular and production ended in 1973.

I've seen a few 7ACA Champs listed in *Trade-A-Plane* over the years. They remain low in price, at least when compared to some of the other classics.

SPECIFICATIONS

Model: 7AC Champ
Engine
    Make: Continental
    Model: A-65
    hp: 65
    TBO: 1800
Seats: 2 tandem
Speed
    Max: 95 mph
    Cruise: 86 mph
    Stall: 38 mph
Fuel capacity: 13 gal
Rate of climb: 370 fpm
Transitions
    Takeoff: 630 ft
    Landing: 880 ft
Weights
    Gross: 1220 lbs
    Empty: 740 lbs
Dimensions
    Length: 21 ft 6 in
    Height: 7 ft
    Span: 35 ft

Model: 7BCM Champ
Engine
    Make: Continental
    Model: C-85
    hp: 85
    TBO: 1800
Seats: 2 tandem
Speed
    Max: 101 mph
    Cruise: 90 mph
    Stall: 42 mph
Fuel capacity: 19 gal
Rate of climb: 620 fpm

Transitions
      Takeoff: 500 ft
      Landing: 850 ft
Weights
      Gross: 1300 lbs
      Empty: 800 lbs
Dimensions
      Length: 21 ft 6 in
      Height: 7 ft
      Span: 35 ft

Model: 7CCM Champ
Engine
      Make: Continental
      Model: C-90
      hp: 90
      TBO: 1800
Seats: 2 tandem
Speed
      Max: 103 mph
      Cruise: 90 mph
      Stall: 42 mph
Fuel capacity: 19 gal
Rate of climb: 650 fpm
Transitions
      Takeoff: 475 ft
      Landing: 850 ft
Weights
      Gross: 1300 lbs
      Empty: 800 lbs
Dimensions
      Length: 21 ft 6 in
      Height: 7 ft 2 in
      Span: 35 ft

Model: 7DC Champ
Engine
      Make: Continental
      Model: C-85-8F
      hp: 85
      TBO: 1800
Seats: 2 tandem
Speed
      Max: 101 mph
      Cruise: 90 mph
      Stall: 42 mph

Fuel capacity: 19 gal
Rate of climb: 620 fpm
Transitions
    Takeoff: 500 ft
    Landing: 850 ft
Weights
    Gross: 1300 lbs
    Empty: 810 lbs
Dimensions
    Length: 21 ft 6 in
    Height: 7 ft 2 in
    Span: 35 ft

Model: 7EC Champ
Engine
    Make: Continental
    Model: C-90-12F
    hp: 90
    TBO: 1800
Seats: 2 tandem
Speed
    Max: 103 mph
    Cruise: 90 mph
    Stall: 42 mph
Fuel capacity: 19 gal
Rate of climb: 650 fpm
Transitions
    Takeoff: 475 ft
    Landing: 850 ft
Weights
    Gross: 1300 lbs
    Empty: 810 lbs
Dimensions
    Length: 21 ft 6 in
    Height: 7 ft 2 in
    Span: 35 ft

Model: 7EC/FC Traveler/Tri-Traveler
Engine
    Make: Continental
    Model: C-90-12F
    hp: 90
    TBO: 1800
Seats: 2 tandem

Speed
    Max: 115 mph
    Cruise: 105 mph
    Stall: 44 mph
Fuel capacity: 24 gal
Rate of climb: 700 fpm
Transitions
    Takeoff over 50 ft obs: 890 ft
    Ground run: 630 ft
    Landing over 50 ft obs: 755 ft
    Ground roll: 400 ft
Weights
    Gross: 1450 lbs
    Empty: 860 lbs
Dimensions
    Length: 21 ft 6 in
    Height: 7 ft 2 in
    Span: 35 ft 2 in

Model: 7ACA
Engine
    Make: Franklin
    Model: 2A-120
    hp: 60
    TBO: 1800
Seats: 2 tandem
Speed
    Max: 98 mph
    Cruise: 86 mph
    Stall: 44 mph
Fuel capacity: 13 gal
Rate of climb: 400 fpm
Transitions
    Takeoff over 50 ft obs: 850 ft
    Ground run: 525 ft
    Landing over 50 ft obs: 755 ft
    Ground roll: 400 ft
Weights
    Gross: 1200 lbs
    Empty: 750 lbs
Dimensions
    Length: 21 ft 11 in
    Height: 7 ft
    Span: 35 ft 1 in

Model: 11AC Chief
Engine
    Make: Continental
    Model: C-65
    hp: 65
    TBO: 1800
Seats: 2 side-by-side
Speed
    Max: 90 mph
    Cruise: 83 mph
    Stall: 38 mph
Fuel capacity: 15 gal
Rate of climb: 360 fpm
Transitions
    Takeoff: 580 ft
    Landing: 880 ft
Weights
    Gross: 1250 lbs
    Empty: 786 lbs
Dimensions
    Length: 20 ft 4 in
    Height: 7 ft
    Span: 36 ft 1 in

Model: 11BC Chief
Engine
    Make: Continental
    Model: C-85
    hp: 85
    TBO: 1800
Seats: 2 side-by-side
Speed
    Max: 95 mph
    Cruise: 85 mph
    Stall: 38 mph
Fuel capacity: 15 gal
Rate of climb: 500 fpm
Transitions
    Takeoff: 520 ft
    Landing: 880 ft
Weights
    Gross: 1250 lbs
    Empty: 790 lbs
Dimensions
    Length: 20 ft 4 in

Height: 7 ft
Span: 36 ft 1 in

Model: 11CC Super Chief
Engine
    Make: Continental
    Model: C-85 8F (metal prop)
    hp: 85
    TBO: 1800
Seats: 2 side-by-side
Speed
    Max: 102 mph
    Cruise: 95 mph
    Stall: 40 mph
Fuel capacity: 15 gal
Rate of climb: 600 fpm
Transitions
    Takeoff: 720 ft
    Landing: 800 ft
Weights
    Gross: 1350 lbs
    Empty: 820 lbs
Dimensions
    Length: 20 ft 7 in
    Height: 7 ft
    Span: 36 ft 1 in

Model: 15AC Sedan
Engine
    Make: Continental
    Model: C-145
    hp: 85
    TBO: 1800
Seats: 4
Speed
    Max: 120 mph
    Cruise: 105 mph
    Stall: 53 mph
Fuel capacity: 36 gal
Rate of climb: 570 fpm
Transitions
    Takeoff over 50 ft obs: 1509 ft
    Ground run: 900 ft
    Landing over 50 ft obs: 1826 ft
    Ground roll: 1300 ft

Weights
    Gross: 2050 lbs
    Empty: 1180 lbs
Dimensions
    Length: 25 ft 3 in
    Height: 7 ft 4 in
    Span: 37 ft 5 in

AIRWORTHINESS DIRECTIVES

Many of the following ADs are old and compliance was probably achieved long ago; however, you should still check for compliance. **Warning:** This AD list is not complete for all the affected airplanes.

47-20-2: replace landing gear oleo piston on 7 and 11 series
47-30-1: replace lift strut wing fittings on 7 and 11 series
48-4-2: inspection of the wing ribs on 7 and 11 series
48-38-1: changes the oil cooler installation on some 15AC Sedans
49-11-2: reinforce wing attach fittings on all Aeronca airplanes
49-15-1: rework the seat anchors on 11 series aircraft
56-4-1: inspect the control stick fittings for cracks on 7EC
61-16-1: periodic inspection of lift strut fittings on 15AC Sedans
64-4-3: rework air door hinges on 7 series air scoop box
68-20-5: inspection of the fuel cells and vents on 15AC Sedans
73-20-8: inspect/rework UNIVAIR propeller tips
74-26-9: inspect Bendix magneto
80-6-5: test magneto impulse coupling on Continental engines
80-21-6: inspect mufflers 100 hrs/12 months Champion before 1973
81-7-6: inspect/replace ac fuel pump on 65–90-hp Continentals
81-16-5: inspect Slick magneto coil on various engines
82-20-1: inspect impulse coupler on some Bendix magnetos
84-26-2: replace paper air filter each 500 hrs

STCs

Owners of airplanes often seek methods to improve their planes, either in performance or for aesthetic reasons. The most popular improvements generally involve the installation of larger engines providing more horsepower.

Wagner Aerial Service has developed and sells STCs (Supplemental Type Certificate) for Aeronca 7 and 11 series owners desiring more power and the addition of an electrical system. For information contact:

Wagner Aerial Service
Box 3
401 1st St. East
Clark, SD 57225

A takeoff run of only 150 feet at gross (400 feet on floats) is possible with a 15AC Sedan by adding a Lycoming 180-hp engine with Hartzell C/S propeller. For more data contact:

Monahan Aircraft Inc.
2311 East Lake Sammamish Pl SE
Issaquah, WA 98027

Fuel tanks that take care of AD 68-20-5 requirements are also available from Monahan Aircraft.

Other STCs for the Aeronca series airplanes follow. The STC number appears first, followed by the item or part modified by the STC, and the name and address of the holder of the STC.

7AC

SA232SO. Installation of Continental C85-12: C.W. Lasher, 4660 Parker Ct., Oviedo, FL 32765

15AC

SA4-567. Glass fabric covering: Glasco-Air Products, County Airport, Oxnard, CA 93030

SA302NW. Installation of Lycoming O-360-A1A: Herman Cantsell, 3645 Kink Ave, Anchorage, AK 99517

SA306GL. Installation of Lycoming O-360-A1F6D: Weber's Aero Repair, Inc., Municipal Airport, Alexandria, MN 56308

SA548CE. Installation of Continental IO-346-B: W.L. Johnson, 7721 Driftwood SE, Grand Rapids, MI 49506

Additional sources for modification information are available from the Aeronca type clubs (see appendix A).

PARTS

Locating parts for Aeroncas can be frustrating, as is the case when repairing and servicing anything nearing 50 years of age. Don't despair though, generic hardware is available from any of the aircraft suppliers mentioned in appendix B and specific parts are available from Wagner Aerial Service. Wagner claims the most complete line of parts for Aeronca airplanes in the world.

Wagner Aerial Service
Box 3
401 1st St. East
Clark, SD 57225

Other excellent sources of hardware and parts specific to Aeronca include:

American Champion Aircraft Corporation
P.O. Box 37
32032 Washington Ave., Hwy D
Rochester, WI 53167
(414) 534-6315

UNIVAIR Aircraft Corporation
2500 Himalaya Rd.
Aurora, CO 80011
(303) 375-8882

Wag-Aero, Inc.
P.O. Box 181
Lyons, WI 53148
(414) 763-9586

3

Cessna

THE PROTOTYPE of the first new two-place Cessnas flew on June 28, 1945 and was the basis for the 120/140 series. Production 120/140s appeared on the market in 1946. This series later became the basis for the very successful model 150 and 152 trainers. The model 170 was the root plane for the super-successful model 172 series (Fig. 3-1). Unfortunately, Cessna stopped all production of small planes during the middle 1980s.

THE CESSNA COMPANY

In 1992 TEXTRON, Inc. purchased Cessna Aircraft Company. TEXTRON also is the current owner of Lycoming, a company that builds small airplane engines. However, even with this interesting sounding marriage, it is unlikely Cessna will ever again manufacture airplanes of interest to the average private pilot/owner. Although still operating in Kansas, its original location, Cessna builds only business and small commercial-size airplanes.

THE NEW 140

The Cessna 140 is an all-metal-fuselage plane with fabric-covered high wings. The planes have forgiving flight characteristics, a snug two-place side-by-side cabin, flaps, control wheels, and hydraulic toe brakes. Of course they are taildraggers (Fig. 3-2).

The 140's landing gear was made of spring steel, an invention by Steve Wittman that Cessna purchased on a royalty basis. This strong, yet simple, landing gear carried through for many years on most of Cessna's single-engine fleet.

The Model 140 was equipped with an electrical system, flaps, rear side windows, and a plush (by postwar standards) cabin. It sold for a base price of $3245 and was built last in April 1949. A Continental C-85-12 engine powered the 140 until 1948 when the Continental C-90-12 became optional for an extra $200.

Cessna Production Numbers

Model	Production total	Serial series
C–120	2172	8000–15074
C–140	4904	same as 120s
C–140A	525	15200–15274
C–170	730	18000–18729
C–170A	1536	18730–20266
C–170B	2916	20267–20999
		& 25000–27169

Fig. 3-1. Cessna production numbers indicating the model numbers, production total, and serial number series.

Cessna

Fig. 3-2. A 1946 Cessna 140. Notice the additional rear window. Many 120s have been modified to look like 140s by addition of this window.

THE 120

The model 120 (Fig. 3-3) came as an afterthought to the 140 and was built to be very inexpensive. It was essentially a stripped-down 140 with no flaps, no rear side window, an austere interior, and an optional electrical system. Many model 120s have been updated to look like 140s by the addition of extra side windows and electric systems.

Fig. 3-3. A 1946 Cessna 120. This airplane actually entered production after the model 140.

THE 140A

In 1949 Cessna introduced the 140A (Figs. 3-4 and 3-5). It was the last Cessna two-place airplane for almost a decade. The 140A was all metal (including the wings) and was powered by a Continental C-85-12 or C-90-12 (after December 1950) engine. About five hundred 140As were built, selling for $3495 ($3695 with 90-hp engine).

Fig. 3-4. A Cessna 140A. The wing struts have been replaced with a single unit and a leading edge landing light has been added.

Fig. 3-5. The instrument panel of a 1949 Cessna 140A.

Production ceased in March 1951, after more than 7000 120/140/140As were manufactured. David Sakrison, editor of the *Cessna Owner*, says the 120/140 series "established Cessna Aircraft as the world leader in the general aviation market." Cessna 120s and 140s now command prices of three to four times that of the original new price.

THE 170 FAMILY PLANE

The Cessna four-place line of airplanes started in 1948 with the introduction of the model 170 (Fig. 3-6). The first 170s, like the two-place 120/140s, had metal fuselages and fabric-covered wings. They also had two wing struts on each side, and, of course, had conventional landing gear.

In 1949 the 170A with all-metal wings and a new fin entered production. It also has single wing struts. The last entry in the 170 series was the 170B, which brought the introduction of the large flaps we have come to associate with Cessnas.

The 170 is a comfortable family airplane with lots of rear seat leg room, large doors for easy entrance, and, for the pilot, is very controllable in crosswinds. The latter is particularly true for the A and B models, (Figs. 3-7 and 3-8) which had larger ailerons than the original 170s.

Fig. 3-6. A Cessna 170. Although old in years, it is as modern as today.

In 1957 the day had come for Cessna, as with Piper and its Pacer series, to end production of old-style conventional-geared airplanes. The flying public's demand for the easy-drive-it airplane had been voiced and Cessna saw sales lagging with

Fig. 3-7. A Cessna 170A. Notice the single wing strut.

Fig. 3-8. A Cessna 170B. This was the end of the line for the 170s. Put a nosewheel on it, and you have a 172.

the 170 and gaining with the 172. Basically, the 172 is a 170 with a nosewheel and a different tail structure. There were 5136 model 170-series airplanes built.

A good 170 will take you just about anywhere, and do it economically. They are considered classics based upon the period of production. However, due to their metal construction, 170s are just as modern as today. As I said before, they are the basis for the Cessna model 172, which is the most produced all-time favorite four-place airplane.

A good 170 will cost more than $15,000 today. The 170 sold new for $5475 in 1948 and the 170B for $8295 in 1956.

SPECIFICATIONS

Model: 120 and 140
Engine
    Make: Continental
    Model: C-85
    hp: 85
    TBO: 1800
Seats: 2 side-by-side
Speed
    Max: 125 mph
    Cruise: 105 mph
    Stall: 49 mph (w/o flaps)
    Stall: 45 mph (with flaps)
Fuel capacity: 25 gal
Rate of climb: 640 fpm
Transitions

Takeoff over 50 ft obs: 1850 ft
Ground run: 650 ft
Landing over 50 ft obs: 1530 ft
Ground roll: 460 ft
Weights
Gross: 1450 lbs
Empty: 800 lbs
Dimensions
Length: 20 ft 9 in
Height: 6 ft 3 in
Span: 32 ft 8 in (120)
Span: 33 ft 3 in (140)

Model: 140-A
Engine
Make: Continental
Model: C-90
hp: 90
TBO: 1800
Seats: 2 side-by-side
Speed
Max: 125 mph
Cruise: 105 mph
Stall: 45 mph
Fuel capacity: 25 gal
Rate of climb: 640 fpm
Transitions
Takeoff over 50 ft obs: 1850 ft
Ground run: 680 ft
Landing over 50 ft obs: 1530 ft
Ground roll: 460 ft
Weights
Gross: 1500 lbs
Empty: 850 lbs
Dimensions
Length: 20 ft 9 in
Height: 6 ft 3 in
Span: 33 ft 3 in

Model: 170
Engine
Make: Continental
Model: C-145-2
hp: 145
TBO: 1800
Seats: 4

Speed
    Max: 140 mph
    Cruise: 120 mph
    Stall: 47 mph
Fuel capacity: 42 gal
Rate of climb: 690 fpm
Transitions
    Takeoff over 50 ft obs: 1820 ft
    Ground run: 700 ft
    Landing over 50 ft obs: 1755 ft
    Ground roll: 790 ft
Weights
    Gross: 2200 lbs
    Empty: 1260 lbs
Dimensions
    Length: 25 ft
    Height: 6 ft 5 in
    Span: 36 ft

Model: 170A
Engine
    Make: Continental
    Model: C-145-2
    hp: 145
    TBO: 1800
Seats: 4
Speed
    Max: 140 mph
    Cruise: 120 mph
    Stall: 49 mph
Fuel capacity: 42 gal
Rate of climb: 690 fpm
Transitions
    Takeoff over 50 ft obs: 1820 ft
    Ground run: 700 ft
    Landing over 50 ft obs: 1755 ft
    Ground roll: 790 ft
Weights
    Gross: 2200 lbs
    Empty: 1260 lbs
Dimensions
    Length: 25 ft
    Height: 6 ft 5 in
    Span: 36 ft

Model: 170B
Engine
    Make: Continental
    Model: C-145-2 or O-300
    hp: 145
    TBO: 1800
Seats: 4
Speed
    Max: 140 mph
    Cruise: 120 mph
    Stall: 52 mph
Fuel capacity: 42 gal
Rate of climb: 690 fpm
Transitions
    Takeoff over 50 ft obs: 1625 ft
    Ground run: 620 ft
    Landing over 50 ft obs: 1145 ft
    Ground roll: 450 ft
Weights
    Gross: 2200 lbs
    Empty: 1260 lbs
Dimensions
    Length: 25 ft
    Height: 6 ft 5 in
    Span: 36 ft

AIRWORTHINESS DIRECTIVES

The following ADs affect Cessna 120/140 and 170 series airplanes. Some are old and most likely have been taken care of. Others will need attention. Check for compliance in the logbooks. **Warning:** This AD list is not complete for all the affected airplanes.

47-50-2: reinforce fuselage bulkhead on 120/140 through SN 14289
50-31-1: reinforce fin spar on 120/140 from SN 8001 to 15035
73-20-8: inspect/rework UNIVAIR propeller tips
74-26-9: inspect Bendix magneto
79-8-3: remove cigar lighter wire/install proper rated device
79-13-8: replace Airborne dry air pumps installed after 5-15-79
81-7-6: inspect/replace ac fuel pump on 65–90-hp Continentals
81-15-3: replace Bracket engine inlet air filter
81-16-5: inspect Slick magneto coil on various engines
82-20-1: inspect impulse coupler on some Bendix magnetos
84-26-2: replace paper air filter each 500 hrs

INSPECTION TIPS

These aircraft are all prone to damage in the gear boxes caused by rough landings. Be sure to inspect this area carefully, or have it inspected by a knowledgeable person such as your mechanic. Another place to look for indications of rough handling is the lower doorposts at the wing attach points. Wrinkling here indicates the need for further investigation.

STCs

The object of airplane modification is to meet the needs and desires of the owner. Many of the currently available STCs for Cessna classics are in the following list. The STC number is first, followed by the part modified and the name and address of the holder of the STC.

120

SA1-39. Metalized wings: Boone County Aviation Inc., P.O. Box 6, Erlanger, KY 41018

120/140

SA1-259. Metalized wings: Skycraft Design, 85 North Main, Yardley, PA 19067

SA4-89. Metalized wings: J.E. Lane, Jr., 3504 Niblick Dr., La Mesa, CA 92041

SA4-95. Installation of Lycoming O-235-C1: H.M. Ruberg, 1300 North 28th St., Springfield, OR 97477

SA4-341. Metalized wings: Frank A. Burdick, 43316 N. 20th St., West Lancaster, CA 93534.

SA4-360 Metalized wings: Carma Manufacturing Co., P.O. Box 11312, Municipal Airport, Tuscon, AZ 85700

SA4-581. Installation of Lycoming O-290-D: H.M. Ruberg, 1300 North 28th St., Springfield, OR 97477

SA4-640. Installation of Lycoming O-290-D2: H.M. Ruberg, 1300 North 28th St., Springfield, OR 97477

SA4-916. Tricycle gear conversion: Met-Co Aire, P.O. Box 2216, Fullerton, CA 92633

SA54CE. Metalized wings: B&W Aircraft Repair, Inc., St. Peters, MO 63376

SA1429GL. Shoulder harness and seat belts: Aero Fabricators, Inc., P.O. Box 181, Lyons, WI 53148

SA3815NM. Tail pull handle: BAS, Inc., P.O. Box 190, Eatonville, WA 98328

SA4338NM. Flap and aileron gap seals: Timothy L. Falen, 86094 Panorama Rd., Springfield, OR 97478

120/140/140A

SA547EA Installation of Continental O-200-A: John T. Lucas & M. David Emmett, RD #2, Emporium, PA 15834

SA648NE. Use Cessna 150 exhaust systems: John E. Stickley & Walter B. Thomas, 6305 Tecumseh Pl., Berwyn Heights, MD 20740

SA3300NM. Use unleaded and leaded automobile gasoline: Wiley's Seaplanes, 13060 SW. Fielding Rd., Lake Oswego, OR 97034

120/140/170

SA331CE. New panel with artificial horizon: Spartacus Industries, P.O. Box 634, Muskegon, MI 49443

SA666NW. Teflon control yoke bushings: George O. Johnson, 10015 S. Meridian, Puyallup, WA 98371

All Cessna classics

SA13GL. Installation of Cleveland wheels and brakes: Aircraft Wheel & Brake Division, Parker Hannifin Corp., 1160 Center Rd., Avon, OH 44011.

140

SA4-79. Metalized wings: Francisco Ochoa, 4836 E. Mercer Way, Mercer Island, WA 98040

SA4-376. Installation of Lycoming O-235-C1: H.M. Ruberg, 1300 North 28th St., Springfield, OR 97477

SA267SW. Installation of Continental O-200-A: S&S Pipeline Patrol, P.O. Box 787, Dickinson, TX 77539

140/170

SA12WE. Fiberglass wing tips: Met-Co-Aire, P.O. 2216, Fullerton, CA 92633

140A/170

SA995SW. STOL modification: Bob Williams, Box 431, Udall, KS 67146
SA1371SW. STOL modification: Bob Williams, Box 431, Udall, KS 67146

170

SA1-13. Metalized wings: General Aviation, Inc., P.O. Box 232, Lost Nation Airport, Willoughby, OH 44094

SA1-240. Installation of Lycoming O-435-C: Fulton Conversion Company, Southbury, CT 06488

SA4-7. Metalized wings: Leo F. Smith & Co. Inc., 225 South Bent, San Marcos, CA 92069

SA4-11. Metalized wings: Aero Sales & Service Inc., Chandler Field, Fresno, CA 93721

SA4-28. Tricycle gear conversion: Met-Co-Aire, P.O. Box 2216, Fullerton, CA 92633

SA4-5.   Auxiliary fuel system: Met-Co-Aire, P.O. Box 2216, Fullerton, CA 92633

SA4-226.   Metalized wings: Frank A. Burdick, 43316 N. 20th St, W., Lancaster, CA 93534

SA236WE.   Use Cessna 210 wing tips: Hudson Aircraft Service, P.O. Box 2471 W A S, Tallahassee, FL 32302

170/170A/170B

SA135CE.   Installation of Lycoming O-320-A1A, -A1B, -A3A, -A3B, or O-320-B1A, -B1B, -B3A, or B3B: KWAD Company, 4530 Jettridge Dr., NW, Atlanta, GA 30327

SA196NW.   One-piece windshield: Jack Shannon, 8451 S.E. 39th, Mercer Island, WA 98040

SA1209GL.   SAF-T-STOP seat stop device: Glen A. Florence, Aero Technologies, 39745 Sylvia, Mt. Clements, MI 48045

SA2345NM.   Addition of SWS-11000 Tundra tires: Richard J. Schneider, 20 Malaspina Dr., Eagle River, AK 99577

SA7441SW.   Installation of Teledyne O-300-D: Ron Massicot, Rt. 6, Box 483, Breaux Bridge, LA 70517

170A/170B

SA3-13.   Installation of Lycoming O-340-A1A: KWAD Company, 4530 Jettridge Drive, NW, Atlanta, GA 30327

SA3-451.   Speed kit: Aircraft Development Co., 1326 N. Westlink Blvd., Wichita, KS 67212

SA3-672.   Installation of Lycoming O-360-A1A, A1D or B1B: KWAD Company, 4530 Jettridge Drive, NW, Atlanta, GA 30327

SA421CE.   Installation of Lycoming O-360-A1A, A1D, or B1B: Bob Williams, P.O. Box 431, Udall, KS 67146

SA806CE.   Installation of Lycoming O-360: Bob Williams, Box 431, Udall, KS 67146

SA989CE.   STOL conversion: Horton STOL-Craft, Inc., Wellington Municipal Airport, Wellington, KS 67152

SA1073CE.   STOL conversion: Bob Williams, Box 431, Udall, KS 67146

SA1664CE.   Speed kit: Aircraft Development Co., 1326 N Westlink Blvd, Wichita, KS 67212

SA2454WE.   Fiberglass wing tips: Madras Air Service, Route 2, Madras, OR 97741

SA2516CE.   Fiberglass wing tips: Horton STOL-Craft, Wellington Municipal Airport, Wellington, KS 67152

SA3548NM.   One-piece windshield: Del-Air, 2121 S Wildcat Way, Porterville, CA 03257

SA3797WE.   Installation of improved muffler: Del-Air, 2121 S Wildcat Way, Porterville, CA 03257

SA4540NM. Modified panel and yoke: Del-Air, 2121 S Wildcat Way, Porterville, CA 03257

170A

SA1614WE. Auxiliary fuel: Flint Aero, Inc., Box 1458, Spring Valley, CA 92077

170B

SA1490CE. Speed kit: Aircraft Development Co., 1326 N Westlink Blvd, Wichita, KS 67212

SA2280CE. Speed kit: Horton STOL-Craft, Wellington Municipal Airport, Wellington, KS 67152

SA2851SW. STOL conversion: Bob Williams, Box 431, Udall, KS 67146

SA293NW. Installation of Franklin 6A0350: Seaplane Flying, Inc., 1111 SE 5th St., Vancouver, WA 98661

SA499NW. STOL conversion: Seaplane Flying, Inc., 1111 SE 5th St., Vancouver, WA 98661

SA637NW. Installation of oil filter: Turbotech, Inc., Box 61586, Vancouver, WA 98666

SA2256WE. STOL conversion: Marshall E. Quackenbush, Box 2421, California City, CA 93505

170 series

SA2067NM. Shoulder harness installation: Bud's Aero Specialties, Inc., Box 190, Eatonville, PA 98328

Additional sources of modification information for Cessnas are the type clubs listed in appendix A.

PARTS

Cessna supports these planes by building and selling parts, issuing needed service bulletins, and providing technical information. Much of the company's printed information, such as that from the Cessna Service Bulletin Listing Program, are available only at a price. The factory claims to be producing the required parts to support its airplanes, maintaining an inventory based upon past orders.

Note that many 150 parts fit the 120/140s and 172 parts often fit the 170s. Additionally, many suppliers of parts, new and used, advertise in *Trade-A-Plane*.

4

Ercoupe

ERCOUPE airplanes are considered among the most foolproof aircraft ever built (Fig. 4-1). They were designed originally with only a control wheel for all directional maneuvering, on the ground and in the air. The wheel operated the ailerons and rudder via control interconnections and steered the nosewheel (Fig. 4-2). No pilot coordination was required to make turns. In addition to the no-need-for-coordination effect, the controls were limited in their amount of travel (elevator authority), thereby preventing stall entry.

SPINPROOF

No stalls meant a spinproof airplane. After all, how can you spin if you can't get into a stall? In fact, the Ercoupe is placarded: "This Airplane Characteristically Incapable of Spinning." Unfortunately, this safety feature led to the issuance of some limited pilot licenses back in the late 1940s. The feeling prevailed, at that time, that the spinproof Ercoupe was not a complete airplane, therefore, its pilots were not complete pilots.

FIGHTER CANOPY

The first Ercoupes had metal fuselages and fabric-covered wings; the later versions were of all-metal design. They all had tricycle landing gear. One particular feature that has always made them popular is the fighter-like canopy that can be opened during flight (Fig. 4-3). Another is the unique way crosswind landings are handled.

CROSSWIND LANDINGS

Due to the cross-connected controls (no coordination needed), crosswind landings are different in the Ercoupe than in other aircraft. It is not possible to slip an Ercoupe, therefore a crab must be maintained to touchdown. The trailing beam main gear takes the shock of a crabbed landing, then makes the directional correction (Figs. 4-4 through 4-6). Landings can be made with up to a 30-degree crab angle. Try that in a taildragger, sports fans!

Ercoupe Production Numbers

Model	Production totals	Serial series
415C	4309	113 – 4422
415D	445	4423 – 4868
415E	127	4869 – 4996
415G	84	4997 – 5081
F–1	114	5600 – 5714
F–1A	49	5715 – 5764
A–2	245	A–1 – A–245
A–2A	63	B246 – B309
M–10	61	690001 – 690011
		& 700001 – 700050

Fig. 4-1. Ercoupe production numbers indicating model numbers, production total, and serial number series.

Fig. 4-2. The wheel. The only control necessary for all directional movement.

Fig. 4-3. Notice the fighter-like appearance of the cabin. Visibility is excellent and the side windows may remain down during flight.

ERCO MODELS

The Ercoupe was the dream child of Fred Weick, who later designed the Piper Cherokee. The planes were manufactured first by Engineering Research Corp. (ERCO) of Riverdale, Maryland in 1940. Like so many of the classic airplanes, the Ercoupe's history is full of bumps.

415C. The 415C was produced first prior to WWII (Figs. 4-7 and 4-8). It was powered with a Continental A-65-8 65-hp engine. There were 112 model 415Cs built before the war. After the war, production of the 415C was restarted. An engine change increased horsepower to 75 by using the Continental C-75-12. As a matter of record, during a nine-month span in 1946 more than 4000 Ercoupes were built. A total of 4520 model 415Cs were produced.

415CD. The 415CD was a basic 415C with slight increase in gross weight (Fig. 4-9).

415D. The 415D model was introduced in 1947 as an update to the 415CD. It was powered by a Continental C-75-12, had electric starter, and a 10-gallon fuel increase.

415E. The 415E appeared in 1948. This model updated the 415D by adding an 85-hp Continental C-85-12 engine. A new 415E sold for $3995.

415F. The 415F was a 415D with a 90-hp Continental C-90 engine.

415G. The 415G was a 415E with rudder pedals installed. It was introduced in 1949 and was the last ERCO airplane to be built. A minor variation of the 415G is the "Club Air," which was equipped with a rear kiddie seat.

415H. The 415H was a step back to lower horsepower engines. It was a 415G powered by a 75-hp Continental.

CROSSWIND TAKE-OFF IN AN ERCOUPE

In taking off cross wind, it is advisable to keep the control wheel well forward, which holds the nose wheel firmly on the ground and gives good steering control. Some excess in forward speed should be gained to allow the airplane to take off very definitely, and at the moment of breaking contact with the ground, the control wheel should be straightened laterally to neutral position. The airplane may weathercock into the wind just after it leaves the ground, but this need cause no concern, as it is merely adjusting itself to true flight with respect to the air, and a straight course of travel is maintained without difficulty. The pilot should not hesitate to make slight turns near the ground in order to maintain the desired path and avoid being drifted off course by the wind.

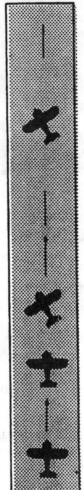

4. A straight course of flight is maintained on the center line of runway during the climb. If plane drifts sideways, make slight turns to get back to center of runway.

3. The airplane weathercocks into the wind just after leaving the ground. Wings are held level.

2. Gain some excess forward speed and take off very definitely. At the moment of breaking contact, straighten the control wheel laterally to neutral position.

1. On ground run, keep forward pressure on the control wheel and some right control necessary to overcome weathervaning. (Tendency to head into the wind.)

UNIVAIR

WIND FROM LEFT

Fig. 4-4. Crosswind takeoff.

OTHER 'COUPES

In 1950 Universal Aircraft purchased the production rights. Universal built no airplanes, but did supply necessary parts to the owners of Ercoupes.

CROSS WIND LANDING IN AN ERCOUPE

In the approach to a cross wind landing, the airplane will be pointing up wind sufficiently to keep the flight path in line with the runway rather than attempt to drop the windward wing as is done in the three control plane. The glide should be continued in this crabbing attitude down until contact is made with the ground. At the moment of contact the airplane should be given its head, and the grip on control wheel relaxed. This allows the nose wheel to caster and line up with the direction of motion of the airplane along the ground. Immediately thereafter ease the control wheel forward slowly and roll down the runway. Prompt application of the brakes or setting the brakes on about half way during the glide approach brings the nose down and completes the change in heading more quickly.

5. During ground run steer like a car.

4. On ground plane will change heading to line up with path along runway.

3. Make contact decisively at low speed with plane still crabbed, but relax grip on control wheel to allow nose to caster and ease forward on control wheel slowly.

2. If plane drifts sideways, make slight turns to get back to center line of runway.

1. Finish turn with ER-COUPE on extended centerline of runway and headed or crabbed into wind just enough to keep its flight path (not heading) on extended centerline.

UNIVAIR

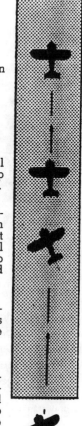

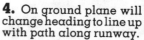

WIND FROM LEFT

PATH OF SHIP

Fig. 4-5. Crosswind landing.

In 1956, the Forney Aircraft Company of Fort Collins, Colorado, become owner of the production rights. Fornair produced the F-1 AirCoupes until 1960. The F-1 was all metal, and powered by the Continental C-90-12F engine. In reality, it was an updated 415G with a new instrument panel. The F-1 sold new for $6995. Forney built 115 F-1s.

For a short period of time in the early 1960s Air Products owned the manufacturing rights and produced about fifty F-1As as an improvement to the F-1. The

Fig. 4-6. The trailing beam landing gear that allows the unique crosswind operations.

gross weight was increased, an improved nosewheel leg was added, and the rear spar strengthened.

Alon Inc., of McPhearson, Kansas, purchased the Ercoupe production rights in 1964 after Air Products gave up. The new A-2 Aircoupe, upgrade of the F-1A, was powered with a 90-hp engine Continental C-90-16F and offered an option of three controls (with rudder pedals) or two controls (without rudder pedals). Also, the canopy was changed to a sliding-type one-piece unit.

Later, Alon modified the main landing gear to spring steel structures and renamed the plane the A-2A. Alon built 308 planes. The price of the A-2 was $7825.

Fig. 4-7. Ercoupe 415C.

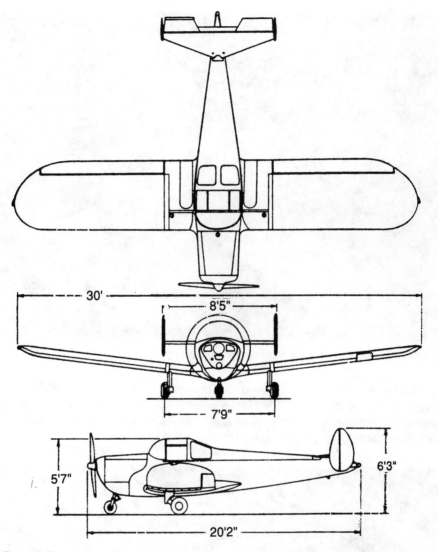

Fig. 4-8. Dimensions of the Ercoupe 415. UNIVAIR

In 1967 Alon sold the production rights to Mooney Aircraft of Kerrville, Texas. Mooney first produced the A-2A as its Cadet. In 1968 Mooney completely redesigned the Ercoupe and redesignated it the M-10 Cadet. The Cadet didn't sell well and was quickly discontinued. Only 61 were built. The last of the Ercoupe line sold for $8995 new.

It is interesting to note that when Mooney redesigned the Ercoupe the stalls and spins were put back in. Also gone was the characteristic twin-boom tail.

In 1970 the last remnants of Ercoupe were purchased by UNIVAIR of Aurora, Colorado. No airplanes were built by UNIVAIR, however, they are producing all the parts required to keep Ercoupes in the air.

Smithsonian Institution Photo No. 92-8007

Fig. 4-9. Ercoupe 415C in flight showing the windows down.

Of the more than 5000 Ercoupes (including Forney, Alon, and Mooney), a large number of these fine little planes are still flying, no doubt due to their small thirst for gasoline, low selling prices, and low taxation of pilot skills. For more details of the airplane, see Figs. 4-10 through 4-12.

Fig. 4-10. Dual fork nosewheel.

Fig. 4-11. Single fork nosewheel on a 415.

SPECIFICATIONS

Model: 415C
Engine
    Make: Continental
    Model: A-65-8
    hp: 65
    TBO: 1800
    Seats: 2 side-by-side
    Speed
    Max: 144 mph
    Cruise: 108 mph
    Stall: 56 mph
Fuel capacity: 14 gal
Rate of climb: 550 fpm
Transitions
    Takeoff over 50 ft obs: 2375 ft
    Ground run: 590 ft
    Landing over 50 ft obs: 1750 ft
    Ground roll: 750 ft
Weights
    Gross: 1260 lbs
    Empty: 800 lbs

RUDDER PEDAL CONTROL KIT

The rudders are completely disengaged from the aileron system and therefore independent of the lateral controls, allowing the airplane to be flown in slips, and misuse of the rudder pedals can be demonstrated in flight. It is not necessary to use the rudder pedals in excess of 70 miles per hour, due to the efficiency of the aileron system.

The three-control Ercoupe is an ideal training airplane for pilots intending to fly Navions and Bonanzas since it provides a cheaper, lighter airplane with tricycle landing gear and similar control set up. It has the hand brake system like the Navion; however, the control of the steering on the ground is still with the control wheel. This provides a more natural means of steering since it is like the automobile and provides a more accruate and delicate control than can be provided with rudder pedals. With the three-control Ercoupe, cross-wind landings may be performed in the conventional Ercoupe manner or with a wing low technique developed for older airplanes. Once on the ground, the airplane is stable, and therefore, still handles like an Ercoupe although directional steering may be performed with the rudders down to about 20 miles an hour.

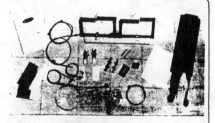

Rudder Pedal Kit consists of foot rest with rudder pedals mounted, cables to connect the rudder pedals to the rudder system with installation parts, hardware and drawings.

The rudder pedals may be installed in approximately eight man hours by the average A & P mechanic. Complete, ready for installation.   4-SK-21

STROBE LIGHT KITS

SINGLE STROBE BEACON. A direct replacement for bottom fuselage WHELEN HR-DF (Double flash) Strobe.   4-SK-20

SINGLE STROBE BEACON. Provides for the installation of a WHELEN HR-DF Strobe unit in the bottom of the fuselage for aircraft that currently has no strobe or beacon unit.   4-SK-20A

TWO STROBE FUSELAGE MOUNTED SYSTEM. Kit includes a power supply and two WHELEN A470 Strobe Lights, (1 Red, 1 Clear).   4-SK-20B

WING TIP MOUNTED 2 STROBE SYSTEM. WHELEN A413 power supply and two A650 Strobe Lights. (This kit must be used in conjunction with the SK-54 or SK-55 kits which must be purchased separately).   4-SK-20C

THREE STROBE WING AND TAIL MOUNTED SYSTEM. Kit includes power supply, two wing-tip strobes, and one tail strobe. (This kit must be used with the SK-54 or SK-55 and the SK-56 which must be purchased separately).   4-SK-20D

SPLIT ELEVATOR KIT

The improved control from the split elevator and the safety of a stall warning cushion can be installed on the older Ercoupes, provided the center quadrant trim control is installed. The Ercoupe can be landed five miles per hour slower with the split elevator. (Labor Estimate, 3 Hours)   4-SK-25

NEW STYLE TAIL CONE

Streamline your Ercoupe with the Alon Tail Cone. Facilitates installation of Tail Mounted Strobe. Gives your Ercoupe that "New Look".   4-SK-56

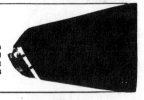

Fig. 4-12. A few of the popular updates and conversions available for the Ercoupe.

Dimensions
  Length: 20 ft 9 in
  Height: 5 ft 11 in
  Span: 30 ft

Model: 415D
Engine
    Make: Continental
    Model: C-75-12F
    hp: 75
    TBO: 1800
Seats: 2 side-by-side
Speed
    Max: 144 mph
    Cruise: 114 mph
    Stall: 56 mph
Fuel capacity: 24 gal
Rate of climb: 560 fpm
Transitions
    Takeoff over 50 ft obs: 2250 ft
    Ground run: 570 ft
    Landing over 50 ft obs: 1750 ft
    Ground roll: 750 ft
Weights
    Gross: 1400 lbs
    Empty: 815 lbs
Dimensions
    Length: 20 ft 9 in
    Height: 5 ft 11 in
    Span: 30 ft

Model: 415E/G
Engine
    Make: Continental
    Model: C-85-12F
    hp: 85
    TBO: 1800
Seats: 2 side-by-side
Speed
    Max: 144 mph
    Cruise: 118 mph
    Stall: 56 mph
Fuel capacity: 24 gal
Rate of climb: 560 fpm
Transitions
    Takeoff over 50 ft obs: 2100 ft
    Ground run: 520 ft
    Landing over 50 ft obs: 1750 ft
    Ground roll: 750 ft

Weights
    Gross: 1400 lbs
    Empty: 830 lbs
Dimensions
    Length: 20 ft 9 in
    Height: 5 ft 11 in
    Span: 30 ft

Model: F-1
Engine
    Make: Continental
    Model: C-90-12F
    hp: 90
    TBO: 1800
Seats: 2 side-by-side
Speed
    Max: 144 mph
    Cruise: 120 mph
    Stall: 56 mph
Fuel capacity: 24 gal
Rate of climb: 600 fpm
Transitions
    Takeoff over 50 ft obs: 2100 ft
    Ground run: 500 ft
    Landing over 50 ft obs: 1750 ft
    Ground roll: 600 ft
Weights
    Gross: 1400 lbs
    Empty: 890 lbs
Dimensions
    Length: 20 ft 9 in
    Height: 5 ft 11 in
    Span: 30 ft

Model: A-2 and A-2A
Engine
    Make: Continental
    Model: C-90-16F
    hp: 90
    TBO: 1800
Seats: 2 side-by-side
Speed
    Max: 128 mph
    Cruise: 124 mph
    Stall: 56 mph
Fuel capacity: 24 gal

Rate of climb: 640 fpm
Transitions
    Takeoff over 50 ft obs: 2100 ft
    Ground run: 540 ft
    Landing over 50 ft obs: 1750 ft
    Ground roll: 650 ft
Weights
    Gross: 1450 lbs
    Empty: 930 lbs
Dimensions
    Length: 20 ft 2 in
    Height: 5 ft 11 in
    Span: 30 ft

Model: M-10
Engine
    Make: Continental
    Model: C-90
    hp: 90
    TBO: 1800
Seats: 2 side-by-side
Speed
    Max: 144 mph
    Cruise: 110 mph
    Stall: 46 mph
Fuel capacity: 24 gal
Rate of climb: 835 fpm
Transitions
    Takeoff over 50 ft obs: 1953 ft
    Ground run: 534 ft
    Landing over 50 ft obs: 1016 ft
    Ground roll: 431 ft
Weights
    Gross: 1450 lbs
    Empty: 950 lbs
Dimensions
    Length: 20 ft 8 in
    Height: 7 ft 8 in
    Span: 33 ft

AIRWORTHINESS DIRECTIVES

The Ercoupes had many ADs issued against them in their early years, and even a few late ones. Be sure to have your mechanic check the logs for compliance. **Warning:** This AD list is not complete for all the affected airplanes.

46-23-3: inspect control wheel/aileron system SN 113 - 1306.

46-38-2: inspect/modify aileron control horn SN 113 - 2706

46-49-1: replacement of nosewheel on early 415-C

47-20-5: reinforcement of belly skin on 415 SN 800 - 2037

47-20-6: reinforcement of aileron skin on most 415s

47-42-20: inspect/replace control column shaft SN 1033 - 1327

52-2-2: inspect aileron hinges and balance assembly on 415s

54-26-2: inspect/replace certain control cables on 415s

55-22-2: inspect/replace fuel tanks on 415s and F-1s

57-2-1: 100 hr inspection rudder horn attachments 415s/F-1s

59-5-4: inspect/replace rear spar center section on 415s

59-25-5: reinforcement of rudder on 415s

60-9-2: replace nosegear bolts all through SN 5678

67-6-3: modify rudder control all through SN 5714

70-17-2: replace hardware attaching rudder pedals on all M10

73-20-8: inspect/rework UNIVAIR propeller tips

74-26-9: inspect Bendix magneto

79-13-8: replace Airborne dry air pumps installed after 5-15-79

81-7-6: inspect AC fuel pump on Continental engines

81-16-5: inspect Slick magneto coil on various engines

82-20-1: inspect impulse coupler on some Bendix magnetos

84-26-2: replace paper air filter each 500 hrs

86-22-9: inspect/replace UNIVAIR fuel nipple 415 and F series.

INSPECTIONS

Before purchasing an Ercoupe, be sure to have a mechanic who is very familiar with the ways of Ercoupes carefully check the plane. These airplanes are nearing 50 years of age and there will always be some metal deterioration (corrosion). Have a mechanic pass judgment before you are financially committed.

STCs

A popular modification to the Ercoupe is the rudder pedal kit which can be installed in about eight hours by a mechanic. It allows the pilot the choice of standard crosswind landings or the "Coupe" method.

Another popular modification is the Double Arm Nose Gear Conversion. It is available for all models of Ercoupes. For information about these modifications contact:

UNIVAIR Aircraft Corporation
2500 Himalaya Road
Aurora, CO 80011
(303) 375-8882

The following listing includes many STCs for the Ercoupe series of airplanes. The STC number appears first, followed by the item or part modified, and the name and address of the holder of the STC.

415 series

SA1-4. Metalized wings: Skycraft Design, Old Star Airport, 85 North Main, Yardley, PA 19067

SA1-208. Landing light installation: Air Service, Inc., Box 189, New Castle, DE 19720

SA1-336. Installation of Continental C-90-14F: Richard Weibley, Skyport, Box 1229, Harrisburg, PA 17105

SA3-512. Metalized wings: Robert Dale, 30030 Minglewood Ln., Famington, MI 48024

SA4-73. Metalized wings: Vern Dell Aircraft Metal Work Co., Box 42, Chula Vista, CA 92010

SA4-285. Addition of propeller spinner: Raymond Stits, 3665 Bloomington Blvd., Riverside, CA 92502

SA4-441. Change to fiberglass nose cowl: Wilbur Thompson, 10617 South Prairie Ave., Inglewood, CA 90306

SA4-839. Metalized wings: Met-Co-Aire, Box 2216, Fullerton, CA 92633

SA4-840. Glass fabric covering: Air Fibre, Inc., Box 244, Altadena, CA 91001

SA341WE. Modified engine mount: Met-Co-Aire, Box 2216, Fullerton, CA 92633

SA465WE. Installation of Continental C-90-12F: R.B. Christianson, 105010 ½ Mather Ave., Sunland, CA 91040

SA4328SW. New instrument panel: Robert Stark, Rt 1, Box 22, Ponca City, OK 74601

SA41254. Add wheel fairings: Kenney Engineering, 4120 Via Solano, Palos Verdes Estates, CA 90275

SA1WE. Installation of fiberglass tail cone: Met-Co-Air, Box 2216, Fullerton, CA 92633

SA3WE. Fiberglass engine cowl: Met-Co-Air, Box 2216, Fullerton, CA 92633

SA319WE. Metalized wings: UNIVAIR Aircraft Corp., Route 3, Box 59, Aurora, CO 80010

415C and up

SA2462WE. Add wheel fairings: FRA Enterprises, Inc., 32032 Washington Ave, Rochester, WI 53167

415C/CD

SA120GL. Cleveland wheels and brakes: Parker Hannifin Corp., Aircraft Wheel and Brake Division, 1160 Center Rd., Avon, OH 44011

SA3502WE. Change to fiberglass nose bowl: FRA Enterprises, Inc., 32032 Washington Ave, Rochester, WI 53167

415C

SA2185WE. Add wheel fairings: FRA Enterprises, Inc., 32032 Washington Ave, Rochester, WI 53167

415D

SA1-440 Installation of Continental C90-12F: Richard Weibley, Skyport, Box 1229, Harrisburg, PA 17105

SA2628WE Installation of Continental O-200-A: Skyport Services Div. FRA Enterprises, Inc., Box 355, Rochester, WI 53167

415/F-1/F-1A

SA127GL Installation of Cleveland wheels and brakes: Parker Hannifin Corp., Aircraft Wheel and Brake Div., 1160 Center Rd., Avon, OH 44011

415D and up

SA1181GL Add wheel fairings: FRA Enterprises, Inc., Box 355, Rochester, WI 53167

F-1/F-1A

SA4-1590 New fuel system: Met-Co-Aire, Box 2216, Fullerton, CA 92633

Other sources for modification information are available from the Ercoupe type clubs (see Appendix A).

PARTS

UNIVAIR, currently the owner of the production rights to the entire series of Ercoupe airplanes, manufactures and sells all parts necessary for the continued operation of Ercoupes. Contact them at:

UNIVAIR Aircraft Corporation
2500 Himalaya Road
Aurora, CO 80011
(303) 375-8882

Another source of Ercoupe parts and knowledge is Skyport Aircoupe Services. Contact them at:

Skyport Aircoupe Services
32032 Washington Ave.
Rochester, WI 53167
(800) 624-5312

5

Luscombe

LUSCOMBE Silvaire airplanes came into being first in 1937. They were designed by Don Luscombe and were powered originally by engines varying from 50-to 75-hp. There are two series of classic Luscombes: the 8 series two-place planes and the 11 series four-place Sedans (Fig. 5-1).

EARLY 8 SERIES

All 8 series Luscombes are all-metal construction, except for fabric-covered wings on some early examples. They seat two side-by-side, albeit a bit cozily, and have stick controls.

The first flight of the production prototype model 8 was on June 6, 1938 and the CAA type certificate was issued on August 11 of that year. It was powered with a 50-hp engine. By late 1938, Continental had introduced the 65-hp Model A-65 engine, resulting in the development of the Luscombe 8A. As a point of interest, the two engines (A-50 and A-65) are basically the same, except for the small compression ratio and rpm increases necessary to develop 65-hp.

PROGRESSION BY MODEL NUMBER

The first model 8A flew in January 1939 and full production started in April (Fig. 5-2). The last model 8 (50-hp) was built in July of that year. Due to the immediate success of the model 8A (Fig. 5-3), a version powered with the less-expensive 65-hp Lycoming 0-145-B engine was introduced. Called the 8B Trainer, it lacked some of the fancier trim found on the 8A.

The model 8C (Fig. 5-4), called the Silvaire Deluxe, was powered by a Continental 75-hp engine and was restyled inside and out. It had an interior of maroon cloth and tan leather, a shock-mounted instrument panel, and contoured control sticks. The exterior showed a restyled engine cowl with grills on the air inlets, maroon striping on the wing leading edges and on the fuselage that streamed back from the letter S on the nose. Production started in July of 1940.

Luscombe Models by Engine

Model	Engine
8	Continental A–50 (50 hp)
8A	Continental A–65 (65 hp)
8B	Lycoming 0–145–B (65 hp)
8C	Continental A–75 (75 hp) fuel–injected
8D	Continental A–75 (75 hp)
8E	Continental C–85 (85 hp)
8F	Continental C–90 (90 hp)

Fig. 5-1. Luscombe models varied by engine power.

The 8D, Silvaire Deluxe Trainer, was the same basic plane as the 8C but had larger fuel tanks, a fuel-injected 75-hp engine, an electrical system, and the instrument panel was redesigned for more instrument and radio space. All this was done with the Civilian Pilot Training Program in mind.

Luscombe production halted in 1942 for the war effort, during which time Luscombe produced assemblies, parts, and pieces on contract. A total of 1125 model 8s were built before the war.

Luscombe Production Numbers

Model	Production total
8A	3695
8B	85
8C	278
8D	97
8E	1038
8F	329

Fig. 5-2. Luscombe production numbers showing models and total built.

Fig. 5-3. Luscombe 8A. This particular airplane has fabric covered wings, note the double wing struts.

Fig. 5-4. Luscombe 8C. Notice the S on the engine cowling; it appears on many Luscombes.

AFTER THE WAR

In 1945 Luscombe once again began producing airplanes. All the old models were available and the 8E with an 85-hp engine was introduced. A newly designed single-strut, all-metal wing became standard.

In 1947 Siflex landing gear was introduced and could be retrofited to older model 8s. The new and stronger gear was designed to reduce damage from ground loops.

The last plane produced by Luscombe in the 8 series was the 8F (Fig. 5-5) powered with a 90-hp Continental C-90 engine. This plane came out in 1948 and can be identified easily by its square-shaped tail.

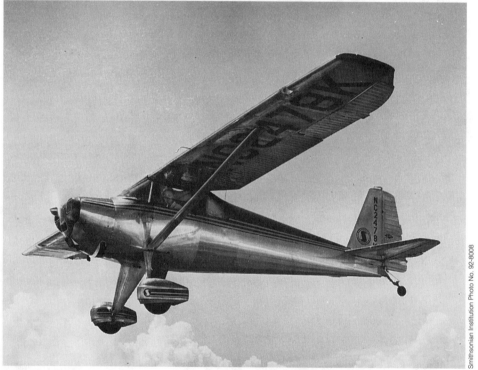

Fig. 5-5. Luscombe 8F. The last of the Luscombes, it was powered with a C-90 engine.

THE BUILDERS

Luscombes were originally built in Trenton, New Jersey. After the war, and through 1949, they were built in Dallas, Texas (Fig. 5-6). In the heyday of postwar aviation, over 1200 Texans proudly worked at the Luscombe factory. Unfortunately, by 1949 Luscombe's financial bubble had burst and the company went into bankruptcy.

In the early 1950s, Texas Engineering and Manufacturing Company (TEMCO) produced the Luscombe model 8F. About fifty were completed.

Fig. 5-6. This 1946 8A is letter-perfect, right down to the wheel pants. Note the single wing struts indicating metal wings.

In 1955 Silvaire Aircraft Corp. was formed in Fort Collins, Colorado, and also produced only the 8F (Fig. 5-7). Production stopped in 1960 and has never been resumed.

Between 1945 and 1951 there were 4560 Luscombe model 8s built (Fig. 5-8). All in all the various manufacturers produced 6057 series 8 Luscombes.

The type certificates for the 8 series planes are currently owned by Larsen Industries, Inc., 7790 Rawsonville Rd., Belleville, MI 48111.

Fig. 5-7. This Luscombe 8F is a 1959 Silvaire Aircraft Corp. product, built in Ft. Collins, Colorado. Notice the square tail.

Fig. 5-8. The instrument panel and sporty curved chrome control sticks inside a 1946 8A.

THE LUSCOMBE SEDAN

Luscombe briefly entered the four-place aircraft field with the family-sized model 11 Sedan (Fig. 5-9). The Sedan was all-metal, had very wide conventional landing gear, and, oddly enough, a rear window (like the modern Cessnas).

The advertising (Figs. 5-10 and 11) describing the Silvaire Sedan likened the airplane to a large family sedan: Deluxe interior; automotive-type walnut-grain instru-

Fig. 5-9. Luscombe Model 11 Sedan. It was really ahead of its time with rear windows and wasp waist. Unfortunately, few were made.

Fig. 5-10. A picture says a thousand words or at least shows how strong the Luscombe wing is.

ment panel with "Silchrome" trimming; all seats quickly removable; spacious glove compartment; wheel controls; hydraulic "instant action" brakes on the pilot's side; parking brake; 3716 square inches of window area; spring interconnected rudder and aileron controls; easy-opening windows in both doors; hat-throw behind the rear seat; exceptionally large doors; easy-clean pinstripe all-wool upholstery, side panels and kick panels; all-wool rug; foam rubber seat cushions; roomy baggage compartment beneath the rear seat; complete soundproofing around the cabin area; cabin heater and four individual fresh air ventilators; overhead front sunshades; sun visor; no-slip cargo strips; normal flight and engine instruments; ignition lock; wheel type elevator tab control; mixture control; three automotive-type individual cigarette lighters and ashtrays (front and rear); metallic bronze deluxe interior trim; hydraulic flap actuating mechanism; individually adjustable front seats; fold-down seat backs; balanced controls; electric starter; wood fixed-pitch propeller; full-swivel steerable tailwheel; Luscombe landing lights; generator; engine primer; position lights; instrument panel lights; dome light; propeller spinner; engine shielding.

Unfortunately, even with all the above, only about eighty Sedans were manufactured in 1948 and 1949. Only about forty survive today according to estimates. They originally sold for $6995.

Currently the type certificate for the model 11 Sedan is owned by Alpha Aviation Service, Majors Field, Box 641, Greenville, TX 75402, (214) 455-9080.

ALL METAL WING- 8A, 8E, 8F

Note: "U" Prefixes on part numbers indicate a *FAA-PMA Approved part.*

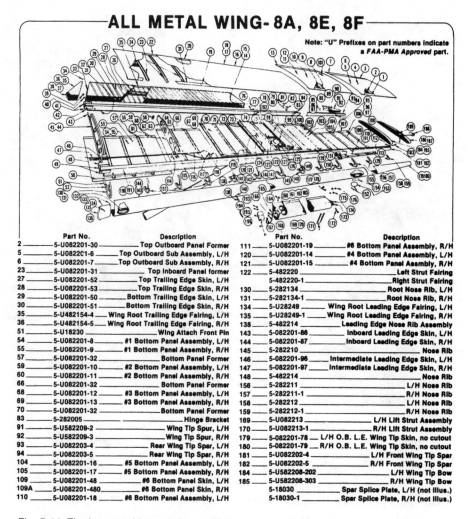

Part No.	Description
2 — 5-U082201-30	Top Outboard Panel Former
5 — 5-U0822C1-6	Top Outboard Sub Assembly, L/H
6 — 5-U082201-7	Top Outboard Sub Assembly, R/H
23 — 5-U082201-31	Top Inboard Panel former
27 — 5-U082201-52	Top Trailing Edge Skin, L/H
28 — 5-U082201-53	Top Trailing Edge Skin, R/H
29 — 5-U082201-50	Bottom Trailing Edge Skin, L/H
30 — 5-U082201-51	Bottom Trailing Edge Skin, R/H
35 — 5-U482154-4	Wing Root Trailing Edge Fairing, L/H
36 — 5-U482154-5	Wing Root Trailing Edge Fairing, R/H
51 — 5-U18230	Wing Attach Front Pin
54 — 5-U082201-8	#1 Bottom Panel Assembly, L/H
55 — 5-U082201-9	#1 Bottom Panel Assembly, R/H
57 — 5-U082201-32	Bottom Panel Former
59 — 5-U082201-10	#2 Bottom Panel Assembly, L/H
60 — 5-U082201-11	#2 Bottom Panel Assembly, R/H
66 — 5-U082201-32	Bottom Panel Former
68 — 5-U082201-12	#3 Bottom Panel Assembly, L/H
69 — 5-U082201-13	#3 Bottom Panel Assembly, R/H
70 — 5-U082201-32	Bottom Panel Former
83 — 5-282005	Hinge Bracket
91 — 5-U582209-2	Wing Tip Spur, L/H
92 — 5-U582209-3	Wing Tip Spur, R/H
93 — 5-U082203-4	Rear Wing Tip Spar, L/H
94 — 5-U082203-5	Rear Wing Tip Spar, R/H
104 — 5-U082201-16	#5 Bottom Panel Assembly, L/H
105 — 5-U082201-17	#5 Bottom Panel Assembly, R/H
109 — 5-U082201-48	#6 Bottom Panel Skin, L/H
109A — 5-U082201-480	#6 Bottom Panel Skin, R/H
110 — 5-U082201-18	#6 Bottom Panel Assembly, L/H

Part No.	Description
111 — 5-U082201-19	#6 Bottom Panel Assembly, R/H
120 — 5-U082201-14	#4 Bottom Panel Assembly, L/H
121 — 5-U082201-15	#4 Bottom Panel Assembly, R/H
122 — 5-482220	Left Strut Fairing
5-482220-1	Right Strut Fairing
130 — 5-282134	Root Nose Rib, L/H
131 — 5-282134-1	Root Nose Rib, R/H
134 — 5-U28249	Wing Root Leading Edge Fairing, L/H
135 — 5-U28249-1	Wing Root Leading Edge Fairing, R/H
138 — 5-482214	Leading Edge Nose Rib Assembly
143 — 5-082201-86	Inboard Leading Edge Skin, L/H
144 — 5-082201-87	Inboard Leading Edge Skin, R/H
145 — 5-282210	Nose Rib
146 — 5-082201-96	Intermediate Leading Edge Skin, L/H
147 — 5-082201-97	Intermediate Leading Edge Skin, R/H
148 — 5-482214	Nose Rib
156 — 5-282211	L/H Nose Rib
157 — 5-282211-1	R/H Nose Rib
158 — 5-282212	L/H Nose Rib
159 — 5-282212-1	R/H Nose Rib
169 — 5-U082213	L/H Lift Strut Assembly
170 — 5-U082213-1	R/H Lift Strut Assembly
179 — 5-082201-78	L/H O.B. L.E. Wing Tip Skin, no cutout
180 — 5-082201-79	R/H O.B. L.E. Wing Tip Skin, no cutout
181 — 5-U082202-4	L/H Front Wing Tip Spar
182 — 5-U082202-5	R/H Front Wing Tip Spar
184 — 5-U582208-202	L/H Wing Tip Bow
185 — 5-U582208-303	R/H Wing Tip Bow
5-18030	Spar Splice Plate, L/H (not illus.)
5-18030-1	Spar Splice Plate, R/H (not illus.)

Fig. 5-11. The inner workings and parts of the super strong Luscombe wing.

SPECIFICATIONS

Model: 8
Engine
    Make: Continental
    Model: A-50
    hp: 50 at 1900 rpm
    TBO: 1800
Seats: 2 side-by-side
Speed
    Max: 107 mph
    Cruise: 94 mph

Stall: 37 mph
Fuel capacity: 14 gal
Oil capacity: 4 qts
Weights
    Gross: 1200 lbs
    Empty: 650 lbs
    Load: 550 lbs
Dimensions
    Length: 19 ft 8 in
    Height: 6 ft 1 in
    Span: 34 ft 7 in

Model: Luscombe 8A/B
Engine
    Make: Continental or Lycoming
    Model: A-65 or O-145-B
    hp: 65 at 2350 rpm
    TBO: 1800
Seats: 2 side-by-side
Speed
    Max: 112 mph
    Cruise: 102 mph
    Stall: 38 mph
Fuel capacity: 15 gal
Rate of climb: 550 fpm
Transitions
    Takeoff over 50 ft obs: 1950 ft
    Ground run: 1050 ft
    Landing over 50 ft obs: 1540 ft
    Ground roll: 450 ft
Weights
    Gross: 1200 lbs
    Empty: 665 lbs
    Load: 535 lbs
Dimensions
    Length: 19 ft 8 in
    Height: 6 ft 1 in
    Span: 34 ft 7 in

Model: 8C/D
Engine
    Make: Continental
    Model: A-75
    hp: 75 at 2600 rpm
    TBO: 1800

Seats: 2 side-by-side
Speed
    Max: 118 mph
    Cruise: 107 mph
    Stall: 40 mph
Fuel capacity: 15 gal
Weights
    Gross: 1260 lbs
    Empty: 720 lbs
    Load: 540 lbs
Dimensions
    Length: 19 ft 8 in
    Height: 6 ft 1 in
    Span: 34 ft 7 in

Model: 8E
Engine
    Make: Continental
    Model: C-85
    hp: 85 at 2575 rpm
    TBO: 1800
Speed
    Max: 122 mph
    Cruise: 112 mph
    Stall: 48 mph
Fuel capacity: 25 gal
Rate of climb: 800 fpm
Transitions
    Takeoff over 50 ft obs: 1875 ft
    Ground run: 650 ft
    Landing over 50 ft obs: 1540 ft
    Ground roll: 450 ft
Weights
    Gross: 1400 lbs
    Empty: 810 lbs
    Load: 590 lbs
Dimensions
    Length: 19 ft 8 in
    Height: 6 ft 1 in
    Span: 34 ft 7 in

Model: 8F
Engine
    Make: Continental

Model: C-90
hp: 90
TBO: 1800
Speed
    Max: 128 mph
    Cruise: 120 mph
    Stall: 48 mph
Fuel capacity: 25 gal
Rate of climb: 900 fpm
Transitions
    Takeoff over 50 ft obs: 1850 ft
    Ground run: 550 ft
    Landing over 50 ft obs: 1540 ft
    Ground roll: 450 ft
Weights
    Gross: 1400 lbs
    Empty: 870 lbs
Dimensions
    Length: 20 ft
    Height: 6 ft 3 in
    Span: 35 ft

Model: 11 Sedan
Engine
    Make: Continental
    Model: C-165
    hp: 165
    TBO: 1800
Seats: 4
Speed
    Max: 140 mph
    Cruise: 130 mph
    Stall: 55 mph
Fuel capacity: 42 gal
Fuel consumption: 9 gph
Rate of climb: 900 fpm
Transitions
    Takeoff run: 800 ft
    Landing roll: 500 ft
Gross Weight: 2280 lbs
Dimensions
    Length: 23 ft 6 in
    Height: 6 ft 10 in
    Span: 38 ft

A LUSCOMBE TALE

The following is excerpted from the Luscombe Association newsletter: From the front page of the *San Francisco Chronicle*, 1953:

Glasgow, Scotland, June 26—Peter Gluckmann flew his tiny single-engined sports plane into Renfrew Airport here today, completing a 7000 mile flight from San Mateo, California, in a final nonstop lap from Iceland. The tall, heavy-set San Francisco watchmaker spanned a continent and an ocean in his peanut-sized plane in just 20 days. The last over-water hop from Reykjavik took him 12 hours. Gluckmann, who has been flying only four years and never crossed a body of water bigger than San Francisco Bay before this jaunt, said his 90-horsepower Luscombe monoplane behaved "just beautifully." "People say this is a tremendous trip to make," Gluckmann told newsmen here, "but to me it was entirely uneventful and just another flight." As soon as he arrived he telephoned his parents in London. He had planned the trip as a surprise for them, but they knew all about his impending arrival as British papers carried news of his multi-stop flight. His journey took him from San Mateo Airport to Arizona, New Mexico, Oklahoma, Michigan, Ontario, Quebec, Labrador, Greenland, and Iceland. Later today he flew south, stopped at Preston, England, for gas, and touched down at Blackpool, on the Irish Sea, to spend the night. Gluckmann said he was planning to land this morning at Prestwick, near the west coast of Scotland, but the field was fogged in, so he flew on to Edinburg, found fog there, too, and finally landed here. Gluckmann's plane, with a wingspan of only 35 feet, and a fuel capacity of only 90 gallons, is one of the smallest to cross the Atlantic. He used overleaded Air Force 110 octane gas instead of the usual 80-87 octane. The big flyer—he's 6 feet 3 inches tall and portly as well—spent a total of 85 hours in the seat of his gold and blue airplane. At Iceland yesterday, authorities at first refused to let him leave because of bad weather conditions. "And when I reached the Scottish coast," he said, "I was a little worried what with all that fog. I wasn't sure I'd have enough gas to find a clear field. But it all worked out."

PREPURCHASE WARNING

Due to the Luscombe's superior handling while in the air, a potential purchaser is cautioned to carefully inspect for damage caused by overstress from aerobatics. This damage might show on the upper wing skins as ripples at a forty-five-degree angle to the wing running from the rear spar to the leading edge. I also strongly recommend a mechanic very familiar with Luscombes inspect the plane for you.

NTSB ACCIDENT RATES

According to National Transportation Safety Board records, the two-place Luscombes have an accident rate of 45 incidents per 100,000 hours of operation, and a fatality rate of 5 incidents for the same period of operation. This is somewhat higher that the Cessna 150 figures of 10 and 1 respectively.

TWO POINTS ABOUT LUSCOMBES

The Luscombe 8s have two reputations they live up to. First, the Luscombe has one of the strongest airframe and wing structures ever manufactured, as demonstrated by the photograph of a Luscombe with 23 persons perched upon the wings and gear leg. This photo, by the way, can be seen (see Fig. 5-10) on the Luscombe Association newsletter.

Second, over the years many stories have circulated about the poor ground-handling characteristics of Luscombes. While it is true that Luscombes are touchy on landings and their landing gear track is rather narrow, any competent pilot can handle one if he stays on his toes.

SIMILAR-LOOKING AIRPLANES

A little-known fact is that Cessna bought a Luscombe 8D and dissected it. The resultant airplane Cessna built had lower aspect ratio wings, a slightly widened cabin, flaps, and control wheels. Some internal structural changes were made and spring steel landing gear and toe brakes were installed. Cessna called their airplane the model 140.

AIRWORTHINESS DIRECTIVES

The Luscombe airplanes have not suffered greatly from ADs, but a couple are notorious:

AD 55-24-1

AD 55-24-1. Concerns corrosion in the superstructure spars and involves the drilling of five holes into each of the spars, through which your mechanic checks for internal corrosion at each annual inspection.

The AD applies to all series 8 airplanes except the 8F models with serial numbers S-1 and up. This particular AD cannot be directly corrected as there are no spars currently being manufactured. However, there is an alternate approach to remedy the problem and eliminate this annual AD inspection (courtesy of the Luscombe Association).

The following modification was made on a FAA Form 337:

1. Removed cabin roof skin (P/N 08011-3).
2. Removed forward spar superstructure (P/N 28018-2) and rear spar superstructure (P/N 28019-2).
3. Constructed new forward and rear spar superstructures from 4130 steel (MIL-S-18729-C) of 0.063-inch thickness. Cold bend all angles to coincide with existing spar superstructures using 0.250 inch radius. All lengths, widths, and dimensions of existing spar superstructures were duplicated, including rivet hole patterns.

4. Primed new spar superstructure with steel metal primer paint (2 coats).

5. Applied zinc chromate tape to areas that come in contact with aluminum parts.

6. Constructed new superstructure skin (cabin roof) leaving out holes required for compliance with AD 55-24-1. Used original rivet hole patterns on .032-inch Alclad aluminum 2024-T3.

7. Installed new front spar superstructure to number 2 bulkhead uprights LH and RH using AN470-AD-6 rivets.

8. Install new rear spar superstructure to number 3 bulkhead uprights LH and RH using AN3-4 bolts; AC945 washers; AN365 self-locking nuts.

For the fortunate Luscombe 8 series owner who had no corrosion showing when inspected, here is another permanent fix (courtesy of the Luscombe Association):

1. Remove the wings, wing attachment fittings, and the superstructure skin (cabin roof), referred to in the AD as the top wing skin. This permits a complete inspection.

2. The spar carry through structures (P/N 28018 and 28019) are inspected and found to be free of any surface corrosion. The spar carry through structures are then cleaned, etched, and painted with Stits Aircraft Coatings brand Epoxy Chromate Metal Primer, in accordance with the manufacturer's instructions.

3. A new superstructure skin (cabin roof) without inspection holes is installed.

As a result of these modifications the FAA allowed discontinuance of the requirements of AD 55-24-01 on both planes.

AD 79-25-5

AD 79-25-5. Pertains to the Luscombe vertical stabilizer forward attach fitting, P/N 28444. This AD is directed at those round-fin Luscombes having cast aluminum fittings. If you have the square-tip fin, or if your round-tip fin has the steel fitting, the AD does not apply. Obviously, if you have the round fin, you must pull the fairing to determine the type of fitting. If it turns out to be cast, then the part must be removed from the plane and checked by dye penetrant. Compliance was required within ten hours of operation from 12-17-79. Thereafter, inspection must be made every 100 hours of operation. This subsequent inspection may be made visually, without removing the part from the plane. UNIVAIR Aircraft Corp., can provide an FAA-PMA approved replacement made of 4130 steel that is attached with machine screws instead of rivets. The part number is P/N U-28444.

In reference to this AD, one member of the Luscombe Association wrote (courtesy of the Luscombe Association): "When I received AD 79-25-05 last winter I thought that this would just be a routine check, probably like many vertical fins, I found a small crack, about ¼ inch long. I was relieved for the AD because I never would have found the crack otherwise. I was even more pleased for the AD when I drilled out the five rivets on the right side and the bracket fell off in my hand. My small ¼-inch crack was actually split all the way up through the five rivets on the left side. To make things worse, the week before I received the AD, I had been practicing spins and loops in the machine. This also puts a little more wood on the fire about the argument of doing aerobatics in old airplanes."

Other ADs

Some less serious ADs that are applicable to Luscombe airplanes are listed here. Most will have been complied with long before this late date; however, they are of interest. Have your mechanic make a complete search for ADs and their compliance as applicable to your individual airplane. **Warning:** This AD list is not complete for all the affected airplanes.

47-10-40: rework of rudder control arm on certain 8As
48-49-1: reinforcement of vertical stabilizer spar on 8 series
49-40-1: rework of trim tab control system on 11 series
49-43-2: inspection of stabilizer spar on all 8 series
49-45-1: reinforcement of landing gear bulkhead on 11 series
50-37-1: modification to the fuel system on 8Cs
51-10-2: inspection/replacement of control cables in 8 series
51-21-3: inspection of rudder bellcrank on 11 series
61-3-5: inspection of fuel lines coming from the wing tanks
74-26-9: inspect some magnetos
79-13-8: replace Airborne dry air pump
80-6-5: test magnetic impulse coupling
81-7-6: inspect/replace ac fuel pump
81-16-5: inspect magneto coil
82-20-1: inspect impulse couplers on Bendix magnetos
84-26-2: replace paper air filter each 500 hrs

STCs

A 150-hp engine conversion STC is available from Larsen Industries. In addition, they also sell parts, hardware, and interior upholstery kits. For further information contact:

Larsen Industries, Inc.
7790 Rawsonville Rd.
Belleville, MI 48111
(313) 482-0694

The following lists many other available STCs for the Luscombe series 8 airplanes: The STC number is followed by the item or part modified, and the name of the holder of the STC.

8 series

SA1-271. Metalized wings: Skycraft Design, 85 North Main, Yardley, PA 19067

SA4-173. Installation of Lycoming O-235 or O-290: H.M. Ruberg, 1300 North 28th St., Springfield, OR 97477

SA4-430. Metalized wings: Aircraft Modification and Repair, Municipal Airport, Hayward, CA 94541

SA4-463. Replacement exhaust system: Universal Aircraft Ind., Box 5306, Terminal Annex, Denver, CO 80217

SA4-560. Glass fabric covering: Glasco-Air Products, Inc, Oxnard-Ventura Airport, Oxnard, CA 93030

SA4-642. Installation of Lycoming O-290-D2: H.M. Ruberg, 1300 North 28th St., Springfield, OR 97477

SA4-840. Glass fabric covering: Air Fibre, Inc., Box 244, Altandena, CA 91001

SA344CE. Installation of Lycoming O-320: Luscombe Aircraft Corp., 3201 Cains Hill Place NW, Atlanta, GA 30305

SA589WE. Oil filter installation: Worldwide Aircraft Filter Corp., 1685 Abram Ct., Box 175B, San Leandro, CA 94577

SA5639SW. Use mogas: Steve Hinckley, 6528 Springriver, Fort Worth, TX 76118

SA2715WE. Carry-through spar beams: William Gratrix, Box 8217, Airport Station, San Fransico, CA 94128

8E

SA379GL. Installation of Lycoming O-235-C2C: Dewey Norton, 1351 Manton Blvd., Canton, MI 48187

8E/8F

SA229GL. Installation of Lycoming O-235-series: Larsen Industries, 7790 Rawsonville Rd., Belleville, MI 48111

SA230GL. Change to a one-piece cowl: Larsen Industries, 7790 Rawsonville Rd., Belleville, MI 48111

PARTS

UNIVAIR stocks most parts and hardware necessary to keep the Luscombe model 8s flying. Contact them at:

UNIVAIR Aircraft Corporation
2500 Himalyaya Road
Aurora, CO 80011
(303) 375-8882

6

Piper

NO OTHER NAME is more associated with small airplanes than Piper. In fact, many people refer to all small airplanes as Piper Cubs.

POSTWAR PIPER

The Piper Aircraft Corporation saw the same humps and valleys in the airplane market as did other airplane builders of the period. During the best of times, 1946, they built the largest number of airplanes ever, and by 1948 Piper was suffering like the other manufacturers (Fig. 6-1). The hayride was over.

As with Cessna, the 1980s took its toll and production of most small airplanes halted. At the time of this writing the company is in limited operation under the oversight of a bankruptcy court and is for sale. The real future of Piper is unknown.

CUBS AND OTHERS

Possibly the most famous Cub (Fig. 6-2) is the J3, actually a prewar plane. The Cub was introduced in 1939 and was produced again after the war (Fig. 6-3). The Army L-4 was really a J3 in olive drab (Fig. 6-4).

At one time J3s were coming out of the factory door at the rate of one every 10 minutes. Production of the J3 ended in 1947, after a total of 14,125 were built.

A simpler flying machine than the J3 has never been made, and it's the basis for other Piper models right through the Super Cub (Fig. 6-5). The J3 Cub is unique in the fact that all solo flight must be done from the rear seat.

Although no J3 Cub is known for great speed, the view from it, and other tandem-seat Cubs, is wonderful. The door is split in half and folds up against the wing, and down along the fuselage, getting out of the way completely.

An interesting side note is the fact some late J3s have aluminum spars in their wings.

Piper Production Numbers

Model	Production total	Serial series
J3	14125	
J4	1251	
J5	1507	
PA11	1541	11–1 – 11–1111
		11–1354 – 11–1678
PA12	3760	12–1 – 12–67
		12–69 – 12–4036
PA14	238	14–1 – 14–204
		14–490 – 14–523
PA15	387	15–1 – 15–388
PA16	736	16–1 – 16–736
PA17	214	17–1 – 17–215
PA18	10282	18–1 – 1–9055
PA20	1120	20–1 – 20–1121
PA22 Tri–Pacer	7670	22–1 – 22–7642
PA22 Colt	1820	22–8000 – 22–9848

* not all numbers in each series were used and in some cases the series appears to be deficient in quantity.

Fig. 6-1. Piper production numbers indicating the model numbers, production total, and serial number series.

J4 CUB COUPE

The J4 Cub Coupe, like the J3, was built before the war, from 1939 to 1941. The Coupe used many J3 parts, which kept costs of design and production to a minimum (Fig. 6-6). No Coupes were built after the war.

The Coupe seated two side-by-side and, as with all planes, specific model numbers varied with engines used. The J4A was powered with a Continental A-65 engine. The B and C models had Franklin or Lycoming engines, respectively, of the same horsepower. The E model used a 75-hp Continental engine.

Many years ago I had a J4A and flew it around West Texas. Let me tell you, many cars passed under my wings, beating me in the race with the wind.

CUB CRUISER

The J5 Cub Cruiser was introduced just before the war, in 1941, and seated three persons. Like the J4, the J5 shared many J3 parts (Fig. 6-7).

The pilot sat in a single bucket seat up front, and two passengers could sit, very cozily, on a bench seat in the rear.

Fig. 6-2. The famous CUB symbol.

After the war the J5C, with an O-235 Lycoming 100-hp engine, was brought out as the Super Cruiser (Fig. 6-8). The PA-12-100 Cruiser followed shortly, as an update to the J5C, and later the PA-12-108 with 108-hp. None of them will fly three adults off the ground on a real hot day unless the original engine has been replaced with something larger.

By the way, the J in the early Piper model numbers indicated Walter C. Jamouneau, Piper's Chief Engineer. Later the PA designator was utilized to indicate Piper Aircraft.

Smithsonian Institution Photo No. A47056A

Fig. 6-3. J3 Cub. For low, slow, and enjoyable flight, it's hard to beat a Cub. Notice the exposed cylinders on the engine.

Fig. 6-4. L4. This was the WWII Army version of the J3. Notice the greenhouse windows for greater visibility.

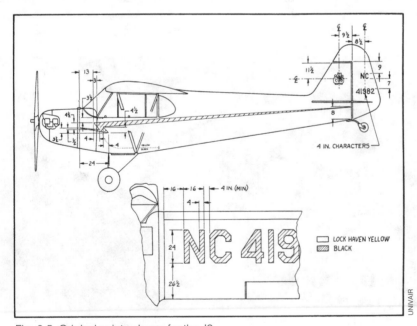

Fig. 6-5. Original paint scheme for the J3.

Fig. 6-6. J4. Using many J3 parts, Piper was able to keep parts development costs down. It seats two side-by-side.

CUB SPECIAL

The PA-11 Cub Special (Fig. 6-9) was introduced in 1947 as an updated version of the J3, allowing the pilot to solo from the front seat. The engine is completely enclosed by a cowling and could be either a 65-hp or 90-hp engine; production stopped in 1949.

VAGABONDS

The PA-15 was introduced as the Vagabond in 1948 (Fig. 6-10), it was a very basic airplane. The PA-15 had the Lycoming O-145 engine, rated at 65-hp, and seated two side-by-side. The main landing gear was solid, with the only shock-absorbing action coming from the finesse of the pilot at landing time.

Fig. 6-7. J5A. Built in 1941, this model seats three. Notice the exposed engine cylinders.

Fig. 6-8. PA-12 Super Cruiser. Built in 1946, this three placer has a 115-hp engine and re-placed the J5s.

A short time later the PA-17, which was also called the Vagabond, came out with more options, such as bungee-type landing gear, floor mats, and the Continental A-65 engine, which is said to have considerably more pep than the Lycoming O-145 (Fig. 6-11). A new PA15 sold for $1990 and the PA17 for $2195.

THE SUPER CUB

The Super Cub, PA-18 (Fig. 6-12), is basically an airplane whose roots can be traced back to the J3. Although built with a completely redesigned airframe, the PA-18 outwardly looks like a J3. It's a fun plane to fly. However, it is usually found working for its keep. These planes are utilized in photography, mapping, fish spotting, spraying, glider towing, bush flying, etc. Production of PA-18s started in 1949 and continued through the early 1980s with a production total in excess of 9000 planes. They were available with a variety of engines from 90- to 150-hp.

Fig. 6-9. PA-11 Cub. Unlike the J3, this plane can be soloed from the front seat.

Fig. 6-10. PA-15 Vagabond. The appearance of this plane is almost identical to the PA-17, also called the Vagabond.

THE COLT

The last entry of a two-place Piper airplane of tube-and-fabric design was the PA-22-108 Colt which was really a two-seat, flapless version of the Tri-Pacer, powered with a 108-hp Lycoming engine (Fig. 6-13). The Colt was meant to be used as a trainer, so if you're looking at one, a careful inspection of the airframe should be made. After all, trainers can be treated mighty rough. Between 1961 and 1963 Piper built 1820 Colts.

FAMILY PLANES

Piper started production of four-place airplanes with the PA-14 Family Cruiser in 1948. The PA-14 is really a modified PA-12, with an extra seat up front. It was small and grossly underpowered. The original price for a new PA-14 was $3825.

Fig. 6-11. PA-17 Vagabond. Much more complete than its predecessor the PA-15.

Fig. 6-12. PA-18 Super Cub. It is the final model for a design that started in the late 1930s, and ended in the mid 1980s. Its true Cub heritage is clearly seen.

The PA-16 Clipper (Fig. 6-14) replaced the Family Cruiser in 1949. The Clipper had shorter wings and fuselage than the PA-14, and was the forerunner of the "short wing" Pipers (PA-20s and 22s). The 16's fuselage is that of a PA-15/17 extended one bay to provide the room for two more side-by-side seats.

Both the PA-14 and the PA-16 are unique from the standpoint of controls (Fig. 6-15). They have sticks rather than the control wheels usually associated with four-place airplanes.

The Clipper was in production only a short time; however, it proved the viability of the particular design, which led to the PA-20 Pacer. The Clipper sold for $3985 and was the lowest priced four-place plane of the period.

Fig. 6-13. PA-22 108. The Piper Colt was really a Tri-Pacer with a smaller engine and without rear seat. It was the last of the Piper rag wings.

Fig. 6-14. PA-16 Clipper. This four-place plane generally is the same as the PA-14 in appearance but with shorter wings. It was the basis for the Pacer and Tri-Pacer series.

PACERS

In 1950 the PA-20 Pacer series appeared (Fig. 6-16). Like the PA-14s and 16s, the original PA-20s were fabric-covered and of conventional gear design. Like their predecessors, they didn't exhibit very exciting performance numbers.

Evolution of the Pacer saw more powerful engines each generation, however, the greatest step was the addition of the nosewheel. The nosewheel version became the PA-22 Tri-Pacer.

The actual PA-20 airframe continued until the end of the Piper tube-and-fabric era.

Fig. 6-15. The panel and controls of a PA-16. Notice the sticks—unusual for a four-place plane. Also note the location of the fuel tank.

Fig. 6-16. PA-20 Pacer. This four-place plane was available with 125 or-135-hp engines.

TRI-PACERS

Billed as an "anyone can fly it" airplane due to the trigear, the PA-22 was sold as an option to the Pacer (Figs. 6-17, 18). Sales of the Tri-Pacer soared, while those of the Pacer fell. General aviation was demanding easier-to-handle airplanes, and in the Tri-Pacer pilots found what they wanted. The Pacer was removed from production in 1954. PA-22s were built from 1951 until 1960 and can be found with 125-, 135-, 150- and 160-hp engines. The Tri-Pacers are good performers, give fair cruise numbers, even when compared to the modern all-metal designs, and can often be bought reasonably, if you are mechanically inclined and wish to do a restoration.

Fig. 6-17. PA-22 Tri-Pacer. One of the most economical four-place aircraft ever built. Based on the PA-20, it was available from 125-through 160-hp engines.

I know of no other airplane that can be purchased for less dollars, become a family project, rise in value with mostly labor being invested, and carry the whole family flying. A total of 7670 PA-22 Tri-Pacers were built before Piper moved on to all-metal airplanes.

See Figs. 6-19 and 6-20 for comparison of entry doors.

Fig. 6-18. The panel and controls of a Tri-Pacer panel. Note that it has the space to be equipped with most avionics.

Fig. 6-19. The fold-up-and-down door is characteristic of all the Piper tandem two-place planes. It opens up to the world and can be found on the J3, PA-11, and PA-18 models. The visibility it affords is outstanding.

Fig. 6-20. A left door is common to all Piper four-place aircraft from the PA-16 through the PA-22.

SPECIFICATIONS

Model: J3C-65
Engine
    Make: Continental
    Model: A-65-8
    hp: 65
    TBO: 1800
Seats: 2 tandem
Speed
    Max: 87 mph
    Cruise: 73 mph
    Stall: 38 mph
Fuel capacity: 12 gal
Fuel consumption: 4 gph
Rate of climb: 450 fpm
Transitions
    Takeoff over 50 ft obs: 730 ft
    Ground run: 370 ft
    Landing over 50 ft obs: 470 ft
    Ground roll: 290 ft

Weights
>   Gross: 1220 lbs
>   Empty: 680 lbs
>   Baggage: 20 lbs

Dimensions
>   Length: 22 ft 4 in
>   Height: 6 ft 8 in
>   Span: 35 ft 2 in

Model: J4A

Engine
>   Make: Continental
>   Model: A-65
>   hp: 65
>   TBO: 1800

Seats: 2 side-by-side

Speed
>   Max: 95 mph
>   Cruise: 80 mph
>   Stall: 42 mph

Fuel capacity: 25 gal

Rate of climb: 450 fpm

Transitions
>   Takeoff over 50 ft obs: 750 ft
>   Ground run: 370 ft
>   Landing over 50 ft obs: 480 ft
>   Ground roll: 300 ft

Weights
>   Gross: 1301 lbs
>   Empty: 650 lbs

Dimensions
>   Length: 22 ft 6 in
>   Height: 6 ft 10 in
>   Span: 36 ft 2 in

Model: J5

Engine
>   Make: Continental
>   Model: A-75
>   hp: 75
>   TBO: 1800

Seats: 3

Speed
>   Max: 95 mph
>   Cruise: 80 mph

Stall: 43 mph
Fuel capacity: 25 gal
Rate of climb: 400 fpm
Transitions
    Takeoff over 50 ft obs: 1250 ft
    Ground run: 750 ft
    Landing over 50 ft obs: 900 ft
    Ground roll: 400 ft
Weights
    Gross: 1450 lbs
    Empty: 820 lbs
Dimensions
    Length: 22 ft 6 in
    Height: 6 ft 10 in
    Span: 35 ft 6 in

Model: J5C
Engine
    Make: Lycoming
    Model: O-235-2
    hp: 100
    TBO: 2000
Seats: three
Speed
    Max: 110 mph
    Cruise: 95 mph
    Stall: 45 mph
Fuel capacity: 20 gal
Rate of climb: 650 fpm
Transitions
    Takeoff over 50 ft obs: 1050 ft
    Ground run: 650 ft
    Landing over 50 ft obs: 950 ft
    Ground roll: 450 ft
Weights
    Gross: 1550 lbs
    Empty: 860 lbs
Dimensions
    Length: 22 ft 6 in
    Height: 6 ft 10 in
    Span: 35 ft 6 in

Model: PA-11-65
Engine
    Make: Continental
    Model: A-65

hp: 65
TBO: 1800
Seats: two tandem
Speed
    Max: 100 mph
    Cruise: 87 mph
    Stall: 38 mph
Fuel capacity: 18 gal
Fuel consumption: 4.0 gph
Rate of climb: 514 fpm
Transitions
    Takeoff run: 350 ft
    Landing roll: 290 ft
Weights
    Gross: 1220 lbs
    Empty: 730 lbs
    Baggage: 20 lbs
Dimensions
    Length: 22 ft 4 in
    Height: 6 ft 8 in
    Span: 35 ft 2 in

Model: PA-11-90
Engine
    Make: Continental
    Model: C-90
    hp: 90
    TBO: 1800
Speed
    Max: 112 mph
    Cruise: 100 mph
    Stall: 40 mph
Fuel capacity: 18 gal
Fuel consumption: 4.7 gph
Rate of climb: 900 fpm
Transitions
    Takeoff over 50 ft obs: 475 ft
    Ground run: 250 ft
    Landing over 50 ft obs: 550 ft
    Ground roll: 290 ft
Weights
    Gross: 1220 lbs
    Empty: 750 lbs
    Baggage: 20 lbs
Dimensions
    Length: 22 ft 5 in

Height: 6 ft 8 in
Span: 35 ft 8 in

Model: PA-12
Engine
    Make: Lycoming
    Model: O-235-C
    hp: 100
    TBO: 2000
Seats: 3
Speed
    Max: 115 mph
    Cruise: 105 mph
    Stall: 49 mph
Fuel capacity: 38 gal
Fuel consumption: 6.5 gph
Rate of climb: 600 fpm
Transitions
    Takeoff over 50 ft obs: 2190 ft
    Ground run: 720 ft
    Landing over 50 ft obs: 1400 ft
    Ground roll: 470 ft
Weights
    Gross: 1750 lbs
    Empty: 950 lbs
    Baggage: 41 lbs
Dimensions
    Length: 22 ft 10 in
    Height: 6 ft 10 in
    Span: 35 ft 6 in

Model: PA-14
Engine
    Make: Lycoming
    Model: O-235-C1
    hp: 115
    TBO: 2000
Seats: 4
Speed
    Max: 123 mph
    Cruise: 110 mph
    Stall: 46 mph
Fuel capacity: 38 gal
Fuel consumption: 6.2 gph
Rate of climb: 540 fpm
Transitions

Takeoff over 50 ft obs: 1770 ft
Ground run: 720 ft
Landing over 50 ft obs: 1410 ft
Ground roll: 470 ft
Weights
Gross: 1850 lbs
Empty: 1020 lbs
Baggage: 80 lbs
Dimensions
Length: 23 ft 2 in
Height: 6 ft 7 in
Span: 35 ft 6 in

Model: PA-15/17
Engine
Make: Lycoming or Continental
Model: O-145 or A-65
hp: 65
TBO: 2000
Seats: 2 side-by-side
Speed
Max: 100 mph
Cruise: 90 mph
Stall: 45 mph
Fuel capacity: 12 gal
Rate of climb: 490 fpm
Transitions
Takeoff over 50 ft obs: 1572 ft
Ground run: 800 ft
Landing over 50 ft obs: 1280 ft
Ground roll: 450 ft
Weights
Gross: 1100 lbs
Empty: 630 lbs
Baggage: 40 lbs
Dimensions
Length: 18 ft 7 in
Height: 6 ft
Span: 29 ft 3 in
Model: PA-16
Engine
Make: Lycoming
Model: O-235-C1
hp: 115
TBO: 2000
Seats: 4

Speed
   Max: 125 mph
   Cruise: 112 mph
   Stall: 50 mph
Rate of climb: 580 fpm
Transitions
   Takeoff over 50 ft obs: 1910 ft
   Ground run: 720 ft
   Landing over 50 ft obs: 1440 ft
   Ground roll: 600 ft
Weights
   Gross: 1650 lbs
   Empty: 850 lbs
   Baggage: 50 lbs
Dimensions
   Length: 20 ft 1 in
   Height: 6 ft 2 in
   Span: 29 ft 3 in

Model: PA-18-90
Engine
   Make: Continental
   Model: C-90
   hp: 90
   TBO: 1800
Seats: 2 tandem
Speed
   Max: 112 mph
   Cruise: 100 mph
   Stall: 42 mph
Fuel capacity: 18 gal
Rate of climb: 700 fpm
Transitions
   Takeoff over 50 ft obs: 750 ft
   Ground run: 400 ft
   Landing over 50 ft obs: 385 ft
Weights
   Gross: 1300 lbs
   Empty: 840 lbs
Dimensions
   Length: 22 ft 5 in
   Height: 6 ft 6 in
   Span: 35 ft 3 in

Model: PA-18-108
Engine

Make: Lycoming
Model: O-235-C1
hp: 108
TBO: 2000
Seats: 2 tandem
Speed
Max: 117 mph
Cruise: 105 mph
Stall: 42 mph
Fuel capacity: 18 gal
Fuel consumption: 6.2 gph
Rate of climb: 850 fpm
Transitions
Takeoff over 50 ft obs: 650 ft
Ground run: 350 ft
Landing roll: 385 ft
Weights
Gross: 1340 lbs
Empty: 875 lbs
Dimensions
Length: 22 ft 5 in
Height: 6 ft 6 in
Span: 35 ft 3 in

Model: PA-18-125
Engine
Make: Lycoming
Model: O-290-D
hp: 125
TBO: 2000
Speed
Max: 125 mph
Cruise: 110 mph
Stall: 38 mph
Fuel capacity: 18 gal
Rate of climb: 1000 fpm
Transitions
Takeoff over 50 ft obs: 510 ft
Ground run: 210 ft
Landing over 50 ft obs: 600 ft
Ground roll: 300 ft
Weights
Gross: 1500 lbs
Empty: 845 lbs
Dimensions
Length: 22 ft 5 in

Height: 6 ft 6 in
Span: 35 ft 3 in

Model: PA-18-135
Engine
    Make: Lycoming
    Model: O-290-D2
    hp: 135
    TBO: 2000
Speed
    Max: 127 mph
    Cruise: 112 mph
    Stall: 38 mph
Fuel capacity: 36 gal
Rate of climb: 1050 fpm
Transitions
    Takeoff over 50 ft obs: 500 ft
    Ground run: 200 ft
    Landing over 50 ft obs: 600 ft
    Ground roll: 300 ft
Weights
    Gross: 1500 lbs
    Empty: 895 lbs
Dimensions
    Length: 22 ft 5 in
    Height: 6 ft 6 in
    Span: 35 ft 3 in

Model: PA-18-150
Engine
    Make: Lycoming
    Model: O-320-A2A
    hp: 150
    TBO: 2000
Speed
    Max: 130 mph
    Cruise: 115 mph
    Stall: 43 mph
Fuel capacity: 36 gal
Rate of climb: 960 fpm
Transitions
    Takeoff over 50 ft obs: 500 ft
    Ground run: 200 ft
    Landing over 50 ft obs: 725 ft
    Ground roll: 350 ft
Weights

Gross: 1750 lbs
Empty: 930 lbs
Dimensions
    Length: 22 ft 5 in
    Height: 6 ft 6 in
    Span: 35 ft 3 in

Model: PA-20-125
Engine
    Make: Lycoming
    Model: O-290-D
    hp: 125
    TBO: 2000
Seats: 4
Speed
    Max: 135 mph
    Cruise: 125 mph
    Stall: 48 mph
Fuel capacity: 36 gal
Fuel consumption: 7.7 gph
Rate of climb: 810 fpm
Transitions
    Takeoff over 50 ft obs: 1788 ft
    Ground run: 1372 ft
    Landing over 50 ft obs: 1187 ft
    Ground roll: 500 ft
Weights
    Gross: 1800 lbs
    Empty: 970 lbs
    Baggage: 50 lbs
Dimensions
    Length: 20 ft 4 in
    Height: 6 ft 2 in
    Span: 29 ft 3 in

Model: PA-20-135
Engine
    Make: Lycoming
    Model: O-290-D2
    hp: 135
    TBO: 1500
Speed
    Max: 139 mph
    Cruise: 125 mph
    Stall: 48 mph
Fuel capacity: 36 gal

Fuel consumption: 7.7 gph
Rate of climb: 620 fpm
Transitions
    Takeoff over 50 ft obs: 1600 ft
    Ground run: 1220 ft
    Landing over 50 ft obs: 1280 ft
    Ground roll: 500 ft
Weights
    Gross: 1950 lbs
    Empty: 1020 lbs
    Baggage: 50 lbs

Model: PA-22-108
Engine
    Make: Lycoming
    Model: O-235-C1B
    hp: 108
    TBO: 2000
Seats: 2 side-by-side
Speed
    Max: 120 mph
    Cruise: 108 mph
    Stall: 54 mph
Fuel capacity: 36 gal
Rate of climb: 610 fpm
Transitions
    Takeoff over 50 ft obs: 1500 ft
    Ground run: 950 ft
    Landing over 50 ft obs: 1250 ft
    Ground roll: 500 ft
Weights
    Gross: 1650 lbs
    Empty: 940 lbs
Dimensions
    Length: 20 ft
    Height: 8 ft 3 in
    Span: 30 ft

Model: PA-22-125
Engine
    Make: Lycoming
    Model: O-290-D
    hp: 125
    TBO: 2000
Seats: 4
Speed

Max: 133 mph
Cruise: 123 mph
Stall: 48 mph
Fuel capacity: 36 gal
Fuel consumption: 7.7 gph
Rate of climb: 810 fpm
Transitions
Takeoff over 50 ft obs: 1788 ft
Ground run: 1372 ft
Landing over 50 ft obs: 1280 ft
Ground roll: 650 ft
Weights
Gross: 1800 lbs
Empty: 1000 lbs
Baggage: 50 lbs
Dimensions
Length: 20 ft 4 in
Height: 8 ft 3 in
Span: 29 ft 3 in

Model: PA-22-135
Engine
Make: Lycoming
Model: O-290-D2
hp: 135
TBO: 1500
Seats: 4
Speed
Max: 137 mph
Cruise: 123 mph
Stall: 48 mph
Fuel capacity: 36 gal
Fuel consumption: 7.7 gph
Rate of climb: 620 fpm
Transitions
Takeoff over 50 ft obs: 1600 ft
Ground run: 1220 ft
Landing over 50 ft obs: 1280 ft
Ground roll: 500 ft
Weights
Gross: 1950 lbs
Empty: 1060 lbs
Baggage: 50 lbs
Dimensions
Length: 20 ft 4 in
Height: 8 ft 3 in

Span: 29 ft 3 in

Model: PA-22-150
Engine
    Make: Lycoming
    Model: 0-320-A1A
    hp: 150
    TBO: 1200
Speed
    Max: 139 mph
    Cruise: 123 mph
    Stall: 49 mph
Fuel capacity: 36 gal
Fuel consumption: 9.0 gph
Rate of climb: 725 fpm
Transitions
    Takeoff over 50 ft obs: 1600 ft
    Ground run: 1220 ft
    Landing over 50 ft obs: 1280 ft
    Ground roll: 500 ft
Weights
    Gross: 2000 lbs
    Empty: 1100 lbs
    Baggage: 100 lbs
Dimensions
    Length: 20 ft 4 in
    Height: 8 ft 3 in
    Span: 29 ft 3 in

Model: PA-22-160
Engine
    Make: Lycoming
    Model: O-320-B2A
    hp: 160
    TBO: 1200
Speed
    Max: 141 mph
    Cruise: 125 mph
    Stall: 49 mph
Fuel capacity: 36 gal
Fuel consumption: 9.0 gph
Rate of climb: 800 fpm
Transitions
    Takeoff over 50 ft obs: 1480 ft
    Ground run: 1120 ft
    Landing over 50 ft obs: 1280 ft

Ground roll: 500 ft
Weights
    Gross: 2000 lbs
    Empty: 1110 lbs
    Baggage: 100 lbs
Dimensions
    Length: 20 ft 4 in
    Height: 8 ft 3 in
    Span: 29 ft 3 in

AIRWORTHINESS DIRECTIVES

Most of the following ADs have been complied with, however, they are of interest. The logs should be checked by a mechanic for assurance of their compliance. **Warning:** This AD list is not complete for all the affected airplanes.

62-2-5: inspect rudder cable PA-18
63-23-2: inspect/replace valves & camshaft Lycoming O-320
64-5-4: inspect upper main oleo bearing PA-22
67-24-2: fuel tank placard PA-22
68-5-1: test exhaust system each 100 hrs J3, PA-12,14,16,18,22
69-23-3: inspect lower longerons PA-18 (150)
72-1-7: install engine mount PA-18 (105,125,135)
72-21-3: replace fuel line PA-20,22
73-9-6: install placard PA-22 (150,160) w/Lycoming O-320
73-20-8: inspect/rework UNIVAIR propeller tips
74-17-4: inspect fabric for failure PA-12,14,15,16,17,20,22
74-26-9: inspect Bendix magneto
75-8-9: replace oil pump shaft & impeller Lycoming O-235,320
76-6-6: inspect pulley flap control guards PA-12
77-3-8: inspect wing struts - most models
78-10-3: rework fuel cap - most models
79-13-8: replace Airborne dry air pumps installed after 5-15-79
80-25-2: inspect valve pushrods Lycoming O-235
81-6-8: inspect fuselage attachment tab PA-18 (150)
81-7-6: inspect ac fuel pump Continental engines
81-15-3: replace Bracket engine inlet air filter
81-16-5: inspect Slick magneto coil on various engines
81-18-4: replace oil pump shaft & impeller Lycoming O-235,320
81-25-5: replace the wing lift strut forks - most models
82-20-1: inspect impulse couplers on Bendix magnetos
84-26-2: replace paper air filter each 500 hrs
85-2-5: install brake placard PA-20,22
85-6-4: install & placard quick fuel drain valve - most models
87-10-6: inspect rocker arm assembly Lycoming O-320
91-14-22: required after propeller strike Lycoming engines

STCs

The Short Wing Piper Club is an excellent source for STC information For example, STC SA805EA, which allows the installation of a Lycoming O-320 150-hp engine in the PA-16 Clipper. Contact them at:

Short Wing Piper Club
c/o Bob Mills, Editor
220 Main
Halstead, KS 67056
(316) 835-2235

UNIVAIR is one of the best sources of information and parts for Piper classic airplanes. They put out a large number of fact sheets and books about these airplanes, including owner's manuals, parts manuals, service manuals, paint schemes, ADs and Service Letters, etc.

UNIVAIR holds numerous STCs of interest to the Piper owner including:

Conversion of a PA-22 Tri-Pacer back to a PA-20 Pacer. This is a very popular conversion, as can be seen at any air show. UNIVAIR sells all the parts, in a kit, for this particular STC.

Installation of a 180-hp Lycoming O-360 engine on the PA-22/20 airframe is a kit, without the engine.

UNIVAIR also holds STCs for the entire Piper classic line for replacement stamped aluminum ribs. For more information contact them at:

UNIVAIR Aircraft Corporation
2500 Himalaya Road
Aurora, CO 80011
(303) 375-8882

All models of the classic Pipers can have their brake systems modernized by Appalachian Accessories, Inc., Tri-City Station, Blountville, TN 37617. Contact them for further information.

Following are other STCs of interest to Piper airplane owners. The STC number appears first followed by the item or part modified, and the name of the holder of the STC.

J3

SA187AL. Installation of Continental C-90: Air Power Overhaul, Box 6025, Airport Annex, Anchorage, AK 99502

SA811SW. Modification to clipped wings and installation of Continental A-75: Keith Rawe, 418 Willow Ln., Baytown, TX 77520

SA1251WE. Add belt driven alternator: Gifford Sherman Co., 2000 Hawkins Way, Spring Valley, CA 92077

SA4-469. Glass fabric cover: Glasco Air Products, County Airport, Oxnard, CA 93030

SA5-13. Add tundra wheels: Ronald Sullivan, Box 110164, Anchorage, AK 99511

J3/PA-11

SA2057SO. Installation of shoulder harnesses: Kosola & Assoc., Inc., 5601 Newton Rd., Albany, GA 31706

J3 & up 2 seat

SA95AL. Installation of Maule tailwheel: Kennedy Air Service, Box 94, Valdez, AK 99686

J3 & up

SA99AL. Add tundra wheels: UNIVAIR Aircraft Corp., Route 3, Box 59, Aurora, CO 80011

SA11RM. Change to Cleveland brakes: UNIVAIR Aircraft Corp., Route 3, Box 59, Aurora, CO 80011

J3/PA-11

SA338CE. Installation of Continental C-90-12F: George Haveman, Home Acres Sky Ranch, Lake City, MI 49651

SA333CE. Omni-view window: George Haveman, Home Acres Sky Ranch, Lake City, MI 49651

J3 & up 2-seat

SA5-65. Add tundra tires: Alaskan Aircraft Equipment Supply, Inc., 4707 Spenard Dr., Anchorage, AK 99503

J3C/PA-11

SA111AL. Add tundra wheels: Jake Bryant, Jake's Aircraft Salvage, 3906 Barbara Dr., Anchorage, AK 99503

SA560GL. Add auxiliary fuel: Aero Fabricators, Inc., Box 181, Lyons, WI 53148

J3C

SA107RM. Installation of Continental O-200: UNIVAIR Aircraft Corp., Route 3, Box 59, Aurora, CO 80011

SA525CE. Clipped wing modification: Alfred Glaser, Box 87, Spaulding, NE 68665

SA457AL. PA-11 conversion: F. Atle Dodge Aircraft Maintenance, Box 6409, Anchorage, AK 99502

SA7435SW. Installation of Teledyne O-200: UNIVAIR Aircraft Corp., Route 3, Box 59, Aurora, CO 80011

SA158GL. Fiberglass cowl: Aero Fabricators, Inc., Box 181, Lyons, WI 53148

SA196GL. Gerdes Products wheels & brakes: Robert Howell, Route 2, Lewisburg, OH 45338

J3C/4/5

SA2NE. Change to Cleveland brakes: William Scherbon, Hadley Rd., Merrimac, MS 01860

J3F

SA394AL. Add tundra wheels: Jake Bryant, Jake's Aircraft Salvage, 3906 Barbara Dr., Anchorage, AK 99503

J4

SA297WE. Change propeller: Dwight Addington, 409 Serenade Way, San Jose, CA 95125

J5

SA320CE. Installation of Lycoming O-290-D2: Aircraft Service Co., 7134 Booth Dr., Prairie Village, KS 66208

J5A

SA305AL. Add auxiliary fuel: W.L. Stoddard, Stoddard Aero Service, 2550 East 5th Ave., Anchorage, AK 99501

SA495AL. Installation of Lycoming O-290-D: UNIVAIR Aircraft Corp., Route 3, Box 59, Aurora, CO 80011

J5A/C

SA396AL. Add tundra wheels: Jake Bryant, Jake's Aircraft Salvage, 3906 Barbara Dr., Anchorage, AK 99503

PA-11

SA3-47. Add auxiliary fuel: Bristow Aircraft Co., Bristow, IA 50611

SA35AL. Installation of PA-18 flaps: UNIVAIR Aircraft Corp., Route 3, Box 59, Aurora, CO 80011

PA-11 & up

SA573SW. Fiberglass wing tips: Harvey Ferguson, Plane Booster, Inc., Box 564, McAllen, TX 78501

SA2127WE. Fiberglass wing tips: Madras Air Service, Route 2, Box 1225, Madras, OR 97741

PA-12

SA1-297. Installation of Lycoming O-290: Central Maine Flying Service, Inc., DeWitt Field, Box 558, Old Town, ME 04468

SA4-456. Installation of Lycoming O-320: Kenmore Air Harbor, Inc., Box 64, Kenmore, WA 98028

SA4-519. Installation of Lycoming O-320: McKenzie Flying Service, 90600 Greenhill Rd., Eugene, OR 97402

SA10EA. Metalized wings: Skycraft Design, Inc., 85 North Main St., Yardley, PA 19067

SA397AL. Add tundra wheels: Jake Bryant, Jake's Aircraft Salvage, 3906 Barbara Dr., Anchorage, AK 99503

SA550EA. Installation of Lycoming O-360-D2A: Lawrence Bradway, North Windham, ME 04062

SA553AL. Installation of Lycoming O-360: Charles Center, 8134 Lake Otis Pkwy, Anchorage, AK 99507

SA644AL. Installation of Avco Lycoming O-320-D2A/B2B: Crosswinds STOL, 8134 Lake Otis Pkwy, Anchorage, AK 99507

SA656AL. Installation of Avco Lycoming O-320-A2B/E2D: Crosswinds STOL, 8134 Lake Otis Pkwy, Anchorage, AK 99507

SA2038WE. Installation of Lycoming O-320: Harold Nelson, 3005 Southwest Marshall St., Pendleton, OR 97801

SA202EA. Installation of Lycoming O-290-D/D2: Wag-Aero, Inc., Box 181, Lyons, WI 53148

SA517AL. Add a skylight: Crosswinds STOL, 8134 Lake Otis Pkwy, Anchorage, AK 99507

SA629AL. Fiberglass wing tips: Charles Center, 8134 Lake Otis Pkwy, Anchorage, AK 99507

SA653AL. Installation of Avco Lycoming O-320-A2B/C2B: Crosswinds STOL, 8134 Lake Otis Pkwy, Anchorage, AK 99507

PA-12/14

SA83AL. Installation of Lycoming O-320: UNIVAIR Aircraft Corp., Route 3, Box 59, Aurora, CO 80011

SA1819AL. Add left side cabin door: M. R. Borer Aircraft Service, 1307 West 39th Pl., Anchorage, AK 99503

PA-12 & up

SA22RM. Strut assemblies: UNIVAIR Aircraft Corp., Route 3, Box 59, Aurora, CO 80011

PA-12/22

SA388SO. Metalized wings: W.F. Robinson, Valley Air Service, Box 241, Lanett, AL 36863

PA-14

SA1-51. Installation of Lycoming O-290-D2: Arthur Barr, 1520 Franklin St., Williamsport, PA 17701

SA1-573. Installation of Lycoming O-320: Susquehanna Aero Marine, c/o Arthur Barr, 1520 Franklin St., Williamsport, PA 17701

SA4-78. Installation of Lycoming O-320: H. M. Ruberg, 1300 North 28th St., Springfield, OR 97477

SA4081. Installation of Lycoming O-290-D2: Marine Air, Inc., Friday Harbor, WA 98250

SA4-410. Installation of Lycoming O-320-A2A: Bates Aviation, Inc., 940 East 120th St., Hawthorne, CA 90250

SA4-412. Installation of PA-18 tail surfaces: Bates Aviation, Inc., 940 East 120th St., Hawthorne, CA 90250

SA57NW. Installation of Lycoming O-320-E2D: Harold Nelson, 3005 Southwest Marshall St., Pendleton, OR 97801

SA398AL. Add tundra wheels: Jake Bryant, Jake's Aircraft Salvage, 3906 Barbara Dr., Anchorage, AK 99503

SA538AL. Special tundra gear legs: Ronald Sullivan, Box 110164, Anchorage, AK 99511

SA541AL. Installation of Lycoming O-360-A2A: Charles Center, 8134 Lake Otis Pkwy, Anchorage, AK 99507

SA630AL. Fiberglass wing tips: Charles Center, 8134 Lake Otis Pkwy, Anchorage, AK 99507

SA657AL. Installation of Avco Lycoming O-320-A2B/E2D: Crosswinds STOL, 8134 Lake Otis Pkwy, Anchorage, AK 99507

PA-14/18/20

SA41AL. Add tundra wheels: Wesley Mathis, 154 North Broad St., Bremen, OH 43107

PA-16

SA399AL. Add tundra wheels: Jake Bryant, Jake's Aircraft Salvage, 3906 Barbara Dr., Anchorage, AK 99503

SA1511SO. Add auxiliary fuel: Swallows of Atlanta, Inc., 5250 Whispering Pines Ln., Conyers, GA 30207

SA1637SO. Installation of Lycoming O-320: Freitag's Aircraft Service, Inc., 107 Airport Entrance, Summerville, SC 29483

SA478AL. Fiberglass wing tips: Robert Sullivan, Box 11064, Anchorage, AK 99501

PA-16/20/22

SA1-282. Metalize cover: Skycraft Design, Inc., 85 North Main St., Yardley, PA 19067

PA-17

SA4-483. Glass fabric cover: Glasco Air Products, Inc., County Airport, Oxnard, CA 93030

PA-18

SA540AL. Special tundra gear legs: Ronald Sullivan, Box 110164, Anchorage, AK 99511

SA682AL. Installation of Lycoming O-320: Crosswinds STOL, 8134 Lake Otis Pkwy, Anchorage, AK 99507

SA1904NM. Schneider wheel skis: Richard Schneider, 20 Malaspina Dr., Eagle River, AK 99577

SA4-364. Glass fabric cover: Glasco Air Products, Inc., County Airport, Oxnard, CA 93030

SA4AL. Add auxiliary fuel: F. Atlee Dodge Aircraft Maintenance, Box 6409, Anchorage, AK 99502

SA143AL. Enlarged instrument panel: F. Atlee Dodge Aircraft Maintenance, Box 6409, Anchorage, AK 99502

SA894WE. Installation of Lycoming O-320-A2B: Sam Flint, Box 332, Holly, CO 81047

SA1588CE. Widen fuselage & increase load: B.A.R.F., Inc., Box 447, Clarence, MO 63437

SA1-349. Glider tow-hook: Schweizer Aircraft Corp., Box 147, County Airport, Elmira, NY 14902

SA1243CE. Change to Cleveland brakes: Flanagan Aircraft Company, 20224 R.D. Mize Rd., Independence, MO 64057

SA2338NM. Add tundra wheels: Richard Schneider, 20 Malaspina Dr., Eagle River, AK 99577

SA427AL. Fiberglass wing tips: Robert Sullivan, Box 110164, Anchorage, AK 99501

SA624AL. Fiberglass wing tips: Flanagan Aircraft Company, 20224 R.D. Mize Rd., Independence, MO 64057

SA490AL. STOL modification: Charles Center, 8134 Lake Otis Pkwy, Anchorage, AK 99507

SA388EA. Installation of Lycoming O-320-A2A/A2B: Wag-Aero, Box 181, Lyons, WI 53148

SA1368CE. Metalized interior, doors, and luggage door: Flanagan Aircraft Company, 20224 R.D. Mize Rd., Independence, MO 64057

SA36RM. Installation of Lycoming O-360-C2A/A3A: Jenson Aircraft, Inc., Peter Holbeny Jr., 8250 Cessna Dr., Peyton, CO 80831

SA532AL. Installation of Lycoming O-360-A2A: Charles Center, 8134 Lake Otis Pkwy, Anchorage, AK 99507

SA554AL. Third seat in baggage compartment: Ronald Sullivan, Box 110164, Anchorage, AK 99511

SA1900NM. Schneider wheel skis: Richard Schneider, 20 Malaspina Dr., Eagle River, AK 99577

SA4-1143. Installation of Lycoming O-320-A3B: Western Commander, Inc., 3011 Airport Ave., Santa Monica, CA 90405

SA92NW. Installation of Lycoming O-360-A2B: Aero Services Northwest, Box 156, Arlington, WA 98223

PA-18/20/22

SA3-654. Fiberglass nose: Dakota Aviation Co., Box 18, Huron, SD 57350

PA-18A

SA886CE. Metalized bottom of fuselage: Flanagan Aircraft Company, 20224 R.D. Mize Rd., Independence, MO 64057

PA-18/16/22

SA589WE. Add oil filter: Worldwide Aircraft Filter Corp., 1685 Abram Ct., San Leandro, CA 94577

PA-20

SA1-167. Installation of Lycoming O-320: Susquehanna Aero Marine, c/o A.E. Barr, 1520 Franklin St., Williamsport, PA 17701

SA401AL. Add tundra wheels: Jake Bryant, Jake's Aircraft Salvage, 3906 Barbara Dr., Anchorage, AK 99503

SA626AL. Fiberglass wing tips: Charles Center, 8134 Lake Otis Pkwy, Anchorage, AK 99507

SA635AL. Installation of Avco Lycoming O-320-A2B: Crosswinds STOL, 8134 Lake Otis Pkwy, Anchorage, AK 99507

SA3518NM. Add a skylight: Steve's Aircraft, 6085 Dodge Rd., White City, OR 97503

PA-20/22

SA1-325. Metalized aircraft cover: Skycraft Design, Inc., 85 North Main St., Yardley, PA 19067

PA-22

SA1-275. Installation of Lycoming O-320: Susquehanna Aero-Marine, c/o A. Barr, 1520 Franklin St., Williamsport, PA 17701

SA3-363. Add wheel fairings: KWAD Co., 4530 Jettridge Dr. NW, Atlanta, GA 30327

SA4-815. Installation of Lycoming O-320: McKenzie Aircraft Repair, 1300 North 27th St., Springfield, OR 97477

SA4-998. Add wheel fairings: Madras Air Service, Madras, OR 97741

SA481WE. Installation of Lycoming O-320-A1A: Kensair Corp., Box 322, County Airport, Broomfield, CO 80020

SA625AL. Fiberglass wing tips: Charles Center, 8134 Lake Otis Pkwy, Anchorage, AK 99507

SA536AL. Add auxiliary fuel: W.L. Stoddard, Stoddard Aero Service, 2550 East 5th Ave., Anchorage, AK 99501

SA181RM. Installation of Lycoming O-360-A4A: UNIVAIR Aircraft Corp., Route 3, Box 59, Aurora, CO 80011

SA453AL. Fiberglass wing tips: Ronald Sullivan, Box 110164, Anchorage, AK 99511

SA3519NM. Installation of skylight: Steve's Aircraft, 6085 Dodge Rd., White City, OR 97503

SA3610NM. Schneider wheel skis: Bushmaster Management Corp., Box 774407, Eagle River, AK 99577

SA847EA. Installation of Lycoming O-320-A/B: Wag-Aero, Inc., Box 181, Lyons, WI 53148

SA1-274. Installation of Lycoming O-320: Wag-Aero, Inc., Box 181, Lyons, WI 53148

SA936NW. Installation of Lycoming O-360-A1A: Milo DeAngeles, 5080 Glen Cairn Dr., North Buraby, BC Canada V5B3C1

SA1027NW. Add auxiliary fuel: Milo DeAngeles, 5080 Glen Cairn Dr., North Buraby, BC Canada V5B3C1

SA95NW. Installation of Lycoming O-360-A1A: Northwest Aero Aircraft Service, 2036 West Bakerview Rd., Bellingham, WA 98225

PA-22/22-108

SA45RM. Conventional gear conversion: UNIVAIR Aircraft Corp., Route 3, Box 59, Aurora, CO 80011

PARTS

At the time of this writing the Piper factory answers the telephone and advises the company is for sale and there is no airplane production. Parts, however, are presently available. Continued availability depends on future ownership of the company.

As an alternative to Piper, most parts and assemblies to maintain and service these aircraft are available from UNIVAIR:

UNIVAIR Aircraft Corporation
2500 Himalaya Road
Aurora, CO 80011
(303) 375-8882

Other suppliers advertise in *Trade-A-Plane* classifieds.

7

Stinson

STINSON airplanes of the postwar era had roots going into and before the war. However, the postwar models were of all new design. Stinson was a division of Convair, producer of many fine airliners and military planes.

THE 108 SERIES

Stinson introduced the 108 series airplanes in 1946. The 108 series were strong and rugged planes, as attested to by the number still in use as bush planes in Canada and Alaska.

The 108s are built of tube and fabric structures, although some have since been metalized, that is fabric removed and a metal skin installed in its place. All structural parts of the fuselage and wing are metal (spars, ribs, etc.). Although these airplanes all had conventional landing gear, they are considered to be extremely docile.

THE MODELS

108. The 108 had metalized flaps, an aluminum vertical fin and metal covered rudder and elevators (Fig. 7-1). It was powered by a 150-hp Franklin engine. The price was $5489.

108-1. The model 108-1 was the same basic airframe, engine, and gross weight, but was approved for floats and had an exterior baggage compartment door. It was marketed as the Voyager 150 with a plush interior and as the Station Wagon for carrying cargo.

108-2. The 108-2 (Fig. 7-2) introduced the same airframe with a 15-hp stronger engine. The gross weight was increased by 80 pounds. Base price was $5849.

108-3. The last of the Stinson classic airplanes was the 108-3. It had a larger fin, rudder trim, and a gross weight increase of 170 pounds. The 108-3 sold for $5989 in the passenger configuration and $6484 in the cargo setup.

With the collapse of the airplane boom in 1947 came the end of Stinson. A total of 5259 Stinson 108s was built before production was completely halted (Fig. 7-3). Many are still flying and a good number are available in various states of disrepair at older airports.

Fig. 7-1. Stinson 108 powered with a Franklin 150-hp engine. These airplanes were designated model 108 and 108-1.

THE ENGINES

Franklin engines were installed in all models of the 108 series. The engines came in two types: heavy case and light case. Only the heavy case is acceptable, as the light case did not stand up, and is claimed to be almost impossible to rebuild. At this late date it is unlikely a light case Franklin will be encountered. The 108 and 108-1 models were powered by 150-hp engines and the 180-2 and 3 models by 165-hp.

VOYAGERS AND STATION WAGONS

When referring to Stinsons, the terms Voyager and Station Wagon are generally used. Both names indicate versions of one basic airframe. The difference is appointments.

Fig. 7-2. Stinson 108 powered with a 165-hp Franklin engine were designated the model 108-2 and 108-3.

Stinson Production Numbers

Model	Serial series
108	108–1 – 108–742 (except 108–11)
108–1	108–11 and 108–743 – 108–2249 (except 108–1474)
108–2	108–1474 and 108–2250 – 108–3501 (except 108–3100)
108–3	108–3502 – 5260

Fig. 7-3. Stinson production numbers indicating the model numbers, production total, and serial number series.

The Voyager cabin is upholstered with cloth and vinyl. During the era it was considered plush. When the rear seat is removed a maximum of 350 pounds of cargo may be carried.

The Station Wagon is finished in wood and vinyl, similar to the "woody wagons" of the same era. The rear seat area has a reinforced floor and sidewalls and can carry 600 pounds with the rear seats removed. (See Figs. 7-4, 5, 6.)

UNIVAIR

Fig. 7-4. The Flying Station Wagon Cabin. (1) Rear safety belts; (2) cargo restrainer straps; (3) rear heater port; (4) map pocket. Notice the *woody* appearance.

Fig. 7-5. The Voyager Cabin. (1) Rear heater port; (2) map pocket. Notice upholstery all around.

PIPER SOLD STINSONS

In late 1948 Piper bought the Stinson Division from Convair. Included in the deal was an inventory of several hundred completed Model 108 airplanes. Piper never built any 108 series airplanes, but did sell off the stockpile.

SPECIFICATIONS

Model: 108
Engine
    Make: Franklin

Fig. 7-6. Typical cargo loading in the 108. (1) Outer front seat support; (2) outer rear safety belt lug; (3) center rear safety belt lug.

Model: 6A4-150-B31 or B3 or B4
hp: 150
TBO: 1200
Seats: 4
Speed
  Max: 148 mph
  Cruise: 117 mph
  Stall: 57 mph
Fuel capacity: 40 gal
Fuel usage: 8.5 to 11.0 gph
Rate of climb: 700 fpm
Transitions
  Takeoff over 50 ft obs: 1750 ft

Landing over 50 ft obs: 1610 ft
Weights
Normal gross: 2150 lbs
Utility gross: 1900 lbs
Empty: 1200 lbs
Baggage: 50 lbs
Dimensions
Length: 24 ft
Height: 7 ft
Span: 33 ft 11 in

Model: 108-1
Engine
Make: Franklin
Model: 6A4-150-B31 or B3 or B4
hp: 150
TBO: 1200
Seats: 4
Speed
Max: 148 mph
Cruise: 117 mph
Stall: 57 mph
Fuel capacity: 40 gal
Fuel usage: 8.5 to 11.0 gph
Rate of climb: 700 fpm
Transitions
Takeoff over 50 ft obs: 1750 ft
Landing over 50 ft obs: 1610 ft
Weights
Normal gross: 2230 lbs
Utility gross: 1925 lbs
Empty: 1250 lbs
Baggage: 100 lbs
Dimensions
Length: 24 ft
Height: 7 ft
Span: 33 ft 11 in

Model: 108-2
Engine
Make: Franklin
Model: 6A4-165-B3 or B4
hp: 165
TBO: 1200
Speed

Max: 153 mph
Cruise: 121 mph
Stall: 57 mph
Fuel capacity: 40 gal
Fuel usage: 9.5 to 13.0 gph
Rate of climb: 750 fpm
Transitions
Takeoff over 50 ft obs: 1400 ft
Landing over 50 ft obs: 1640 ft
Weights
Normal gross: 2230 lbs
Utility gross: 1925 lbs
Empty: 1250 lbs
Baggage: 100 lbs
(Voyager 350 w/o rear seats)
(Station Wagon 600 w/o rear seats)
Dimensions
Length: 24 ft
Height: 7 ft
Span: 33 ft 11 in

Model: 108-3
Engine
Make: Franklin
Model: 6A4-165-B3 or B4
hp: 165
TBO: 1200
Speed
Max: 158 mph
Cruise: 126 mph
Stall: 61 mph
Fuel capacity: 50 gal
Fuel usage: 9.6 to 13.0 gph
Rate of climb: 750 fpm
Transitions
Takeoff over 50 ft obs: 1400 ft
Landing over 50 ft obs: 1640 ft
Weights
Normal gross: 2400 lbs
Utility gross: 2000 lbs
Empty: 1250 lbs
Baggage: 100 lbs
(Voyager 350 w/o rear seats)
(Station Wagon 600 w/o rear seats)

Dimensions
    Length: 25 ft 2 in
    Height: 7 ft 6 in
    Span: 34 ft

AIRWORTHINESS DIRECTIVES

As with all the other classic airplanes, the ADs are old, however, compliance still is required. **Warning:** This AD list is not complete for all the affected airplanes. The STC number appears first followed by the part or item modified, and the name of the holder of the STC.

51-15-2: inspect the Franklin 6A4-165-B3 crank case for cracks
63-22-3: rework Marvel carburetor
73-20-8: inspect/rework UNIVAIR propeller tips
79-13-8: replace Airborne dry air pumps installed after 5-15-79
82-20-1: inspect impulse couplers on Bendix magnetos
84-26-2: replace paper air filter each 500 hrs

STCs

Due to the difficulty of maintaining the Franklin engines found in most Stinsons, UNIVAIR has developed STC SA1552NM for the 108-3 model calling for a Hartzell constant-speed propeller and Lycoming IO-360-A1A engine combination. This 200-hp conversion gives 35 additional horsepower over the 165 Franklin, hence improved performance. UNIVAIR claims greater fuel economy also. A complete kit, except for engine, is available.

UNIVAIR also sells a 180-hp STC with a fixed pitch Sensenich propeller for all models. As with the 200-hp STC, a complete installation kit is available. For further information contact:

UNIVAIR Aircraft Corporation
2500 Himalaya Road
Aurora, CO 80011
(303) 375-8882

Other STCs for the 108 series include:

108 series

SA1-374.   Add an oil filter: Fram Aerospace, Division of Fram Corp., 750 School St., Pawtucket, RI 02860

SA1-258.   Metalized control surfaces: Skycraft Design, 85 North main, Yardley, PA 19067

SA3-27.   Metalized wings: Howard Aviation, Inc., Box 1287, Peoria, IL 61601

SA4-46.   Installation of Lycoming O-435-1: Serv- Aero Engineering, Inc., Box 84409, 861 South Bringham Ave., Los Angeles, CA 90073

SA4-284.   Add a propeller spinner: Raymond Stits, 3665 Bloomington Blvd., Riverside, CA 02502

SA4-840.   Glass fabric covering: Air Fibre, Inc., Box 244, Alradena, CA 91001

SA4-1195.   Metalized wings: Air-Mod, 11379 Playa St., Culver City, CA 90230

SA327SO.   Tricycle gear conversion: W.F. Robinson, Box 241, Lanett, AL 36863

SA463CE.   Metalized fuselage: David Waldemer, Flying W Ranch, Fairdealing, MO 63936

SA666NW.   Teflon control yoke bushings: George Johnson, 10015 South Meridian, Puyallup, WA 98371

108-1/2

SA963NW.   Installation of Lycoming O-360-A1A: Alpine Aviation, 62270 Powell Butt Rd., Bend, OR 97701

180-2/3

SA4-398.   Installation of Lycoming O-435-C: Serv-Aero Engineering, Inc., Salinas Municipal Airport, Salinas, CA 93901

108-2/2

SA1199WE.   Installation of Continental O-470 series: Seaplane Flying, Inc., 1111 SE 5th St., Vancouver, WA 98661

108-2/3

SA1666NM.   Installation of Franklin 6A-335 series: Seaplane Flying, Inc., 1111 SE 5th St., Vancouver, WA 98661

108-3

SA238NW.   Fiberglass wing tips: Madres Air Service, Route 2, Box 1225, Madras, OR 97741

SA313NW.   Installation of Franklin 6A-350-C1: Seaplane Flying, Inc., 1111 SE 5th St., Vancouver, WA 98661

PARTS

UNIVAIR is the best source of information and parts for Stinson airplanes. They put out a large number of fact sheets and books about Stinsons, including owner's manuals, parts manuals, service manuals, and paint schemes.

8

Taylorcraft

THE HISTORY of Taylorcraft airplanes is interwoven with Piper Aircraft. C. Gilbert Taylor and his brother founded Taylorcraft and built several models before William Piper joined the firm and later bought it. After a split between Piper and Taylor, the latter set out on his own and built his factory in Alliance, Ohio.

BEFORE THE WAR

In 1939 and 1940 Taylorcraft built the BL-65, BC-65, and BF-65 planes. They were alike except for the engines, Lycoming, Continental, or Franklin, which are indicated by the second letter of the model designator. The engines were not fully cowled, and the planes appear similar to the Piper J3 with the cylinders protruding out each side. In 1940 the price for a Taylorcraft was $1495 and up.

In 1941 the model BC-12 was introduced. It saw a very short production life due to the start of WWII and the end of all civil airplane activities.

According to Joseph P. Juptner's book *U.S. Civil Aircraft Vol. 7*, a Taylorcraft BL-65 was the first U.S. aircraft to be fired upon in WWII. This was on December 7, 1941, at Pearl Harbor.

AFTER THE WAR

After the war, Taylorcraft, like all the other aircraft companies, restarted production. The new plane was the BC-12D, an updated version of the prewar BC-12. The BC-12D (Fig. 8-1) was a tube-and-fabric, side-by-side two-place airplane powered by a Continental 65-hp engine. Even though it was side-by-side and provided a larger cross section to wind resistance than the Piper J3, the Taylorcraft could outdistance the Cub by better than 20 miles in an hour.

Taylorcraft built four versions of the BC-12D:

Ace. The Ace had a single 12-gallon fuel tank, a single control wheel, and only one door. It sold for $1995 in December 1946.

Standard. The Standard sported dual controls (Fig. 8-2), an upgraded interior, and two doors. It sold for $2400.

Fig. 8-1. Taylorcraft BC-12D as it looked the day it was new.

Custom. held 18 gallons of fuel, had a radio, lights, and battery. It sold for $2500.

Deluxe. The Deluxe, with 24 gallons of fuel on board, sold for $2600.

The Deluxe carried extra fuel in 6-gallon wing tanks. The wings had spruce spars and tube steel drag struts. The landing gear was built of steel tubing and used shock cord for shock absorption. The cockpit featured dual control wheels and heel-operated mechanical brakes on the pilot's side.

Fig. 8-2. You could fly either by stick or wheel in the Taylorcrafts.

Production of the BC-12D (Fig. 8-3) continued through 1950, with better than 3000 planes delivered. Unfortunately, the Taylor airplanes never enjoyed Piper-like popularity.

Fig. 8-3. A stored BC-12D nearly fifty years old.

OTHER TAYLORCRAFTS

By late 1950 the original Taylorcraft Aviation Corporation, of Alliance, Ohio, was a thing of the past. A new company, Taylorcraft Incorporated, was started in Conway, Pennsylvania, and introduced the model 19. Also called the Sportsman, the model 19 was powered by an 85-hp Continental engine. A skylight, 24 gallons of fuel, and better brakes were the features of the 19. About 200 were built between 1950 and 1957.

When Taylorcraft again folded, the production rights were sold to UNIVAIR. From then until 1965 only parts were produced. UNIVAIR does not build airplanes.

In 1965 Charles and Dorothy Feris, pre-WWII Taylorcraft dealers, purchased the Taylorcraft rights and returned the production of the airplane to its original home of Alliance, Ohio (Fig. 8-4). Many of the Taylorcraft employees had airplane building experience dating back to the days of C. Gilbert Taylor.

In 1974 the model F(Feris)-19 was introduced. The F-19 was powered with the Continental O-200 engine and, other than slight updating, was little changed from the BC-12D airplanes. It really is difficult to improve upon something that is as good, and time-proven, as the postwar T-craft airplanes.

Charles Feris passed away in 1976, and his wife, Dorothy, took over and operated the company until it was again sold in 1985.

TODAY'S T-CRAFT

Although not true "classics" as defined by years of production, the Taylorcraft name continues to appear on new airplanes. A limited number of Taylorcraft's model F-21s (Fig. 8-5) were built by the Taylor Aircraft Corporation of Lock

Taylorcraft Production Numbers

Model	Production total	Serial series
BC/BL/BF–65(60)	2401	1000–3400
BC–12D	4191	6400–10590
BC–12D–1	22	10779–10800
BD–12D–85	41	12000–12038 & 12500–12501
19	n/a	unknown
F–19	153	F001–F153
F–21	22	F1001–F1022
F–21A	6	F1501–F1506
F–21B	17	F1507–F1523
F–22 series	n/a	F2203–and up

Fig. 8-4. Taylorcraft production numbers indicating the model numbers, production total, and serial number series.

Haven, Pennsylvania. The factory is housed in the old Piper plant where the famous Cubs were built.

In a 1990s bid for more of the market, Taylorcraft introduced the F-22A (Fig. 8-6), a tri-geared version of the basic Taylorcraft airframe. The F-22A is powered with a 118-hp Lycoming, has flaps (other models did not), and can operate from the most basic of airstrips. A more powerful version, the F-22C,(Fig.8-7), is pulled through the air powered by a 180-hp engine. Conventional geared versions are available. Prices range from $62,900 to $72,900.

Fig. 8-5. The F-21B was in production only a short time. The basic lines are unchanged from the BC-12D. Notice the extra side windows.

Fig. 8-6. The 1990s bid for part of the market includes this F-22A with a nosewheel.

EFFICIENCY

Taylorcrafts are good performers and very economical to operate. The BC-12Ds, if in good condition, are about the most efficient (cheap) airplanes you can fly. They use a little over four gallons of fuel per hour in the 65-hp versions.

MODEL DIFFERENCES

BC-65. The BC-65 powered by Continental 65-hp engine—prewar.

BF-60. This model is powered by Franklin 60-hp engine—prewar.

BL-65. The BL-65 is powered by Lycoming 65-hp engine—prewar.

BC-12. The BC-12 is powered by Continental 65-hp engine—immediately prewar.

BC-12D. The BC-12D model was the postwar version of the BC-12.

BC-12D-85. This model is a BC-12D powered by a Continental 85-hp engine.

BC-12D-4-85. The BC-12D-4-85 is a BC-12D-85 with additional rear side windows.

Model 19 was a BC-12D-4-85 with a Continental C-85-12 engine and modified side windows.

F-19. The F-19 was a model 19 with a Continental O-200 engine and increase in gross weight.

F-21. The model F-21 was an F-19 with a Lycoming O-235-l 118-hp engine and increase in gross weight.

F-21A. The F-21A was an F-19 with 40-gallon fuel tanks in the wings and increase in gross weight.

F-21B. The B version was an F-21A with 42 gallons of fuel in the wings and a metal belly skin and increased gross weight.

Fig. 8-7 The F-22, also available as the F-22C powered by 180 horses.

F-22. With flaps and a 118-hp engine, the F-21B became F-22.
F-22A. The F-22A is tri-gear version of the F-22.
F-22B. This model is the 180-hp version of the F-22.
F-22C. The F-22C is a tri-gear version of the F-22B.

SPECIFICATIONS

Model: BC-65 (and BF-60 & BL-65)
Engine
    Make: Continental
    Model: A-65
    hp: 65
    TBO: 1200
Seats: 2 side-by-side
Speed
    Max: 105 mph
    Cruise: 90 mph
    Stall: 38 mph
Fuel capacity: 12 gal
Rate of climb: 500 fpm
Weights
    Gross: 1150 lbs
    Empty: 640 lbs
Dimensions
    Length: 22 ft
    Height: 6 ft 8 in
    Span: 36 ft

Model: BC-12
Engine
    Make: Continental
    Model: A-65
    hp: 65
    TBO: 1200
Seats: 2 side-by-side
Speed
    Max: 105 mph
    Cruise: 95 mph
    Stall: 40 mph
Fuel capacity: 12 gal
Rate of climb: 600 fpm
Weights
    Gross: 1200 lbs
    Empty: 730 lbs
Dimensions
    Length: 21 ft 10 in
    Height: 6 ft 8 in
    Span: 36 ft

Model: BC-12D
Engine
    Make: Continental
    Model: A-65-8A
    hp: 65
    TBO: 1200
Seats: 2 side-by-side
Speed
    Max: 100 mph
    Cruise: 95 mph
    Stall: 38 mph
Fuel capacity: 12–24 gal
Fuel consumption: 4.2 gph
Rate of climb: 500 fpm
Transitions
    Takeoff run: 350 ft
    Landing roll: 300 ft
Weights
    Gross: 1200 lbs
    Empty: 750 lbs
Dimensions
    Length: 21 ft 9 in
    Height: 6 ft 10 in
    Span: 36 ft

Model: 19
Engine
    Make: Continental
    Model: C-85
    hp: 85
    TBO: 1800
Seats: 2 side-by-side
Speed
    Max: 120 mph
    Cruise: 110 mph
    Stall: 41 mph
Fuel capacity: 24 gal
Rate of climb: 700 fpm
Transitions
    Takeoff over 50 ft obs: 400 ft
    Ground run: 300 ft
    Landing roll: 300 ft
Weights
    Gross: 1500 lbs
    Empty: 860 lbs
Dimensions
    Length: 22 ft 4 in
    Height: 6 ft 10 in
    Span: 36 ft

Model: F-19
Engine
    Make: Continental
    Model: O-200
    hp: 100
    TBO: 1800
Seats: 2 side-by-side
Speed
    Max: 127 mph
    Cruise: 118 mph
    Stall: 43 mph
Fuel capacity: 24 gal
Rate of climb: 775 fpm
Transitions
    Takeoff over 50 ft obs: 350 ft
    Ground run: 200 ft
    Landing over 50 ft obs: 350 ft
    Ground roll: 275 ft
Weights
    Gross: 1500 lbs

Empty: 900 lbs
Dimensions
    Length: 22 ft 1 in
    Height: 6 ft 10 in
    Span: 36 ft

: 350 ft

s: 350 ft

Make: Lycoming
Model: O-235-L2C
hp: 118
TBO: 2000
Speed
    Max: 125 mph
    Cruise: 115 mph
    Stall: 48 mph
Fuel capacity: 42 gal
Fuel consumption: 6.0 gph
Range at 75% power: 732 mi
Rate of climb: 750 fpm

Service ceiling: 18,000 ft
Transitions
    Takeoff: 450 ft
    Landing: 500 ft
Weights
    Gross: 1750 lbs
    Empty: 1025 lbs
Dimensions
    Length: 22 ft 3 in
    Height: 6 ft 6 in
    Span: 36 ft

AIRWORTHINESS DIRECTIVES

As with all the other classic airplanes, the ADs are old, however, compliance still is required: **Warning:** This AD list is not complete for all the affected airplanes.

74-26-9: inspect Bendix magneto
75-18-5: inspect engine mount bolts F-19s
78-20-11: inspect aileron stop pins F-19
79-4-4: rewire starter solenoid F-19
79-13-8: replace Airborne dry air pumps installed after 5-15-79
81-7-6: inspect ac fuel pump Continental engines
81-16-5: inspect Slick magneto coil on various engines
82-20-1: inspect impulse couplers on Bendix magnetos
84-26-2: replace paper air filter each 500 hrs
87-3-8: inspect oil gauge hose F-19,21,21A
88-2-4: check Marvel carburetors on Lycoming O-235 series.

STCs

For information about an STC for installing a Continental C-85 on your BC-12D, contact:

Jack Gilbert
Box 246
Aliquippa, PA 15881
Phone: (412) 375-5396

Other STCs for Taylorcraft planes include the following. The STC number is listed first, followed by the item or part modified, and the name of the holder of the STC.

BC series

SA4-294. Installation of propeller spinner: Raymond Stits, 3665 Bloomington Blvd., Riverside, CA 92502

SA4-613. Add fiberglass wheel fairings: Richard Grunsven, Route 2, Box 187, Forest Grove, OR 97116

SA4-840. Glass fabric cover: Air Fibre, Inc., Box 244, Altadena, CA 91001

BC12D

SA661AL. Add a skylight: Gregory Clayton, Box 73204, Fairbanks, AK 99707

SA1901SW. Clipped wings modification: Swick Aircraft Corp., Route 1, Box 163B, Louisville, TX 75067

SA2891SW. Stick controls: Swick Aircraft Corp., Route 1, Box 163B, Louisville, TX 75067

For other modification ideas and information contact the type club listed in appendix A.

PARTS

Taylorcraft is currently producing the model F-22 series and can supply some parts for older models. At a point in the future the company plans to produce all the parts necessary to keep the classics in the air. Contact them at:

Taylorcraft Aircraft Company
P.O. Box 480
820 E. Bald Eagle St.
Lock Haven, PA 17745
(717) 748-8262

UNIVAIR is the most comprehensive source of information and parts for Taylorcraft airplanes. They put out a number of fact sheets and books about them including owner's manuals, parts manuals, and service manuals. Nearly all parts are available from them. For further information contact:

UNIVAIR Aircraft Corporation
2500 Himalaya Road
Aurora, CO 80011
(303) 375-8882

9

Engines

YOU ARE completely dependent on the integrity of your airplane's engine for your life, and the lives of your passengers. The more you know about it the better.

DEFINITIONS

Here are a few definitions to help you understand engines better:

TBO. TBO stands for time between overhaul and is the engine manufacturer's recommended maximum engine life and has no legal bearing for airplanes not used in commercial service. However, the TBO is certainly an indicator of engine life expectancy. Many well-cared-for engines last hundreds of hours beyond TBO, but not all. Poorly maintained engines do not reach TBO.

Overhaul. Overhaul means disassembly, repair, inspection, cleaning, and reassembly of an engine. The work may be done to new limits or to service limits—there is no standard. Some engine repair centers refer to an engine overhauled to new limits as **remanufactured**, a term having no official validity.

Rebuild. The term rebuild means the disassembly, repair, alteration, inspection, cleaning, and reassembly of an engine, including bringing all specifications back to factory-new limits. Only the engine's manufacturer can rebuild an engine. When so done, the engine is zero timed and comes with a new log book.

Top overhaul. Top overhaul means the rebuilding of the head assemblies, but not of the entire engine. In other words, the case of the engine is not split, only the cylinders are pulled. Top overhauls are utilized to bring oil burning and/or low compression engines within specifications. This kind of overhaul is a method of stretching the life of an otherwise-sound engine. A top overhaul is not necessarily an indicator of a poor engine. Its need might have been brought on by such things as pilot abuse, lack of care, lack of use of the engine, or plain abuse, such as hard climbs and fast letdowns. An interesting note: The term top overhaul does not indicate the extent of the rebuild job (i.e., number of cylinders rebuilt or the completeness of the job).

New limits. New limits indicate the dimensions and specifications used when constructing a new engine. Parts meeting these specifications will normally reach TBO with no further attention, except for routine maintenance.

Service limits. Service limits show dimensions and specifications below which use is forbidden. Many used parts fit into this category, making their use legal. It is unlikely, however, such parts will last the full TBO as they are already partially worn.

Nitriding. Nitriding is a method of hardening cylinder barrels and crankshafts to reduce wear, thereby extending the useful life of the part.

Chrome plating. Chrome plating is a process that brings the internal dimensions of a cylinder back to specifications by producing a hard, machinable, and long-lasting surface. Due to the hardness of chrome, break-in time for chromed cylinders is longer than for normal cylinders. An advantage of chrome plating is resistance to destructive oxidation (rust) within combustion chambers.

Cermicrome. Cermicrome is a trademarked process of chrome plating combined with an oil wettable silicon carbide impregnated coating.

Magnaflux/Magnaglow. These methods are used in examinations to detect invisible defects (cracks) in ferrous metals. Engine parts normally examined by these means are crankshafts, camshafts, piston pins, rocker arms, and cases.

Zygloe. Zygloe is used for detection of defects in aluminum parts.

ENGINE MODEL CODES

The model number of an aircraft engine usually describes either the horsepower—such as Continental C-85 (85 hp) or Continental A-65 (65 hp)—or the number will indicate the cubic-inch displacement of the engine rounded off to the nearest number divisible by 5 as in this example: Lycoming O-235 (233-cubic-inch displacement).

The O that appears as part of many airplane engine model numbers merely indicates that the engine is horizontally opposed in configuration, the only type that you will find in the classics.

Suffix codes describe individual models of engines differing in magnetos used, timing set, balancing, etc. Example: Lycoming O-235-L2C is an opposed cylinder engine of 235 cubic inch displacement. The suffix L2C indicates this particular model is the 118-hp version, which burns low-lead fuel.

CYLINDER COLOR CODES

Cylinder color codes are applied via paint or by banding a portion of the lower cylinder barrel. Orange indicates a chrome-plated cylinder barrel. Blue indicates a nitrided cylinder barrel. Green means that the cylinder barrel is bored .010 oversize, and yellow means .020 oversize.

SPARK PLUG COLOR CODES

Spark plug color codes identify the reach length of the required plugs. The color will be seen in the fin area of the cylinder between the plug and the rocker box. Grey or unpainted indicates short-reach plugs. Yellow indicates long-reach plugs.

USED ENGINES

Unless you're purchasing an airplane with a brand-new engine on it, you'll need to concern yourself with various phrases and facts. Many airplane ads proudly state the hours on the engine (i.e., 876 SMOH). Basically this means that there have been 876 hours of use since the engine was overhauled. Not stated is how it was used or how completely it was overhauled. There are few standards.

TIME VS. VALUE

The time (hours) since new or overhaul is an important factor when placing a value on an airplane. The recommended TBO, less the hours currently on the engine, is the time remaining. This is the span you will have to live in. Three basic terms are usually used when referring to time on an airplane engine:

Low Time—first ⅓ of TBO
Mid Time—second ⅓ of TBO
High Time—last ⅓ of TBO

Naturally, other variables come into play when referring to TBO and answers should be sought to the following questions:

Are the hours on the engine since new, rebuild, or overhaul?
What type of flying has the engine seen?
Was it flown on a regular basis?
Lastly, what kind of maintenance did the engine get?

Airplanes that have not been flown on a regular basis, and maintained in a like fashion, will never reach full TBO. The logbooks should be of some help in determining any questions about maintenance.

REGULAR USAGE

Manufacturers refer to regular usage as 20 to 40 hours monthly. However, there are few privately owned airplanes meeting the upper limits of this requirement. Let's face it, most of us don't have the time or money required for such constant use. This 20 to 40 hours monthly equates to 240 to 480 hours yearly. That's a lot of flying for the recreational pilot. When an engine isn't run, acids and moisture in the oil oxidize (rust) engine components. In addition, lack of lubrication movement causes the seals to dry out. Left long enough, the engine will seize and no longer be operable.

ENGINE ABUSE

Just as hard on engines as no use is abuse. Hard climbs and fast descents, causing abnormal heating and cooling conditions, are extremely destructive to air-cooled engines. Aircraft used for training often exhibit this trait, due to their type of usage (i.e., takeoff and landing practice).

MAINTENANCE

Naturally, preventive maintenance should have been accomplished and logged throughout the engine's life (i.e., oil changes, plug changes, etc.). Note that according to regulation, all maintenance must be logged.

BEWARE

Beware of the engine that has accumulated only a few hours use since an overhaul. Perhaps something is not right with the overhaul, or it was a very cheap job, just to make the plane more saleable. Remember, not all overhauls are created equal. Find exactly what was done during the overhaul and who did the work.

When it comes to overhauls I always recommend the large shops that specialize in aircraft engine rebuilding. I'm not saying that the local FBO can't do a good job. I just feel that the large organizations, specializing in this work, have more experience and better equipment with which to work.

Engines are expensive to rebuild or overhaul; even a Continental C-series, found on many of the smaller classics, will cost $6000 to $7000. And usually the cost is more than $8000 on the engines from the four-placers.

USING YOUR ENGINE

The following information is reprinted by permission of AVCO Lycoming, as found in their *Key Reprints* (*Key Reprints* are available by writing to AVCO Lycoming):

> We have received many inquiries from the field expressing concern over the limited availability of 80/87 grade fuel, and the associated questions about the use of higher leaded fuel in engines rated for grade 80/87 fuel. The leading fuel suppliers indicate that in some areas 80/87 grade aviation fuel is not available. It is further indicated that the trend is toward phase-out of 80/87 aviation grade fuel. The low-lead 100LL Avgas, blue color, which is limited to 2 ml tetraethyl lead per gallon, will gradually become the only fuel available for piston engines. Whenever 80/87 is not available you should use the lowest lead 100 grade fuel available. Automotive fuels should never be used as a substitute for aviation fuel in aircraft engines.
>
> The continuous use, more than 25 percent of the operating time, with the higher leaded fuels in engines certified for 80 octane fuel can result in increased engine deposits both in the combustion chamber and in the engine oil. It may require increased spark plug maintenance and more frequent oil changes. The frequency of spark plug maintenance and oil drain periods will be governed by the amount of lead per gallon and the type of operation. Operation at full rich mixture requires more frequent maintenance periods; therefore it is important to use properly approved mixture leaning procedures. To reduce or keep engine deposits at a minimum when using the higher leaded fuels, 100LL Avgas blue, or 100 green, it is essential that the following four conditions of operation and maintenance are applied.
>
> A. Fuel management required in all modes of flight operation. (See A, General Rules.)

B. Prior to engine shutdown run up to 1200 rpm for one minute to clean out any unburned fuel after taxiing in. (See B, Engine Shutdown.)

C. Replace lubricating oil and filters each 50 hours of operation, under normal environmental conditions. (See C, Lubrication Recommendations.)

D. Proper selection of spark plug types and good maintenance are necessary. (See D, Spark Plugs.) The use of economy cruise engine leaning whenever possible will keep deposits to a minimum. Pertinent portions of the manual leaning procedures as recommended in Avco Lycoming Service Instruction No. 1094 are reprinted here for reference.

A. General rules

(1) Never lean the mixture from full rich during takeoff, climb or high-performance cruise operation unless the airplane owner's manual advises otherwise. However, during takeoff from high elevation airports or during climb at higher altitudes, roughness or reduction of power may occur at full rich mixtures. In such a case the mixture may be adjusted only enough to obtain smooth engine operation. Careful observation of temperature instruments should be practiced.

(2) Operate the engine at maximum power mixture for performance cruise powers and at best economy mixture for economy cruise power, unless otherwise specified in the airplane owner's manual.

(3) Always return the mixture to full rich before increasing power settings.

(4) During let-down and reduced power flight operations it may be necessary to manually lean or leave the mixture setting at cruise position prior to landing. During the landing sequence the mixture control should then be placed in the full rich position, unless landing at high elevation fields where leaning may be necessary.

(5) Methods for manually setting maximum power or best economy mixture.

a. Engine tachometer —airspeed indicator method:

The tachometer and/or the airspeed indicator may be used to locate, approximately, maximum power and best economy mixture ranges. When a fixed-pitch propeller is used, either or both instruments are useful indicators. If the airplane uses a constant-speed propeller, the airspeed indicator is useful. Regardless of the propeller type, set the controls for the desired cruise power as shown in the owner's manual. Gradually lean the mixture from full rich until either the tachometer or the airspeed indicator are reading peaks. At peak indication the engine is operating in the maximum power range.

b. For cruise power:

Where best economy operation is allowed by the manufacturer, the mixture is first leaned from full rich to maximum power, then leaning slowly continued until engine operation becomes rough or until engine power is rapidly diminishing as noted by an undesirable decrease in airspeed. When either condition occurs, enrich the mixture sufficiently to obtain an evenly firing engine or the regain of most of the lost airspeed or engine rpm. Some slight engine power and airspeed must be sacrificed to gain best economy mixture setting.

c. Exhaust gas temperature method (EGT):

Refer to Service Instruction No. 1094 for procedure.

Recommended fuel management Manual leaning, will not only result in less engine deposits and reduced maintenance cost, but will provide more economical operation and fuel saving.

B. Engine shutdown

The deposit formation rate can be greatly retarded by controlling ground operation to minimize separation of the non-volatile components of the higher leaded aviation fuels. This rate can be accelerated by (1) Low mixture temperatures and (2) Excessively rich fuel/air mixtures associated with the idling and taxiing operations. Therefore, it is important that engine idling speeds should be set at their proper 600 to 650 rpm range with the idle mixture adjusted properly to provide smooth idling operation. Shutdown procedure recommends setting rpm at 1200 for one minute prior to shutdown.

C. Lubrication recommendations

Many of the engine deposits formed by the use of the higher leaded fuel are in suspension within the engine oil and are not removed by a full flow filter. When sufficient amounts of these contaminants in the oil reach high temperature areas of the engine they can be baked out, resulting in possible malfunctions such as in exhaust valve guides, causing sticking valves. When using the higher leaded fuels, the recommended oil drain period of 50 hours should not be extended, and if occurrences of valve sticking is noted, all guides should be reamed using the procedures as stated in Service Instruction No. 1116, and a reduction in the oil drain periods and oil filter replacement used.

D. Spark plugs

Spark plugs should be rotated from the top to bottom on a 50-hour basis, and should be serviced on a 100-hour basis. If excessive spark plug lead fouling occurs, the selection of a hotter plug from the approved list in Service Instruction No. 1042 may be necessary. However, depending on the type of lead deposit formed, a colder plug from the approved list may better resolve the problem. Depending on the lead content of the fuel and the type of operation, more frequent cleaning of the spark plugs may be necessary. Where the majority of operation is at low power, such as patrol, a hotter plug would be advantageous. If the majority of operation is at high cruise power, a colder plug is recommended.

AVIATION FUELS

All of the classic airplanes have engines that were designed to use 80/87 octane avgas. Currently there is great concern about the limited availability of 80/87 fuel and the use of a higher grade fuel in the older engines designed for its use.

Most fuel suppliers state that there are some geographical areas where 80/87 grade fuel is not generally available. A few readily admit that the trend is towards a complete phaseout of 80/87 grade aviation fuel. The fuel suppliers state that in the absence of 80/87 grade fuel, the next highest grade available should be used. This means using 100LL. However, with continual use (defined as more than 25% of operating time) the higher rated fuel can cause an increase in engine deposits both in the combustion chamber and in the crank case oil. This equates to increased spark plug maintenance and more frequent oil changes at a minimum. Internal engine damage in the valve train is also common (and expensive).

Fuel suppliers claim that low-lead 100LL Avgas, blue in color, which contains 2 ml (milliliters) tetraethyl lead per gallon, will gradually become the only fuel available for piston-powered aircraft engines.

COLOR CODING OF AVGAS

Aviation fuels are color coded to reduce confusion among the various fuels:

Red: 80 octane containing .50 ml lead/gal.
Blue: 100 octane containing 2 ml lead/gal.
Green: 100 octane containing 3 ml lead/gal.

VALVE MODIFICATIONS

Valve modifications that you should watch for have been made to some Continental engines. These changes are to relieve the valve erosion problems encountered when using 100LL Avgas.

A-65/A-75: Replace the intake valves with part #639661, and the exhaust valves with part #639662.

C-75/C-85/C-90/C-145/O-200/O-300: Replace the intake valves with part #641792, and intake valve seats with part #641793.

There are similar modifications available for the AVCO Lycoming engines. These modifications will be noted in the engine log. Check for them.

Fine wire spark plugs, if approved for your engine, are claimed to be less prone to lead fouling.

USE OF AUTO FUELS

An alternative to the use of expensive avgas is automobile fuel, commonly referred to as mogas. Although the use of mogas was quite common some years ago and many classic airplanes used it regularly, it was not legal at that time.

STCs

The use of auto fuel in an airplane can be legalized by purchasing a Supplemental Type Certificate (STC) for your particular airplane. An STC is an authorization allowing a proven modification to be made to your airplane. In the case of an auto fuel STC the modification generally consists of a logbook entry, by a licensed mechanic, and slight fuel system adjustments.

GOOD NEWS

There are pluses and minuses to mogas use and the subject should be explored carefully before making a decision for its use. On the positive side is economy. Unleaded auto fuel is certainly less expensive than 100LL. At the time of this writing mogas is selling for $1.02 at the pumps and avgas is at $2.25.

Auto fuel appears to operate well in the older engines that were designed for 80/87 octane fuel with a reduction of the problems associated with 100LL avgas use. If you have a private gas tank you will most likely find it easier to locate a jobber willing to keep it filled with auto fuel than avgas. Most avgas dealers refuse to make small deliveries.

BAD NEWS

On the negative side is the lack of consistent formulation among the various brands. Most damaging is the inclusion of alcohol, which is chemically destructive to aircraft fuel systems and some auto systems too.

Some FBOs are reluctant to make mogas available for liability reasons, reduced profit, arbitrary rules from airport commissions, or a threat of supply cutoff by a displeased avgas distributor. Lycoming and Continental both state that the use of mogas will void all warranties and recommend against its use in all cases.

If you decide to use mogas, be sure your fuel complies with Specification D-439 and D-4814 by ASTM (American Society for Testing Materials). Compliance should be no problem if you select from major brand names, however, some lesser brands in the 17 states not requiring compliance with these standards should be checked before use. States that do not require compliance with the ASTM standards:

Alaska	Missouri	New York	Texas
Kentucky	Nebraska	Ohio	Vermont
Maine	New Hampshire	Oregon	Washington
Michigan	New Jersey	Pennsylvania	West Virginia

The FAA says any automotive fuel is okay except those containing ethanol or methanol (IAW AC 23.1521) and declares that auto fuels can lead to reduced maintenance costs (FAA AC 91-33). The FAA also advises not to use fuels containing MTBE (synthetic alcohol substitutes) in aircraft engines (AC 91-40). The latter is generally found only as an octane booster in premium grade fuels

MORE BAD NEWS

It is possible that legislation requiring 10% oxygenates in auto fuels (alcohol) to reduce air pollution could have an adverse affect upon the STCs for auto fuels. As formulas are changed they might no longer meet the requirements of D-439.

STC SOURCES

There are two suppliers of auto fuel STCs. For further information about the legal use of auto fuels in your airplane, contact:

Experimental Aircraft Association
Wittman Field
Oshkosh, WI 54903
(414) 426-4800

or

Petersen Aviation, Inc.
Auto Fuel STCs
RR #1 Box 18
Minden, NE 68959
(308) 237-9338

APPROVED AIRPLANES

Both the EAA and Petersen Aviation have ongoing programs for testing airplanes and obtaining STCs for the use of auto fuel. Currently the following airframes and engines are approved:

Aeronca

7AC
7BCM
7CCM
7DC
7EC
7FC
11AC
11CC
15AC

Cessna

120
140
140A
170A
170B

Luscombe

8
8A
8B
8C
8D
8E
8F

Piper

J3C
J4A
PA-11
PA-12
PA-14
PA-15
PA-16

PA-18-105/125/135/150
PA-20-115/135
PA-22-108/135/150/160

Stinson

108
108-1
108-2
108-3

Taylorcraft

BC-65
BC-12D
BC-12D-85
BC-12D-4-85
19
F-19

TESTING FOR ALCOHOL IN MOGAS

If you are a user of mogas, and you suspect that your choice of fuel might contain alcohol (used as a volatility booster), here is a simple test to do:

(1) Mix 9 parts of fuel with 1 part water.

(2) Shake the mixture and let it stand for a few minutes.

After the mixture settles out, look for a dividing line between the water and the gas. The water and any alcohol will settle to the bottom of the test solution. You have real gasoline if you still have 9 parts gasoline and one part water. If you have tested a fuel containing alcohol, you will have 8 parts gasoline and 2 parts of a water/alcohol mixture. Alcohol readily mixes with water, causing it to separate from the gasoline and settle to the bottom.

NEVER USE ANY
MOGAS THAT CONTAINS ALCOHOL!

For testing purposes, a chemist's graduate is recommended. These instruments, consisting of marked plastic or glass tubes, are available from chemical supply houses and swimming pool supply stores. For ease of use, obtain one marked in divisions of 10s that holds 10 ounces of liquid.

ENGINE APPLICATIONS AND SPECIFICATIONS

The following indicates model numbers, horsepower, fuel required, takeoff rpm, recommended TBO, and the airplanes the engines were originally installed in. The model number appears first, followed by the hp of the engine, the octane level of fuel required, takeoff rpm and finally the TBO. Below each listing are names of aircraft in which the engines are installed.

Continental

Model	hp	Fuel	T/O rpm	TBO
A-65-8	65	80	2300	1800 hrs (Fig. 9-1)

Model	hp	Fuel	T/O rpm	TBO
Aeronca 7AC/11AC				
Ercoupe 415C				
Luscombe 8A				
Piper J3C/J4A/PA-11/PA-17				
Taylorcraft BC-12D				
A-75	75	80	2600	1800
Luscombe 8C/8D				
Piper J5				
C-75-12	75	80	2275	1800
Ercoupe 415D				
C-85-8F	85	80	2575	1800
Aeronca 7DC/11CC				
C-85-12	85	80	2575	1800 (Fig. 9-2)
Aeronca 7BCM				
*Alon				
Cessna 120/140				
Ercoupe 415E/415G				
Luscombe 8E				
Taylorcraft BC-12D-85				
C-90-12F	90	80	2625	1800
Aeronca 7CCM/7EC				
Alon				
Cessna 140 series				
Forney F1/F1A				
Luscombe 8F				
Piper PA-18				
C-90-16F	90	80	2625	1800
Alon				
Cessna 140 series				
Mooney M-10				
C-145-2	145	80	2700	1800
Aeronca 15				
Cessna 170 series				
O-200	100	80	2750	1800 (Fig. 9-3)
Taylorcraft F-19				
O-300	145	80	2700	1800
Cessna 170B				

Fig. 9-1. This Continental 65-hp engine is mounted on a Piper J3 Cub. Notice the magneto on the rear of the engine, the unshielded spark plugs, exhaust pipes, and how the engine mounts are attached to the fire wall.

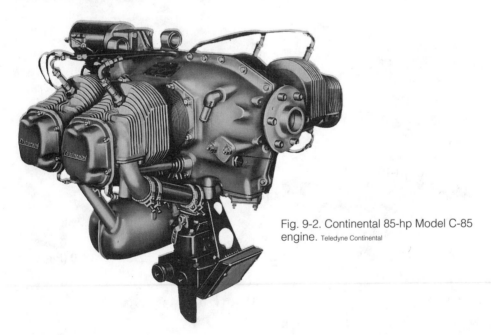

Fig. 9-2. Continental 85-hp Model C-85 engine. Teledyne Continental

Fig. 9-3. The Continental O-200 engine. This engine is popular for use in aircraft modification for increased engine power and performance. Teledyne Continental

Model	hp	Fuel	T/O rpm	TBO
Franklin				
2A-120B	60	80	N/A	1500
Champion 7-ACA				
6A4-150	50	80	2600	1200
Stinson 108				
6A4-165	165	80	2800	1200
Stinson 108				
Lycoming				
O-145-B	65	80	N/A	N/A
Luscombe 8B				
O-235-C1B	115	80	2800	2000
Piper J5C/PA-11/ PA-12/PA-14/ PA-16/PA-18				
O-235-C2	115	80	2800	2000 (Fig. 9-4)
Piper PA-18/PA-22				
O-235-L2C	118	100	2800	2000
Taylorcraft F-21				

Model	hp	Fuel	T/O rpm	TBO
O-290-D	130	80	2800	2000
Piper PA-18/PA-20/PA-22				
O-290-D2	140	80	2800	1500
Piper PA-18/PA-20/PA-22				
O-320-A1A	150	80	2700	1200(Fig. 9-5)
Piper PA-22				
O-320-A2A	150	80	2700	1200(Fig. 9-6)
Piper PA-18/PA-22				
O-320-A1B	150	80	2700	1200
Piper PA-22				
O-320-A2B	150	80	2700	1200
Piper PA-18/PA-22				
O-320-B2A	160	91	2700	1200
Piper PA-22				

O-320 series engines may have the TBO extended to 2000 hrs by installing ½-inch exhaust valves.

ENGINE STORAGE

Earlier I mentioned that a healthy engine must be exercised and should see 20 to 40 hours of use monthly. But, I did not mention what to do if the plane is to be parked for long periods of time, such as over the winter.

The following information is provided courtesy of Teledyne Continental, applies to all aircraft engines, and shows to what extent you must go to care for your engine investment.

GENERAL

Engines in aircraft that are flown only occasionally tend to exhibit cylinder wall corrosion more than engines in aircraft that are flown frequently.

Of particular concern are new engines or engines with new or freshly honed cylinders after a top or major overhaul. In areas of high humidity, there have been instances where corrosion has been found in cylinders after an inactive period of only a few days. When cylinders have been operated for approximately 50 hours, the varnish deposited on the cylinder walls offers some protection against corrosion.

Obviously, proper steps must be taken on engines used infrequently to lessen the possibility of corrosion. This is especially true if the aircraft is based near the coast or in areas of high humidity and flown less than once a week.

In all geographical areas the best method of preventing corrosion of the cylinders and other internal parts of the engine is to fly the aircraft at least once a week long enough to reach normal operating temperatures, which will vaporize moisture and other byproducts of combustion. Aircraft engine storage recommendations are broken down into the following categories:

Flyable storage (7 to 30 days)
Temporary storage (up to 90 days)
Indefinite storage

FLYABLE STORAGE (7 TO 30 DAYS)

(a) Service aircraft per normal airframe manufacturer's instructions.

(b) Each seven days during flyable storage, the propeller should be rotated by hand without running the engine. Rotate the engine six revolutions, stop the propeller 45 to 90 degrees from the original position. For maximum safety, accomplish engine rotation as follows:

(1) Verify magneto switches are OFF.

(2) Throttle position CLOSED.

(3) Mixture control IDLE CUTOFF.

(4) Set brakes and block aircraft wheels.

(5) Leave aircraft tiedowns installed and verify that the cabin door latch is open.

(6) Do not stand within the arc of the propeller.

(c) If at the end of 30 days the aircraft is not removed from storage, the aircraft should be flown for 30 minutes, reaching, but not exceeding, normal oil and cylinder temperatures. If the aircraft cannot be flown it should be re-preserved in accordance with "B" (Temporary Storage) or "C" (Indefinite Storage).

TEMPORARY STORAGE (UP TO 90 DAYS)

(a) Preparation for storage

(1) Remove the top spark plug and spray atomized preservative oil (lubrication oil-contact and volatile corrosion-inhibited, MIL-L-46002, Grade 1) at room temperature, through upper spark plug hole of each cylinder with the piston in approximately the bottom dead center position. Rotate crankshaft as each pair of opposite cylinders is sprayed. Stop crankshaft with no piston at top dead center.

Note: Approved preservative oils recommended for use in Teledyne Continental engines for temporary and indefinite storage are MIL-L-46002, Grade 1 Oils such as NOX RUST VCI-105, available from Daubert Chemical Co., 4700 S. Central Ave., Chicago, IL 60600 and TECTYL 859A from Ashland Oil, Inc., 1401 Winchester Ave., Ashland, KY 41101.

Fig. 9-4. Lycoming O-235 engine.
AVCO Lycoming

(2) Respray each cylinder without rotating crank, to thoroughly cover all surfaces of the cylinder interior, move the nozzle or spray gun from the top to the bottom of the cylinder.

(3) Reinstall spark plugs.

(4) Apply preservative to engine interior by spraying the above specified oil (approximately two ounces) through the oil filler tube.

Fig. 9-5. Lycoming O-320 engine installed in a Piper Tri-Pacer. Notice the baffles that control the air flow around the engine. Lower left is the alternator, lower center is the oil cooler, lower right is the starter.

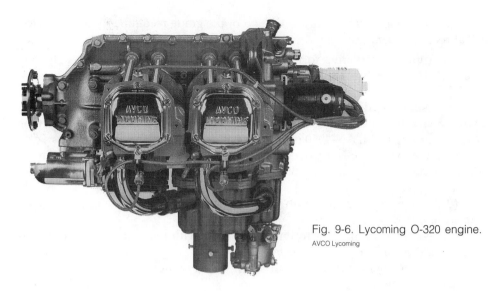

Fig. 9-6. Lycoming O-320 engine.
AVCO Lycoming

(5) Seal all engine openings exposed to the atmosphere using suitable plugs, or moisture resistant tape, and attach red streamers at each point.

(6) Engines, with propellers installed, that are preserved for storage in accordance with this section should have a tag affixed to the propeller in a conspicuous place with the following notation on the tag: "DO NOT TURN PROPELLER—ENGINE PRESERVED."

(b) Removal from storage

(1) Remove seals, tape, paper, and streamers from all openings.

(2) With bottom spark plugs removed from the cylinders, hand turn propeller several revolutions to clear excess preservative oil, then reinstall spark plugs.

(3) Conduct normal start-up procedure.

(4) Give the aircraft a thorough cleaning and visual inspection. A test flight is recommended.

INDEFINITE STORAGE

(a) Preparation for storage

(1) Drain the engine oil and refill with MIL-C-6529 type 2. Start engine and run until normal oil and cylinder head temperatures are reached. The preferred method would be to fly the aircraft for thirty minutes. Allow engine to cool to ambient temperature. Accomplish steps a. described in flyable storage and(a)(1 through 6) listed in temporary storage.

Note: MIL-C-6527 type 2 may be formulated by thoroughly mixing one part compound MIL-C-6529 type 1 (ESSO Rust-Ban 628, Cosmoline No. 1223, or equivalent) with three parts new lubricating oil of the grade recommended for service, all at room temperature.

(2) Apply preservative to engine interior by spraying approximately two ounces MIL-L-46002, grade 1 oil through the oil filler tube.

(b) Install dehydrator plugs MS27215-2, in each of the top spark plug holes, making sure that each plug is blue in color when installed. Protect and support the spark plug leads with AN-4060 protectors.

(c) If the carburetor is removed from the engine place a bag of desiccant in the throat of the carburetor air adaptor. Seal the adaptor with moisture-resistant paper and tape or a cover plate.

(d) Place a bag of desiccant in the exhaust pipes and seal the openings with moisture-resistant tape.

(e) Seal the cold air inlet to the heater muff with moisture-resistant tape to exclude moisture and foreign objects.

(f) Seal the engine breather by inserting a dehydrator MS27215-2 plug in the breather hose and clamping in place.

(g) Attach a red streamer to each place on the engine where bags of desiccant are placed. Either attach red streamers outside the sealed area with tape or to the inside of the sealed area with safety wire to prevent wicking of moisture into the sealed area.

(h) Engines with propellers installed that are preserved for storage in accordance with this section should have each propeller tagged in a conspicuous place with the following notation on the tag: "DO NOT TURN PROPELLER—ENGINE PRESERVED."

As an alternative method of indefinite storage, the aircraft may be serviced in accordance with the procedures under the section temporary storage providing the airplane is run up at maximum intervals of 90 days and then reserviced per the temporary storage requirements.

Procedures necessary for returning an aircraft to service are as follows:

(a) Remove the cylinder dehydrator plugs and all paper, tape, desiccant bags, and streamers used to preserve the engine.

(b) Drain the corrosion preventative mixture and reservice with recommended lubricating oil.

Warning: When returning the aircraft to service do not use the corrosion preventive oil referenced in indefinite storage (a)(1) for more than 25 hours.

(c) With bottom plugs removed, rotate propeller to clear excess preservative oil from cylinders.

(d) Re-install the spark plugs and rotate the propeller by hand through the compression strokes of all the cylinders to check for possible liquid lock. Start the engine in the normal manner.

(e) Give the aircraft a thorough cleaning, visual inspection and test flight per airframe manufacturer's instructions.

Aircraft stored in accordance with the indefinite storage procedures should be inspected per the following instructions:

(a) Aircraft prepared for indefinite storage should have the cylinder dehydrator plugs inspected visually every 30 days. The plugs should be changed as soon as their color indicates unsafe conditions of storage. If the dehydrator plugs have changed color in one-half or more of the cylinders, all desiccant material on the engine should be replaced.

(b) The cylinder bores of all engines prepared for indefinite storage should be resprayed with corrosion preventative mixture every six months, or more frequently if bore inspection indicates corrosion has started earlier than six months. Replace all desiccant and dehydrator plugs. Before spraying, the engine should be inspected for corrosion as follows: Inspect the interior of at least one cylinder on each engine through the spark plug hole. If cylinder shows start of rust, spray cylinder corrosion preventative oil and turn prop six times, then respray all cylinders. Remove at least one rocker box cover from each engine and inspect the valve mechanism.

LOADS OF WORK

As you can see, the proper steps for engine preservation are tedious, however, the work can be financially rewarding. Don't forget how much an engine overhaul costs.

I always wonder just how many planes really get the care outlined here? Just go out to any small airport on a warm spring day and see if there isn't at least one pilot that looks to the beckoning blue yonder, checks the oil, unties, and goes. So wrapped up in getting in the air, he never heard the hundreds of dollars he spent when the engine turned over, all dry and full of oxidation from months of neglect.

10

Propellers

YOUR CONNECTION with the air you move in is the propeller. Without it you have no means of transforming the power from the engine into motion. In short, without it, you don't fly. The propellers you see on classic airplanes are either metal or wood, with most being fixed-pitch. The following information is provided courtesy of Sensenich Corp. Look for its name on the propellers of classics. More often than not, the prop you see is a Sensenich product; the company has been around since the 1930s (Fig. 10-1).

TECHNICAL DEFINITIONS

Pitch, geometric. The geometrical pitch of an element of a propeller is the distance which the element would advance along a helix of slope equal to its blade angle. The nominal or standard pitch of Sensenich propellers is the geometric pitch as determined at 75 percent of the radius.

Pitch, effective. The effective pitch of a propeller is the distance an aircraft actually advances along its flight path in one revolution of the propeller.

Rotation. The rotation of the propeller is determined when viewing the propeller from the slipstream. A right-hand propeller is one which rotates clockwise when viewed from the slipstream, that is, from the cockpit in a tractor installation. A left-hand propeller is one which rotates counterclockwise when viewed in the same manner.

Minor repair. A minor repair would be rounding out a shallow nick or cut, as long as the strength, weight, and stiffness of the blade are not materially affected.

Major repair. Major repairs include diameter reduction to repair tip damage, repairs to deep cuts and nicks, and straightening of bent blades.

WOODEN PROPELLERS

Your Sensenich wood propeller was manufactured from aircraft-quality selected lumber. The laminations are bonded with high-strength, waterproof, resorcinol glue and were assembled under closely controlled factory conditions. Propeller balance was maintained strictly during manufacture and verified before shipment

Fig. 10-1. The Sensenich factory as it appeared in the days of the great postwar airplane boom.
Sensenich

from the factory (Fig. 10-2). Assembly of the Type Certificated propeller/engine/ aircraft must be accomplished by personnel holding the appropriate FAA license.

INSTALLATION

The propellers covered by these instructions are all of the two-blade, fixed-pitch type constructed of laminated birch wood. They have metal leading edge strips which protect the wood against abrasion. The metal strips are attached to the wood with wood screws and rivets. In addition to the metal strips, 10 to 15 inches of the outer area of each blade is covered with sturdy fabric as further protection against damage from stones during takeoff or landing. Some of the propellers covered by these instructions have integral spinners constructed of molded plywood.

INSTALLATION OF HUB

(1) Make sure the threads on the bolts are free from metal chips and other foreign matter.

(2) Coat the threads with light engine oil.

(3) Insert the bolts in holes so that nuts will be on front face of propellers. On some flange-mounted installations, it might be necessary to install the bolts with heads on front face of propeller. Use a soft-headed hammer, if necessary, to drive the bolts through the hub.

(4) Put on the hub bolt nuts and draw up evenly, a little at a time, moving back and forth across the hub from one bolt to another. This method helps prevent throwing the propeller out of track and pitch.

(5) Use a torque wrench to tighten the nuts to a torque reading as recommended in the torque table. A tolerance of plus or minus 25 inch pounds can be allowed on these values. It is important that the nuts are not tightened beyond the recommended values, in order that the surface of the wood propeller not be fractured. Any fracture of the wood allows moisture to enter the wood, thus leading to checking of the wood and consequent early rejection from service.

BOLT DIAMETER RECOMMENDED TORQUE

The recommended torque for propeller bolts is dependent upon the bolt's diameter:

⅜ inch—200 inch-pounds
⅞₁₆ inch—250 inch-pounds
½ inch—300 inch-pounds

TRACK

(1) After the hub has been installed, the complete assembly should be placed on a conventional checking stand and checked to determine if the blades track within ¹⁄₁₆ of each other.

(2) If the blades do not track, the hub bolts should be loosened and hard paper, pasteboard, or thin metal shims placed between the fixed hub flange and the propeller hub face, so as to bring the tips of the blades into alignment within ¹⁄₁₆ inch of each other. Tighten the hub bolt nuts with the recommended torque when checking the track.

BALANCE

All propellers should be checked for balance before installation on an engine. This is especially true of propellers coming from spare propeller stocks. Propellers that have been in stock any length of time might have lost their balance and, therefore, should be checked and corrected before installation on an engine.

Fig. 10-2. An original wood propeller, as it appeared on many classics. This kind of propeller is currently manufactured and available.

INSTALLATION ON ENGINE

(1) General After balance has been corrected and cotter pins or safety wire installed through the hub bolts, the propeller is ready for installation on the engine.

(2) Preinstallation operations Observe, where applicable, the following operations:

(a) Recheck entire surface of propeller including fabric covering and tipping.

(b) Clean shaft threads and splines thoroughly, removing all nicks, burns, and galls from the shaft.

(c) In the case of spline shaft installations, clean the rear cone and place it on shaft.

(d) Clean thoroughly and coat the threads of the propeller shaft and nut with an approved antiseize compound.

(e) Locate propeller on the shaft, being careful not to damage the shaft, shaft threads, or rear cone seat.

(f) On spline shaft installations make certain the halves of the front cone are mates. Place them on the nut. If the cone is new it may come in one piece, in which case it will be necessary to saw the halves apart and carefully remove the metal left in the split.

(g) Carefully start the nut on the threads of the engine shaft. Tighten the nut by means of a three-foot bar placed through the holes in the nut. This applies to the No. 20 shaft only. On the No. 0 taper shaft and the No. 10 splines shaft, use an 18-inch bar. **Caution**: Hammering on the bar should be avoided.

(h) Install the snap ring and safety the shaft nut in the manner provided on the particular hub being used.

(i) When installing propellers on the integral hub flange shafts, place the propeller on the stub shaft, insert bolts in the flange and tighten, as explained previously.

STORAGE

If the propeller does not go into service immediately after repair, it should be stored in a horizontal position, supported by the hub and not at the blades. Propellers should never be allowed to stand against a wall, or be stored in such a manner that the weight is taken by the blades. Propellers should not be stored where they are close to, or in a direct line with, the flow of air from any heating or cooling equipment. If at all possible, a relative humidity of from 30 to 60 percent should be maintained in the storage room.

REPAIRS

We strongly recommend that propellers needing repairs be sent only to approved propeller repair stations or propeller manufacturers or their branches.

Operating tips

The following practices will add to the service life of your wood propeller:

(1) Do not use the propeller as a tow-bar to move your aircraft.

(2) Avoid running-up in areas containing loose stones and gravel.

(3) Place the propeller in a horizontal position when parked.

(4) Inspect frequently for bruises, scars, or other damage to wood and blade leading-edge protection. It is good practice to conduct preflight and postflight inspections.

(5) Protect your propeller from moisture by waxing with an automotive paste wax. Keep the drain holes in metal tipping open.

(6) Assume that your propeller is unairworthy after any kind of impact until it has been inspected by qualified personnel.

(7) Inspect and check propeller attaching bolts for tightness at least every 100 hours or annually. More frequent inspection might be necessary when climatic changes are extreme.

(8) All wood and metal tipping repairs must be made at the factory or by an approved propeller repair station. If your propeller was manufactured with recessed synthetic leading edge protection, a kit is available from the factory for repair of minor damage to the plastic material.

(9) Check propeller balance whenever you notice evidence of roughness in operation. If your propeller begins to show any of the following damage, it should be retired from service:

(a) Cracks in hub bore

(b) A deep cut across the wood grain

(c) A long, wide, or deep crack parallel to the grain

(d) A separated lamination

(e) Oversize or elongated hub bore or bolt holes

(f) An appreciable warp, which might be discovered by inspection or through rough operation

(g) An appreciable portion of wood missing

(h) Obvious damage or wear beyond economical repair

WOOD PROPELLER MODEL NUMBERS

The Sensenich simplified model or part number system can be explained by use of the following examples:

(a) 86C-67

(b) 86CA-67

(c) 86CASP-72

(d) 86CS-72

(e) 86CAL-67

The first two figures, 86, indicate the propeller diameter in inches. The following letter, C, designates one basic blade design selected from a group applicable to the particular diameter. All of the above listed propellers have the same basic blade design. A letter other than L or S following the first letter in the model designation indicates a variation in hub dimensions from another model having the same diameter and same basic blade design. The letter L following in any position after the first letter in the model designation indicates a left-hand rotating propeller. All other propellers are right-hand rotation.

Example (e) is the same as example (b) except that it is left-handed. The letter S following in any position after the first letter in the model designation indicates that the propeller has a built-in spinner. If the letter S is followed by the letter P the spinner is constructed of plywood.

Example (c) is of the same basic blade design, fits the same hub and differs from example (b) only in so far as it has an integral spinner constructed of plywood.

If the letter P does not follow the letter S then the integral spinner is of solid wood construction as in example (d). The last two numbers indicate the pitch of the propeller in inches. Examples (a), (b), and (e) have a pitch of 67 inches. Examples (c) and (d) each have a pitch of 72 inches. This is the geometric pitch measured at 75 percent of the radius. If the model number is preceded by the letter W, the propeller was manufactured after April 25, 1968.

APPLICATIONS

Model	Engine	Propeller
Aeronca		
7AC	Continental A-65	72CK42
11AC	Continental A-65	72CK42
7BCM	Continental C-85	72GK50
7CC	Continental C-90	72GK48
7DC	Continental C-85	72GK44
7EC	Continental C-90	72GK48
15AC	Continental C-145	73BR44
Cessna		
120/140	Continental C-85	74FK49
140	Continental C-90	74FK51
170/170A	Continental C-145	73BR50
Champion		
7EC	Continental C-90	72GK48
Ercoupe		
415C	Continental A-65	72CK44
415C-G	Continental C-75	72FKT48
Luscombe		
8A	Continental A-65	76CK44

Model	Engine	Propeller
8B	Lycoming O-145-B	70LY38
8C/D	Continental A-75	72GK46
8E	Continental C-85	72GK50
8F	Continental C-90	72GK52
11A	Continental E-165	80EY80

Piper

J3C-65	Continental A-65	72CK42
J3L-65	Lycoming O-145-B	70LY34
J4	Continental A-65	72CK42
J5	Continental A-75	70D40
J5C	Lycoming O-235	74FE46
PA-11	Continental A-65	72CK42
PA-11	Continental C-90	72GK50
PA-12	Lycoming O-235-C	76RM44
PA-14	Lycoming O-235-C1	74FM52
PA-15	Lycoming O-145B	70LY36
PA-16	Lycoming O-235-C1	74FM52
PA-17	Continental A-65	72CK42
PA-18	Continental C-90	72GK50
PA-18	Lycoming O-235-C1	74FM52
PA-18	Lycoming O-290-D	74FM52
PA-20	Lycoming O-290-D	74FM57

Stinson

108	Franklin 6A4-150	76JA53
108-1	Franklin 6A4-150	76JR53
108-2/3	Franklin 6A4-165	76JR53

Taylorcraft

BC12D	Continental A-65	72CK44
19	Continental C-85	72GK46

METAL PROPELLERS

Metal propellers are manufactured under closely controlled conditions to the approved design in accordance with the applicable FAA Regulations. Stamped on the propeller hub face are the model and serial numbers, the type certificate number, and the production certificate number.

METAL PROPELLER MODEL NUMBERS

The Sensenich Metal Propeller Designation System is a coded means of telling all about a particular propeller. The number 74DM6S5-2-60 is broken down as:

74—Basic propeller diameter (inches)

D—Blade design
M6—Propeller hub design
    C SAE ARP-502 flange
    K SAE No. 1 flange
    M SAE No. 2 flange
    R SAE No. 3 flange
    M6 hub drilled for SAE No. 2 flange with $\frac{5}{16}$" bolts
    M8 hub drilled for SAE No. 2 flange with $\frac{3}{8}$" bolts
    S5 designates a $\frac{5}{4}$" spacer
    S6 designates a $\frac{6}{4}$" spacer
    S8 designates a $\frac{3}{4}$" spacer
2—Allowable reduction (inches) from basic diameter
60—Blade pitch at 75 percent radius

THE RIGHT WAY

(1) Have your propeller installed by an A&P mechanic. For convenience, the proper installation bolt torque is shown on the blade decal near the hub. Always have the blade track checked after the hub bolts are tightened. **Note**: Every propeller is accurately balanced at the factory. If the propeller-engine combination feels rough in flight, ask your mechanic to remove the propeller, rotate it 180 degrees on the engine crankshaft flange, and reinstall. Again check the blade track. If the blades track, this will verify trueness of the crankshaft flange.

(2) Inspect the blades of your propeller before each flight for nicks, cuts, and stone bruises. Have the minor repairs performed promptly by an A&P mechanic. If a crack is discovered, the propeller must be removed immediately from service.

(3) Have major repairs performed by an FAA Certified Propeller Repair Station or by the factory.

(4) Conform to applicable rpm limitations and periodically have your tachometer checked for accuracy.

(5) Frequently wipe the propeller blades clean with an oily rag. This oily wipe off will remove corrosive substances, and the oily residue will repel water and corrosives.

(6) The recommended flight time between reconditioning for your Sensenich fixed-pitch metal propeller is 1000 hours provided it has not received prior damage requiring immediate attention. This accomplishes the removal of fatigued surface metal and the accumulation of small nicks and cuts too numerous to be repaired individually.

DO NOT

(1) Do not permit installation of a propeller unless it is the model approved under the aircraft type certificate and has been obtained from a reliable source. Beware of a propeller of unknown service history.

(2) Do not push or pull on the propeller when moving the aircraft by hand.

(3) Do not run up your engine/propeller over loose stones or gravel.

(4) Do not paint over corroded or damaged blades. This hides the defect and may deter needed repair.

(5) Do not permit repair of blade damage by peening or welding. These practices will lead to early blade failure.

(6) Do not fly your aircraft under any circumstances before a thorough inspection by qualified personnel if the propeller has been subject to impact.

(7) Do not have your propeller straightened except by an FAA Certified Propeller Repair Station or the factory. Even partial straightening of blades for convenience of shipping to a repair station may cause hidden damage which, if not detected, could result in the return to service of a non-airworthy propeller. Report anything of this nature before repair is initiated.

APPLICATIONS

Model	Engine	Propeller
Aeronca		
7AC	Continental A-65	74CK-0-46
11AC	Continental A-65	74CK-0-46
11CC	Continental C-85	74CK-2-44
Cessna		
120/140	Continental C-85	76AK-2-44
Ercoupe		
415C/D	Continental C-75	76AK-2-48
415C-G	Continental C-85	76AK-2-46
Piper		
J3C	Continental A-65	74CK-0-46
J4	Continental A-65	74CK-0-46
PA-11	Continental A-65	74CK-0-46
PA-11	Continental C-90	76AK-2-42
PA-11	Lycoming O-235-C	76AM6-2-46
PA-12	Lycoming O-235-C	76AM6-2-46
PA-12	Lycoming O-235-C1	76AM6-2-48
PA-14	Lycoming O-235-C1	76AM6-2-48
PA-16	Lycoming O-235-C1	76AM6-2-50
PA-17	Continental A-65	74CK-2-48
PA-18	Continental C-90	76AK-2-42
PA-18	Lycoming O-235-C1	76AM6-2-48
PA-18	Lycoming O-290-D	74DM6-0-50
PA-18	Lycoming O-290-D2	74DM6-0-52
PA-18	Lycoming O-320	74DM6-0-56
PA-20	Lycoming O-235-C1	76AM6-2-50
PA-20	Lycoming O-235-C1	76AM6-2-50

Model	Engine	Propeller
PA-20	Lycoming O-290-D	74DM6-0-56
PA-20	Lycoming O-290-D2	74DM6-0-57
PA-22 Colt	Lycoming O-235-C1B	76AM6-2-48
PA-22	Lycoming O-320	74DM6-0-60
Taylorcraft		
BC12D	Continental A-65	74CK-0-48
F21	Lycoming O-235-L2C	72CK-0-50

STANDARD/CLIMB/CRUISE

When referring to propellers, you often hear the terms climb prop or cruise prop. These terms refer to an improvement in the rate of climb or cruise speed as compared to the standard propeller. The tables seen in this chapter give only standard propellers. However it is easy to convert from standard to optional cruise or climb propellers:

Cruise—add 2 inches of pitch.
Climb—reduce the pitch by 2 inches.

When climb/cruise propellers are recommended, the lower pitch (climb propeller) can be expected to offer better takeoff, climb, and high-altitude performance. The higher pitch (cruise) propeller should be chosen only if takeoff and climb are not critical.

CARE OF PROPELLERS

Take care of your propeller—a wood propeller costs more than $600 to replace. A metal propeller commands a price nearly three times that.

As many planes live outside, due to the scarcity and expense of hangars, it is recommended that covers be used to protect the windshield and the cabin. Additionally, everyone knows to plug the cowlings to keep the birds out. But how about covering the propeller when the plane is parked?

Covers can range from a piece of heavy-duty transparent waterproof material tied over the propeller to sock-type devices, made of Lycra-Spandex-acrylic fabric, that slide over the blades of a propeller. The latter are available from:

Accurate Knitting Mills, Inc.
16 W. 19th Street
New York, NY 10011
(212) 675-9066

11

Avionics

BACK IN the introduction, I mentioned the "classic" style of flying. VFR navigation was all done by pilotage, or looking out the window to see where you were. But, alas, times have changed. Today's modern airway system requires at least a required minimum of avionics on board to freely travel where you want to go.

DEFINITIONS

A-panel. Audio Panel allows centralized control of all radio equipment

ADF. ADF stands for automatic direction finder

CDI. A course deviation indicator is a panel-mounted device providing visual output of the NAV radio.

COM. COM is short for a VHF transceiver for voice radio communications (see Fig. 11-1).

ELT. These letters stand for emergency locator transmitter (required by FARs for all but local flying).

LOC/GS. LOC and GS mean localizer/glideslope. Visual output is via a course deviation indicator (CDI), with the addition of a horizontal indicator.

LORAN. LORAN is a long range radio navigation receiver.

MBR. MBR stands for marker beacon receiver.

NAV. NAV is short for a VHF navigation receiver for utilizing VORs.

NAV/COM. A combination of COM and NAV in one unit is referred to as NAV/COM (see Figs. 11-2 and 3).

XPNDR. Transponder is often shortened to XPNDR (might or might not have altitude encoding).

WHAT IS REQUIRED

The minimum requirement is an ELT, which is completely self-contained and useable on any airplane, even if the plane does not have an electrical system.

Although you might not need it at your home base, a COM radio is necessary for operations to or from controlled airports. Without one, you are relegated to

Fig. 11-1. The COM 760 TSO communications transceiver. This unit is currently the least expensive COM available, yet offers full features.

Fig. 11-2. The famous King KX17B NAV/COM, one of the most widely used NAV/COMs in general aviation.

operating only from uncontrolled airports and won't even be able to use UNICOM at those. A COM radio offers additional safety in case you have problems between airports.

If you do very much cross-country flying, a NAV radio would be nice; after all, those VOR signals are already out there, so why not put them to use, at least as a backup to pilotage. Generally, the NAV and COM radio are packaged as one unit called a NAV/COM (see Figs. 11-4 through 8).

The transponder (Figs. 11-9 and 10) is the remaining basic piece of equipment to complete your lineup. It enhances your image on the FAA air traffic controller's radar screen and can identify your airplane by digital means. If you have altitude reporting capabilities on your transponder, it will even tell the controller that too.

IFR flying is not generally within the purview of classics, although it is completely possible if the airplane is equipped for such operations.

YOUR NEEDS

It all costs money; money to purchase the equipment, money to install it, and money to maintain it. It's quite easy to spend more for avionics than you originally spent for your classic airplane. In fact, that could be said for many airplanes. Determine your flying needs and habits and apply them to avionics.

Fig. 11-3. Narco MK 12D NAV/COM. This digital readout unit features an active/standby switch allowing instant frequency change between the right and left displays.

The casual flyer doing mostly local flying with only occasional cross-country trips can get by with a minimum of equipment ranging from an ELT only to a package of ELT, XPNDR, and NAV/COM.

If you will be flying all over the country on extensive trips, you might want to add an extra NAV/COM as a backup.

The addition of a LORAN receiver to the lineup is a good choice.

The occasional IFR pilot needs dual NAV/COM with LOC/GS, a MBR, and ADF. Most of the classics don't have the space available or the electric power for this lineup.

ELECTRICAL POWER

Some of the classics don't have electrical systems, so you might wonder what you do in that case for electric power. Really it's quite simple—a wind generator is installed under the fuselage to supply power to a small battery. A wind generator has a small propeller on it that is mounted directly to the armature shaft. As you move forward, the propeller turns the shaft, and electricity is generated (Figs. 11-11 and 12).

Wind generators were designed originally to power only a single COM radio. Remember, when that old COM radio was built it had vacuum tubes in it, drew lots of power, and was all the wind generator system could handle. With today's new solid-state electronics, that same wind generator/battery combination can power an amazing amount of avionics.

By the way, there is a wind generator system on the ultra-modern Boeing 767 airliner. It deploys in case of electrical failure, and provides the power necessary for a safe landing.

FILLING THE PANEL

There are several ways of going about filling those vacant spots on your instrument panel (Fig. 11-13). Some are more expensive than others and some are less advisable than others.

KX 165 NAV/COMM with Digital radial

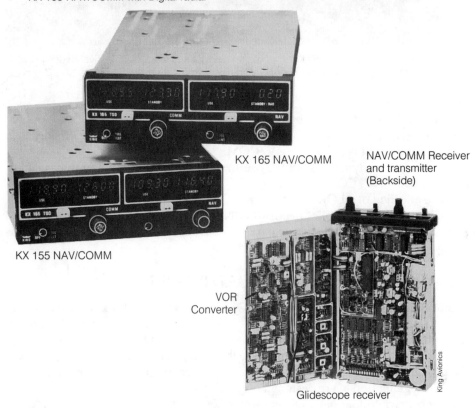

KX 165 NAV/COMM

NAV/COMM Receiver
and transmitter
(Backside)

KX 155 NAV/COMM

VOR
Converter

Glidescope receiver

Fig. 11-4. King Silver Crown lineup of the KX165 and KX155 NAV/COMs.

NEW EQUIPMENT

New equipment is state-of-the-art, offering the newest innovations, best reliability, smallest size, lowest power requirements, and a warranty. New avionics can be purchased from your local avionics dealer or through a discount house, and many advertise in *Trade-A-Plane*.

You can visit your local avionics dealer and purchase all the equipment you want and have the dealer install it. Of course, this method is the most expensive. However, you'll have new equipment, expert installation, and service backup.

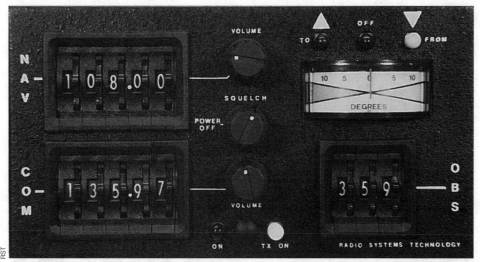

Fig. 11-5. The Radio Systems Technology (RST) NAV/COM you build from a kit. After completion, you return the finished kit to the factory for complete testing.

The discount house saves you money at the time of the initial purchase, but you might be left out when the need for warranty service arises. Some manufacturers do not honor warranty service requests unless the equipment was purchased from and installed by an authorized dealer. This might not seem fair to the consumer, but it is an effective method for a manufacturer to protect the authorized dealers.

USED EQUIPMENT

Used avionics can be purchased from dealers or individuals. The aviation magazines and *Trade-A-Plane* are good sources of used equipment. I recommend against purchasing any equipment with tubes in it, that is more than six years old, was built by a now defunct manufacturer, or is described "as is" or "working when removed."

Used equipment can be a wise investment, but it is very risky unless you happen to be an avionics technician or have access to one. In most cases, I recommend against the purchase of used avionics unless you are very familiar with the source and have the opportunity to test the equipment prior to purchase.

A few purists purchase and completely rebuild vintage equipment for their classic. They do so for cosmetic reasons only, and unless you are going after prizes at air shows, I do not suggest it. Even when completely rebuilt, this old equipment is very limited, and often unreliable, as was sometimes the case when new.

RECONDITIONED EQUIPMENT

Several companies advertise reconditioned avionics at bargain, or at least low, prices. This equipment has been removed from service and completely checked

Fig. 11-6. This Narco Escort II fits a standard 3" instrument panel hole, weighs only 3 pounds and is 3.25 × 3.25 × 10.75 inches (WHD). It features automatic omni, digital RMI, an electronic CDI, digital OBS, high visibility display, and a 5-watt transmitter. It saves space and uses very little electrical power.

out by an avionics shop. Parts that have failed, are near failure, or are likely to fail, have been replaced.

These radios offer a fair buy for the airplane owner, and are normally warranteed by the seller for a specified period of time. However, reconditioned is not new. Everything in the unit has been used but not everything will be replaced during reconditioning. You will have some new parts and some old parts.

RADIO KITS

The latest method of purchasing avionics is kit construction. You purchase a complete kit and build it yourself. Radio Systems Technology offers a limited line of avionics from audio panels to a 720 channel NAV/COM in kit form.

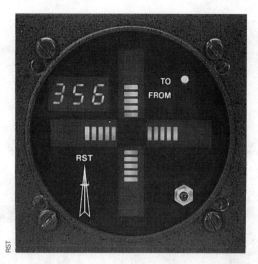

Fig. 11-7. Digital electronic CDI uses no moving parts. Note the digital numeric display of the direction and the LED indicator for TO and FROM.

For certification purposes, you build it, then ship it back to the manufacturer for checkout and certification. By building your equipment you save money and learn about the inside of these complex boxes (so say the kit manufacturers). RST will also service it at a later date, should you need it. This is certainly an interesting way for the budget-minded individual to acquire avionics.

PURCHASING ADVICE

I have many years of experience in electronics and strongly recommend that when contemplating the purchase of avionics, save your money until you can purchase new equipment. If you have equipment on board that is currently working properly, keep it and save your money. Above all, if it works, don't fix it. As soon as

Fig. 11-8. This KI 203, a standard type of analog display, shows only VOR information.

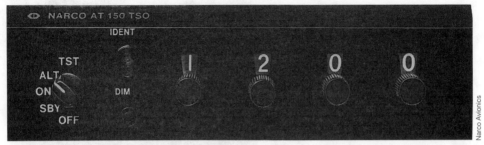

Fig. 11-9. Narco AT 150 Transponder.

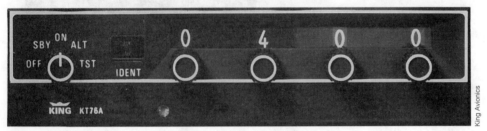

Fig. 11-10. KT 76A Transponder.

someone gets into these boxes to realign, or just to "touch up" the tuning, the box thinks it's found a new mama, and will holler for her at all inconvenient times.

If you decide to replace your older avionics equipment, either keep the older working stuff as a second system, spares, or make an outright sale. You won't get real dollar value on a trade-in, and dual systems are nice to have.

NEW CHOICES

The field of avionics is constantly moving forward in state-of-the-art equipment. Units of smaller physical size, greater capability, and easier use are in the forefront.

Fig. 11-11. Ward Aero wind generator used to provide electrical power when the engine is not equipped with an alternator or generator.

Fig. 11-12. Phoenix Wind Charger available from Brite Flight Aviation, Inc., 1910 W. Deer Valley Rd., Phoenix, AZ 85027 (602) 582-1710.

Brite Flight Aviation

HANDHELD RADIOS

If your plane does not have an electrical system, or you are looking for radio back-up without the expense of installation, consider a handheld NAV/COM.

The HT (Fig. 11-14), as handheld radios are generally called, requires no installation, mechanical or electrical, and is independent of the airplane's electrical system, unless you want to plug it into the cigarette lighter.

Fig. 11-13. The panel of this 1941 Piper J5A shows a functional mix of new and old.

Fig. 11-14. Narco HT 800 full-featured COM that operates on battery power and displays the frequency digitally.

Narco Avionics

Typically, a handheld portable NAV/COM radio has full 760 COM and 200 NAV channel capabilities—something lacking in many panel mounted COMs—a VOR display, push button frequency entry, memory functions, rechargeable batteries, and a headphone jack (Fig. 11-15). Capability-wise, HTs are great as they are. However, to increase the usable range, some owners have external antennas installed on their planes that can be connected to the HT.

LORAN

LORAN, specifically LORAN C, has gained popularity because of the computer-based system of operation. LORAN was designed initially for marine navigation and the first aviation LORAN C units were actually reworked marine systems.

The capabilities of the new generation LORAN Cs are based on a combination of computer microprocessing and radio propagation factors at the frequencies used by LORAN.

Fig. 11-15. King KX 99 portable NAV /COM.

Narco Avionics

The accuracy and usability of LORAN offers distinct advantages over normal VHF NAV-aids such as VORs. LORAN, due to low operating frequencies, in the range from 100 to 110 kHz, is usable hundreds of miles from the transmitting site. The VHF line-of-sight limitation does not exist with LORAN. This opens some very interesting possibilities for usage.

A considerable amount of small plane flying is conducted below 2000 feet and in very isolated areas. Until the advent of LORAN C, low-altitude flying was the limiting factor of radio navigation. Low altitude meant that VORs were of little or no use, as the line-of-sight VHF signals often were blocked by mountains and horizons. LORAN shines here, undaunted by mountains of horizon distances. It is usable right down to the ground.

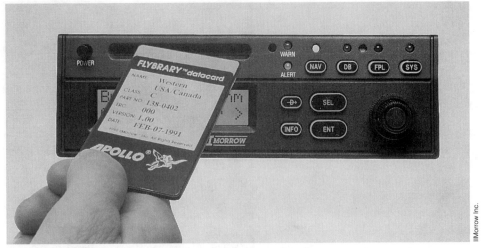

Fig. 11-16. Apollo LORAN with the "Flybrary Card." The card is a removable database that can be updated.

Without going into extensive theory about internal operations, the LORAN C operates by receiving several LORAN signals at one time and comparing them to determine an exact location.

Navigation is accomplished by the use of waypoints, which are geographical coordinates entered by the user or placed in a manufactured data base. The LORAN compares its determined position to that of selected waypoints and gives output pertaining to the progress of a flight. This includes: location, ETA, direction of travel, ground speed, time enroute, distance traveled/remaining, etc. All this from one little box that in some cases is battery-operated and completely portable.

The many makes/models of LORAN Cs on the market vary primarily in the number and types of features included(Figs.11-16 and 17). Prices vary accord-

Fig. 11-17. The RST Long Ranger LORAN.

ingly. However, on the bright side, due to the extensive use of computer technology and parts in the LORAN C units, the prices keep dropping. As of this writing several manufacturers offer very complete and feature-loaded units for well under $1000.

SMALL LIFESAVER

The ELT is a piece of equipment required by FARs for just about all general aviation operations. The purpose of the ELT is to emit a traceable radio signal after a crash.

Unfortunately, the record shows that ELTs are among the most unreliable pieces of avionics on today's market. They have a habit of falsing when not wanted and failing when needed. Check your ELT's trip switch and battery often and test it as prescribed in the FARs. Be sure you have an ELT that works.

NOISE POLLUTION

The FAA recently issued Advisory Circular AC 91-35, partially reprinted here:

SUBJECT: NOISE, HEARING DAMAGE, AND FATIGUE IN GENERAL AVIATION PILOTS

Modern general aviation aircraft provide comfort, convenience, and excellent performance. At the same time that the manufacturers have developed more powerful engines, they have given the occupants better noise protection and control, so that today's aircraft are more powerful, yet quieter than ever. Still, the levels of sound associated with powered flight are high enough for general aviation pilots to be concerned about participating in continuous operations without some sort of personal hearing protection.

Like carbon monoxide, noise exposure has harmful effects that are cumulative—they add together to produce a greater effect on the listener both as sound intensity is increased, and as the length of time he listens is increased. A noise that could cause a mild hearing loss to a man who heard it once a week for a few minutes, might make him quite deaf if he worked in it for eight hours.

HEADSETS

The FAA puts forth a convincing argument in favor reducing the amount of noise reaching our ears. There is no doubt that classic airplanes are noisy and that you really should do something to protect your hearing. Possibly the best method of reducing the level of damaging noise is to wear ear protectors such as rifle and pistol shooters wear. However, this is impractical when there is a need to use the radios.

Noise reducing headsets (Fig. 11-18) act like the ear protectors that shooters use by sealing the noise out. Additionally, they allow you to hear the COM radio, or even your passengers (if your airplane is equipped with an intercom system).

I am not sure if this is a new idea, or just an improvement of what I did years ago when I listened to a portable radio with a set of good quality stereo headphones while flying over the vast reaches of West Texas. They effectively sealed out the engine noise. Of course I had to take them off for rare use of the COM.

Fig. 11-18. David Clark Mode 1
H10-20 Headset/Microphone.
David Clark Co.

Fig. 11-19. David Clarke
intercom system allows easy
conversation between pilot and
passengers. David Clark Co.

INTERCOM SYSTEMS

Intercom systems (Figs. 11-19 and 20) come in various types with assorted capabilities. They can be wired into the aircraft's audio panel and connected directly to the radios or they can be standalone (intercoms that are completely portable) and used only for chatter among the occupants of the airplane.

Intercoms for talking to other occupants of the airplane are nice to have. They negate the need for the pantomime acting, screaming, and pointing that goes on in an airplane just to say, "Look over there!"

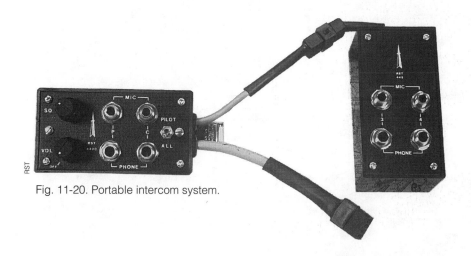

Fig. 11-20. Portable intercom system.

Fig. 11-21. HEADS UP!, a stick on CO (carbon monoxide) detector, although not avionics equipment and having no moving parts, is a recommended safety item. Available from Sims Marketing, 23 N. Gore, Ste 002, St.. Louis, MO 63119-2300 (314) 961-0896.

12

Buying your classic

FINDING A good used airplane can be very difficult, especially if you're looking for one particular make and model. You could have an airplane broker do the search for you, but most potential classic purchasers prefer to do their own searching. After all, that's part of the fun of airplane ownership—going out looking for an airplane and talking to airplane people. Besides, nobody would want to miss going to many airports looking for that elusive one-of-a-kind airplane, because you might just see something else of interest.

THE SEARCH

Searching for a classic airplane can be viewed as an experience in frustration or education. There are a large number of qualifying airplanes generally available, however, the difficult task is to locate the right plane for you; the plane you will enjoy flying and can afford to keep in top condition.

WHERE TO LOOK

The search can begin, and end, with the local Fixed Base Operator (FBO). However, many FBOs are more likely to be concerned with newer airplanes having a high dollar value than with a classic.

Visit all the local airports and check the bulletin boards for airplanes for sale. Ask around while you're there and walk around looking for airplanes with for sale signs in the windows (Figs. 12-1 through 12-5).

The best airports for classics are the uncontrolled grass strips and those with a single paved runway. These fields normally will be well away from any major metropolitan area, and might even appear run-down and out of date by today's hi-tech standards.

Used airplane ads are sometimes seen in local newspapers and always in the various flight-oriented magazines (**AOPA Pilot**, **Flying**, **Private Pilot**, etc.). Unfortunately, the magazine ads are usually out of date due to the 60 to 90 days of lag time between ad placement and printing. There are, however, other recommended sources of timely advertising.

Fig. 12-1. Looking for something really sharp? Then attend local air shows. You can learn lots of good information from owners.

TRADE-A-PLANE

Trade-A-Plane has been printing its yellow-colored paper three times monthly for 50 years. Nearly everything you would ever need for aviation, including airplanes, parts, service, insurance, avionics, and much more is advertised in it. It is safe to say that if you don't see it in *Trade-A-Plane*, it probably is not available. For more information contact:

Trade-A-Plane
P.O. Box 509
Crossville, TN 38555
(615) 484-5137

Fig. 12-2. No, No, No! this Stinson needs far more than a quick oil change, fresh battery, and a questionable annual. Unless you have thousands of dollars and hours to spend, you don't want this sad airplane. For most pilots, it would not be a bargain if it were free.

Fig. 12-3. The only purpose this all-metal Luscombe serves is as home to a family of birds and a few mice. You could buy a showstopper for what it will cost to put this plane safely back in the air.

If you are looking for bargains, you have to be at the head of the line, meaning you must get *Trade-A-Plane* before the rest of the world. For those really serious about making a purchase, I recommend a first class U.S. mail subscription, or better yet, a Federal Express 2nd day air priority subscription.

Fig. 12-4. It needs only an engine . . . Yep! And that will set you back more than a currently flying Ercoupe will. To say nothing of the missing cowl, rotted tires, vermin infested interior, and instrument panel ready for the local landfill.

Fig. 12-5. Seek only an airplane that has been carefully maintained, such as this award winning Piper Colt.

GENERAL AVIATION NEWS AND FLYER

General Aviation News and Flyer is a twice-monthly newspaper carrying up-to-the-minute news affecting general aviation and a considerable amount of regional details from all over the nation. "You read it here months before the magazines print it" is a phrase I have heard more than one pilot say about *General Aviation News and Flyer*. Its classifieds are printed on pink paper and carried as an insert to the newspaper and will typically number more than twenty pages. Contact them at:

General Aviation News and Flyer
P.O. Box 98786
Tacoma, WA 98498-0786
(206) 588-1743

OTHER PUBLICATIONS

Other recommended publications containing timely airplane listings are:

Atlantic Flyer
Civil Air Terminal
Hanscom Field
Bedford, MA 01730
(617) 274-7208

Aviators Hot Line
1003 Central Ave.
Fort Dodge, IA 50501
(515) 955-1600

A/C Flyer
P.O. Box 609
Hightstown, NJ 08520
(609) 426-7070

In Flight
P.O. Box 620477
Woodside, CA 94062
(415) 364-8110

If you have decided on a particular make and model, then join the appropriate owners' club and read the classified ads in their newsletters. Information about these clubs is included in Appendix A.

AIRPLANE POPULATION

The largest populations of general aviation aircraft are based in the following states (in descending order):

California
Texas
Florida
Ohio
Michigan
Alaska
Illinois
Washington
New York
Pennsylvania

Of course, there are small airplanes in every state.

READING THE ADS

Most ads of airplanes for sale make use of various more-or-less standard abbreviations. These abbreviations describe the airplane. A telephone number for contact, with an area code, can generally be a clue as to where the airplane is located. A sample ad:

49 C170,2309TT,605 SMOH,Nov ANN,
KX170 NAV/COM,ELT, polished, Ceconite
wings, NDH. Asking $17,900.
915-555-1234

Translated, this ad reads: For sale, a 1949 Cessna 170 airplane with 2309 total hours on the airframe and an engine with 605 hours since a major overhaul. The next annual inspection is due in November. The plane is equipped with a King KX170 Nav/Com, has an emergency locator transmitter, is polished aluminum and has Ceconite covered wings. Best of all, the airplane has no history of damage. The price is $17,900, and the seller will bargain, as most do. Last is the telephone number with an area code indicating West Texas.

As you can see, there sure was a lot of information inside those four little lines. Here are two lists that can help you when reading airplane ads:

COMMONLY USED ABBREVIATIONS

AD Airworthiness Directive
ADF Automatic Direction Finder
AF Airframe
AF&E Airframe and engine
AI Aircraft inspector
ALT Altimeter
ANN Annual inspection
AP Autopilot
ASI Airspeed indicator
A&E Airframe and engine
A/P Autopilot
BAT Battery
CAT Carburetor air temperature
CHT Cylinder head temperature
COM Communications radio
COMM Communications radio
CS Constant speed propeller
C/S Constant speed propeller
C/W Complied with
DBL Double
DG Directional gyro
FAC Factory
FBO Fixed Base Operator
FGP Full gyro panel
FWF Firewall forward
G Gravity
GAL Gallons
GPH Gallons per hour
GS Glideslope
HD Heavy duty
HP Horsepower
IFR Instrument flight rules
INSP Inspection
INST Instrument
KTS Knots
L Left
LDG Landing
LED Light emitting diode

LH Left-hand
LIC License
LOC Localizer
LTS Lights
L&R Left and right
MB Marker beacon
MBR Marker beacon
MP Manifold pressure
MPH Miles per hour
MOD Modification
NAV Navigation
NAV/COM Navigation/communication radio
NDH No damage history
OAT Outside air temperature
PMA Parts manufacture approval
PROP Propeller
R Right
RC Rate of climb
REMAN Remanufactured
RH Right-hand
RMFD Remanufactured
RMFG Remanufactured
ROC Rate of climb
SAFOH Since airframe overhaul
SCMOH Since chrome major overhaul
SEL Single engine land
SFACNEW Since factory new
SFN Since factory new
SFNE Since factory new engine
SFREM Since factory remanufacture
SFREMAN Since factory remanufacture
SFRMFG Since factory remanufacture
SMOH Since major overhaul
SN Serial number
SNEW Since new
SPOH Since propeller overhaul
STC Supplemental Type Certificate
STOH Since top overhaul
STOL Short takeoff and landing
TAS True airspeed
TBO Time between overhaul
TC Turbocharged
TNSP Transponder
TNSPNDR Transponder
TSN Time since new
TSO Technical Service Order

TT   Total time
TTAF   Total time airframe
TTA&E   Total time airframe and engine
TTE   Total time engine
TTSN   Total time since new
TXP   Transponder
T&B   Turn and bank
VAC   Vacuum
VFR   Visual Flight Rules
VHF   Very high frequency
VOR   Visual omnidirectional range
XC   Cross-country
XMTR   Transmitter
XPDR   Transponder
XPNDR   Transponder

TELEPHONE AREA CODES

Don't forget the area code in the telephone number. It usually tells where the airplane is located. The location is important, as you might not be interested in traveling a couple of thousand of miles to see a particular plane. Also, location indicates the climatic conditions the plane currently lives in.

For example, a plane based near the New England coast might have serious corrosion or finish problems, due to the salt air and/or acid rain. In the Southwest blowing sands take their toll on the gyros, moving parts, and paint, and the cold of the North can be hard on engines and plastic materials.

Generally, these problems can be avoided if the airplane is well cared for. All the better if the airplane was stored inside.

201   New Jersey north (Newark)
202   District of Columbia (Washington)
203   Connecticut
204   Manitoba, Canada
205   Alabama
206   Washington west (Seattle)
207   Maine
208   Idaho
209   California central (Fresno)
212   New York southeast (New York City)
213   California southwest (Los Angeles)
214   Texas northeast (Dallas)
215   Pennsylvania southeast (Philadelphia)
216   Ohio northeast (Cleveland)
217   Illinois central (Springfield)
218   Minnesota north (Duluth)
219   Indiana north (South Bend)

301 Maryland
302 Delaware
303 Colorado
304 West Virginia
305 Florida southeast (Miami)
306 Saskatchewan, Canada
307 Wyoming
308 Nebraska west (North Platte)
309 Illinois northwest (Peoria)
310 California southwest (Los Angeles)
312 Illinois northeast (Chicago)
313 Michigan southeast (Detroit)
314 Missouri east (St. Louis)
315 New York north central (Syracuse)
316 Kansas south (Wichita)
317 Indiana central (Indianapolis)
318 Louisiana northwest (Shreveport)
319 Iowa east (Dubuque)

401 Rhode Island
402 Nebraska east (Omaha)
403 Alberta, Canada
404 Georgia north (Atlanta)
405 Oklahoma west (Oklahoma City)
406 Montana
407 Florida east (Melbourne)
408 California northwest (San Jose)
409 Texas southeast (Galveston)
410 Maryland Baltimore & eastern shore
412 Pennsylvania southwest (Pittsburgh)
413 Massachusetts west (Springfield)
414 Wisconsin southeast (Milwaukee)
415 California central (San Francisco)
416 Ontario, Canada
417 Missouri southwest (Springfield)
418 Quebec, Canada
419 Ohio northwest (Toledo)

501 Arkansas
502 Kentucky west (Louisville)
503 Oregon
504 Louisiana southeast (New Orleans)
505 New Mexico
506 New Brunswick, Canada
507 Minnesota south (Rochester)
508 Massachusetts east (except Boston)
509 Washington east (Spokane)

510 California central (Oakland)
512 Texas south (San Antonio)
513 Ohio southwest (Cincinnati)
514 Quebec, Canada
515 Iowa central (Des Moines)
516 New York southeast (Long Island)
517 Michigan central (Lansing)
518 New York northeast (Albany)
519 Ontario, Canada

601 Mississippi
602 Arizona
603 New Hampshire
604 British Columbia, Canada
605 South Dakota
606 Kentucky east (Lexington)
607 New York south central (Binghamton)
608 Wisconsin southwest (Madison)
609 New Jersey south (Trenton)
612 Minnesota central (Minneapolis)
613 Ontario, Canada
614 Ohio southeast (Columbus)
615 Tennessee east (Nashville)
616 Michigan west (Grand Rapids)
617 Massachusetts east (Boston)
618 Illinois south (Centralia)
619 California south (San Diego)

701 North Dakota
702 Nevada
703 Virginia north & west (Arlington)
704 North Carolina west (Charlotte)
705 Ontario, Canada
707 California northwest (Santa Rosa)
708 Illinois north (Chicago)
709 Newfoundland, Canada
712 Iowa west (Council Bluffs)
713 Texas southeast (Houston)
714 California southwest (Orange)
715 Wisconsin north (Eau Claire)
716 New York west (Buffalo)
717 Pennsylvania central (Harrisburg)
718 New York southeast (Brooklyn)
719 Colorado south (Pueblo)

801 Utah
802 Vermont
803 South Carolina

804 VA southeast (Richmond)
805 California west central (Bakersfield)
806 Texas northwest (Amarillo)
807 Ontario, Canada
808 Hawaii
809 Bermuda, Puerto Rico, Virgin Islands, & other islands
812 Indiana south (Evansville)
813 Florida southwest (Tampa)
814 Pennsylvania northwest (Altoona)
815 Illinois northwest (Rockford)
816 Missouri northwest (Kansas City)
817 Texas north central (Fort Worth)
818 California southwest (Pasadena)
819 Quebec, Canada

901 Tennessee west (Memphis)
902 Nova Scotia, Canada
903 Mexico
904 Florida north (Jacksonville)
905 Mexico City, Mexico
906 Michigan northwest (Escanaba)
907 Alaska
908 New Jersey central
912 Georgia south (Savannah)
913 Kansas north (Topeka)
914 New York southeast (White Plains)
915 Texas southwest (San Angelo)
916 California northwest (Sacramento)
918 Oklahoma northeast (Tulsa)
919 North Carolina east (Raleigh)

TALKING TO THE OWNER

The very first question to ask is: Why are you selling your airplane? Fortunately, most people are honest, and you'll usually get a truthful answer. Very often the owner is moving up to a larger plane, is wanting to start another rebuild/restoration project, or perhaps has other commitments (i.e.: spouse says sell, or perhaps the present owner can no longer afford the plane). Ask questions and take notes on the following:

What is the general appearance and condition of the plane?
How many total hours on the airframe?
What is the make and model of engine?
How many hours on the engine since new?
How many hours since the last overhaul?
What type of overhaul was done?
Who did the overhaul?

Is there any damage history?
What is the asking price?

Remember, this telephone inquiry is to determine if you would like to see the airplane or eliminate it from further consideration.

BEFORE YOU BUY

After you locate an airplane and have purchase in mind, you'll have to inspect it. The object of the prepurchase inspection is to determine if the airplane you are looking at is really worth consideration as a possible purchase.

I consider the prepurchase inspection of a used airplane as the most important single step in the process of buying. If the inspection is not completed in an orderly, well-planned manner, you could end up purchasing someone else's troubles, and be spending a lot more money than planned. This is particularly true with classics due to their age.

DEFINITIONS

Airworthy. The airplane must conform to the original type certificate, or those Supplemental Type Certificates (STCs) issued for a particular airplane. In addition, the airplane must be in safe operating condition relative to wear and deterioration.

Annual inspection. All small airplanes not in commercial use must be inspected annually by an FAA certified Airframe & Powerplant mechanic who holds an Inspection Authorization license (IA), by an FAA certified repair station, or by the airplane's manufacturer. This is a complete inspection of the airframe, powerplant, and all subassemblies. The object of the annual inspection is to assure that the airplane is safe to fly. This inspection is required every twelve months; without it, you don't fly.

Preflight inspection. The preflight is a thorough inspection, by the pilot, of an aircraft prior to flight. The purpose is to determine if the aircraft is indeed airworthy. The pilot makes this decision by looking for discrepancies while inspecting the exterior, interior, and engine of the airplane. The preflight is required by FARs, and as with all inspection requirements, it shows that safety is of great importance.

Preventive maintenance. FAR Part 43 lists a number of maintenance operations that a certificated pilot may perform on an airplane he/she owns, provided the airplane is not flown in commercial service. (These maintenance operations are described elsewhere in this book.)

Repairs and alterations. There are two classes of repairs and/or alterations: major and minor. Major repairs/alterations must be approved for a return to service by an FAA certified Airframe & Powerplant mechanic holding an IA authorization, repair station, or by the FAA. Minor repairs/alterations may be returned to service by an FAA certified Airframe & Powerplant mechanic, or any of the above.

Airworthiness Directives. Airworthiness Directives (ADs) are covered under FAR Part 39, and must be complied with. An AD can be a simple one-time inspection, a periodic inspection such as every 50 hours of operation, or a major modification to the airframe/engine of a particular airplane or group of airplanes (make/model). Notice of an AD will be placed in the Federal Register and sent by mail to registered owners of the aircraft concerned. In an emergency, the information will be sent by telegram to registered owners. Either way, its purpose is to assure the integrity of your flying machine and your safety.

THE FOUR-STEP INSPECTION

Now let's examine the proper way to inspect a potential purchase. There are four steps to a prepurchase inspection:

(1) The walk-around inspection
(2) The logbook check
(3) The test flight
(4) The mechanic's inspection

The walk-around inspection

The walk-around is really a very thorough preflight (Fig. 12-6). It's divided into three logical parts: cabin, airframe, and engine.

The first part of the walk-around is to check that all required paperwork is with the airplane. This includes the Airworthiness Certificate, Aircraft Registration Certificate, flight manual or operating limitations, and logbooks for airframe, engine, and propeller. If the airplane is equipped with communications equipment, look for a Federal Communications Commission (FCC) station license.

While you're inside the airplane looking for the paperwork, notice the general condition of the interior. Does it appear clean, or has it just been scrubbed after a long period of inattention? Look in the corners, just as you would if you were buying a used car.

The care given the interior can be a good indication of what care was given to the remainder of the airplane. However, beware of cosmetic fixes. Often an older airplane will have a new interior, tires, and wax job, but hidden under this skin of beauty lurks a monster with red eyes just waiting for the unwary buyer. This is the reason, in a later step, I recommend you have a mechanic check the plane over also.

In the cabin check the following:

Windows for crazing, yellowing, and damage
Doors for proper operation
Seats for condition and ease of adjustment
Headliner and side walls for condition
Floor for damage and condition
Fuel cutoff for leaks
Primer for leaks
Controls for proper movement
Instrument appearance
Under the instrument panel for loose wires, hoses, etc.

SERVICE MEMO

Service Memo No. 65

SAFETY PRECAUTIONS

Operational carelessness is increasing at an alarming rate and has become a matter of great concern to the aircraft manufacturers as well as the Civil Aeronautics authorities. The modern airplanes which are being built today are far superior to those of yesteryear in that they require less maintenance and almost reach the everyday dependability of the automobile. These two factors alone are primarily responsible for the apparent indifferent attitide toward basic operational safety precautions.

The Service Department would like to put particular emphasis on the following safety procedure instructions which must become an integral part of the aircraft owner's operational routine and/or preflight inspection.

Before each flight, visually inspect the airplane, and/or determine that:

1. The tires are satisfactorily inflated and not excessively worn.
2. The landing gear oleos and shock struts operate within limits.
3. The propellers are free of detrimental nicks.
4. The ground area under propeller is free of loose stones, cinders, etc.
5. The cowling and inspection opening covers are secure.
6. There is no external damage or operational interference to the control surfaces, wings or fuselage.
7. The windshield is clean and free of defects.
8. There is no snow, ice or frost on the wings or control surfaces.
9. The tow-bar and control locks are detached and properly stowed.
10. The fuel tanks are full or are at a safe level of proper fuel.
11. The fuel tank caps are tight.
12. The fuel system vents are open.
13. The fuel strainers and fuel lines are free of water and sediment by draining all fuel strainers once a day. (See Manual for location.)
14. The fuel tanks and carburetor bowls are free of water and sediment by draining sumps once a week.
15. There are no obvious fuel or oil leaks.
16. The engine oil is at proper level.
17. The brakes are working properly.
18. The radio equipment is in order.
19. There is adequate carburetor heat.
20. The weather is satisfactory for the type of flying you expect to do.

End.

PIPER AIRCRAFT CORPORATION, LOCK HAVEN, PA., U. S. A.

Fig. 12-6. These Safety Precautions are what we generally refer to as a preflight.

For wetness or indications of water leaks
Note any avionics installed
Look for rodent damage

Outside the airplane walk around the plane and look at its general condition. Is the paint in good condition, or is some of it laying on the ground under the airplane? Paint jobs are expensive, yet necessary for the protection of the metal/fabric surfaces.

Look for dents, wrinkles, tears, or repairs to the metal or fabric skin. They may indicate prior damage or just careless handling. Each discrepancy must be examined very carefully.

Most tube and fabric planes you will encounter today are covered with a synthetic material of Dacron or Fiberglass designed for long service. This means the internal airframe and wing structures will not be completely inspected, except through small inspection holes, for many years. Some mechanics feel the covering should be removed after 12 to 15 years to see what's going on underneath, at least to inspect and varnish the spars, if they are wood.

Look for signs of rust on the tail section. This is quite common among taildraggers, as moisture seeks low spots, and the tailwheel area of a conventional geared airplane is a low spot. One sign of rust is the discoloration of fabric in the area. A complete check, including the removal of inspection plates, is recommended.

Corrosion or rust on surfaces, or on control systems, is cause for concern. Corrosion is to aluminum as rust is to iron. It is very destructive. Any corrosion or rust should be brought to the attention of a mechanic for his judgement.

The landing gear should be checked for evidence of being sprung. Check the tires for signs of unusual wear that might indicate other structural damage. Also look at the oleo struts for signs of fluid leakage and check the tires for tread depth. If the plane has bungee cords, check them for condition.

Move all the control surfaces, and check each for damage. They should be free in movement. Pay close attention to control surface hinges when looking for rust. When the controls are centered, the surfaces should also be centered. If they are not, a problem in the rigging of the airplane may exist.

As much as possible, check the cables that operate the control surfaces. Look for frayed or broken strands and assure that the pulleys actually turn.

Operate the lights, if equipped with an electrical system.

Open the engine cowling and look for signs of oil leakage. Do this by looking at the engine, inside the cowl cover, and on the firewall. If the leaks are bad enough, there will be oil dripping to the ground. Naturally the seller has probably cleaned away all the old oil drips; however, oil leaves stains. Look for them.

Check the engine mount. It must be free of rust and show no cracks or other weaknesses. Watch for touch-up paint covering flaws. Use a magnifying glass when inspecting welded joints.

Examine all hoses and lines for signs of deterioration or chafing and check all connections for tightness and indications of leakage.

Look at the engine's wiring. Is it secure and routed properly? Are there any worn/chaffed wires?

Check the baffles for security; they route cooling air around the engine. If they are faulty the engine will not cool properly.

Verify freedom of control linkage and cable movement and look for obvious damage.

Look at the cylinders for cracks, broken or missing fins, and indications of oil leaks. Tap each fin with a small metallic tool and listen for a ring. If you hear a thud or clunk, the cause may be a cracked fin or jug.

Check the battery box and battery for corrosion. On some classics you won't have this problem, as there is no electrical system.

Carefully examine the propeller for damage such as nicks, cracks, or gouges. Often these small defects cause stress areas on the prop. Therefore visible damage must be checked by a mechanic. Inflight catastrophic blade separation resulting from stressed areas is not fun.

Check for propeller movement that would indicate looseness at the hub.

Check the exhaust pipes for rigidity, then reach inside them and rub your finger along the inside wall. If your finger comes back perfectly clean, someone has washed the inside of the pipes, possibly to remove the oily deposits that form there when an engine is burning a lot of oil. Black oily goo indicates problems for your mechanic to check. A light grey dusty coating shows proper operation. Look for exhaust stains on the belly of the plane to the rear of the stacks. This area has probably been washed, but look anyway. If you find black oily goo, see your mechanic.

The logbook check

If you are satisfied with what you've seen up to this point, then go back to the cabin and have a seat. Pull out the logbooks and start reading them.

The owner of an aircraft is required to keep aircraft maintenance records that contain a description of the work performed on the aircraft, the date the work was completed, and the signature and FAA certificate number of the person approving the aircraft for return to service. The owner's aircraft records must contain additional information required by FAR Section 91.173.

(a) There must be records of maintenance, alterations and annual or other inspections. These records may be discarded when the work is repeated or superseded by other work, or one year after the work is performed.

(b) There must also be records of:

(1) The total time in service of the airframe

(2) The current status of life-limited parts of each airframe, engine, propeller, and appliance

(3) The time since the last overhaul of all items included on the aircraft which are required to be overhauled on a specific time basis

(4) The identification of the current inspection status of the aircraft including the time since the last required inspection

(5) The current status of applicable ADs including the method of compliance, AD number, revision date

(6) A list of the current major alterations to each airframe, engine, propeller, and appliance

These records must be retained by the owner/operator and must be transferred with the aircraft when ownership changes.

Be sure you're looking at the proper logs for the aircraft and that they are the original logs. Sometimes logbooks get lost and are replaced with new ones. The new logs may be lacking very important information, or could be outright frauds. Be on your guard if the original logs are not available, although this is not uncommon among airplanes 30 to 50 years old.

Start with the airframe log, and look in the back for the AD compliance section. Check that it's up-to-date, and that any required periodic inspections have been made. Now go back to the most recent entry; it probably is an annual inspection. The annual inspection will be a statement that reads:

July 27, 1993 Total Time: 2435 hrs.

I certify that this aircraft has been inspected in accordance with an annual inspection and was determined to be in airworthy condition.

signed here
IA # 0000000

From this point back to the first entry in the logbook you'll be looking for similar entries, always keeping track of the total time for continuity purposes and to indicate the regularity of usage, such as the number of hours flown between inspections. Also you will be looking for indications of major repairs and modifications. This will be signaled by the phrase, Form 337 filed. A copy of this form may be with the logs, and will tell what work was done. The work should be described in the logbook. Be sure there is a current weight and balance sheet with the logbook.

The engine log will be quite similar in nature to the airframe log, and will contain information from the annual. Total time will be given, and possibly an indication of time since a major overhaul (you may have to use your basic math skills here).

Pay particular attention to the numbers that indicate the results of a differential compression check. These numbers give a good indication of the overall health of the engine. Each is given as a fraction, with the lower number always being 80. The 80 indicates the air pressure that was utilized for the check. 80 PSI (pounds per square inch) is the industry standard. The upper number is the air pressure that the combustion chamber was able to maintain while being tested; 80 would be perfect, but it isn't attainable. The figure will always be less. The reason for the lower reading is the air pressure loss that results from loose, worn, or broken rings; scored or cracked cylinder walls; or burned, stuck, or poorly seated valves. There are methods mechanics use to determine which of the above is the cause and, of course, repair the damage. Normally repairs made to an engine to remedy any of the above faults equate to large dollar amounts.

Normal readings would be no less then 70/80, and should be uniform—within 2 or 3 PSI—for all cylinders. A discrepancy between cylinders could indicate the need of a top overhaul of one or more cylinders. The FAA says that a loss in excess of 25 percent is cause for further investigation. That would be a reading of 60/80. I think that a reading such as this indicates a very tired engine in need of much work.

By the way, the results of the latest compression check for each cylinder should be written on the valve cover of that cylinder. Look for them.

Read the information from the last oil change. It may contain a statement about debris found on the oil screen. However, oil changes are often performed by owners, and may or may not be recorded in the log even though required by the

FARs. If they are recorded, how regular were they? I prefer every 25 hours, but 50 is acceptable. Oil is cheap insurance for long engine life.

If the engine has been top overhauled or majored, there will be a description of the work performed, a date, and the total time on the engine when the work was accomplished. If this is not the original engine for this aircraft, then there will be an indication in the logbook giving a date when it was installed.

Check to see if the ADs have been complied with, and the appropriate entries made.

The test flight

The test flight is only a short flight to determine that the airplane feels right to you. It is not meant to be a rip-snort'n, slam-bang, shakeout ride. Remember, you are looking at a classic, not a hot rod.

I suggest that either the owner or a flight instructor accompany you. The latter may be difficult to find, as there are increasingly fewer instructors competent in taildraggers. This may eliminate problems of currency, ratings, etc., with the FAA and the owner's insurance company.

After starting the engine, pay particular attention to the gauges. Do they jump to life, or are they sluggish? Are they indicating as should be expected? Watch these gauges again during the takeoff and climbout. Do the numbers match those called for in the operations manual?

Pay attention to the gyro instruments, if there are any installed, and be sure they are stable. Operate all the avionics, if there are any.

Check the ventilation and heating system for proper operation. Usually ventilation will be no problem in these old birds, but heat may well be nonexistent.

Do a few turns, stalls, and some level flight. Does the airplane perform as expected? Can it be trimmed for hands-off flight?

Return to the airport for a couple of landings. Check for proper brake operation, and for tailwheel or nosewheel vibration/shimmy.

After returning to the parking ramp, open the engine compartment and look again for oil leaks. Also check along the belly for indications of oil leakage and blow-by.

The mechanic's check

If you are still satisfied with the airplane and want to pursue the matter further, then have it inspected by an A&P or AI. This will cost you a few dollars, however, it could save you thousands. The average for a prepurchase inspection is three to four hours labor, at shop rates.

The mechanic's inspection will include a search of ADs and SDRs, a complete check of the logs, and an overall check of the plane. A compression check and a borescope examination must be made. If the plane is fabric-covered, then have that tested also.

POINTS OF ADVICE

Use your own mechanic for the prepurchase inspection, not someone who may have an interest in the sale of the plane (i.e., employee of the seller). Have the plane checked even if an annual was just done, unless you know and trust the AI who did the inspection.

You may be able to make a deal with the owner over the cost of the mechanic's inspection, particularly if an annual is due.

I said this in my other books, and I'll say it again here: If an airplane seller refuses anything that has been mentioned in this chapter, then thank him (optional) for his time, walk away, and look elsewhere. Never let a seller control the situation. Your money, your safety, and possibly your very life are at stake. Airplanes are not hot sellers, regardless of the hype you might have read elsewhere, and there is rarely a line forming to make a purchase. You are the buyer and have the final word.

PURCHASING PAPERWORK AND RESPONSIBILITIES

The day has finally arrived. You're going to take the big step and purchase an airplane. Assuming that you have completely inspected your prospective purchase and found it acceptable at an agreeable price, you're ready to sit down and complete the paperwork that will lead to ownership.

TITLE SEARCH

The first step in purchasing an airplane is to be sure that a clear title exists. A clear title means there are no encumbrances, such as liens, mortgages, or other claims, against the aircraft. This is done by a title search. Just because an airplane is 30 to 50 years old doesn't mean it can't have a lien or two against it.

A title search is accomplished by checking the aircraft's individual records at the Mike Monroney Aeronautical Center in Oklahoma City, Oklahoma. These records include title information, chain of ownership, Major Repair/Alteration (Form 337) information, and other data pertinent to your particular airplane. The FAA files this information by N-number.

The title search may be done by you, your attorney, or other representative selected by you.

Since most of us would find it rather inconvenient to travel to Oklahoma City to do the search ourselves, it is advisable to contract with a third party specializing in this service to do our bidding for us, such as:

King Aircraft Title, Inc.
1411 Classen Blvd. Suite 114
Oklahoma City,OK 73106
(800) 688-1832

or

Aircraft Owners and Pilots Association
Aircraft and Airmen Records Dept.
P.O. Box 19244
Southwest Station
Oklahoma City, OK 73144
(800) 654-4700

WHAT YOU MUST GET

The following documents must be given to you with your airplane:

(1) Bill of sale
(2) Airworthiness Certificate (Fig. 12-7)
(3) Logbooks

(a) Airframe
(b) Engine
(c) Propeller

(4) Equipment List (including weight and balance data)
(5) Operating Limitations and/or Flight Manual

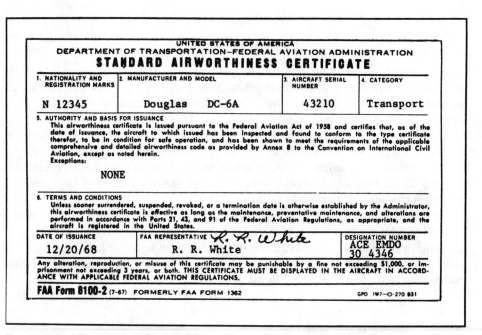

Fig. 12-7. FAA Form 8100-2, Standard Airworthiness Certificate. It must be displayed in the aircraft.

FORMS TO BE COMPLETED

The FAA has forms for changing airplane ownership. They are the only means acceptable for use.

AC Form 8050-2. This is the bill of sale (Figs. 12-8A and 12-8B).

AC Form 8050-1. This form is the aircraft registration (Figs. 12-9A and 12-9B). It is filed with the bill of sale. The pink copy of the form is retained by you and will remain in the airplane until the new registration is issued by the FAA. If you are purchasing the airplane under a contract of conditional sale, then that contract must accompany the registration application in lieu of the AC Form 8050-2.

AC 8050-41. The AC 8050-41 is a release of lien (Fig. 12-10). It must be filed by the seller, if he still owes money on the airplane, to clear any liens on file.

AC 8050-3. This form is the certificate of aircraft registration that you will receive from the FAA (Fig. 12-11).

AC 8050-64. This form is required if there is an assignment of special registration number. All N-numbers consist of the prefix N, and are followed by: one to five numbers, one to four numbers and a letter suffix, or one to three numbers and a two-letter suffix. Special registration numbers are similar to personalized license plates for automobiles.

Federal Communications Commission Form 404. Application for Aircraft Radio Station license is made on this form. It must be completed if you have any radio equipment, capable of transmitting, on the airplane (Figs. 12-12A through 12-12C). The application tears in two; with one portion mailed to the FCC, along with the appropriate application fee, and the other remaining in your airplane as temporary authorization until the new license is sent to you.

Most forms you send to the FAA or FCC will result in the issuance of a document to you. Be patient; it all takes time. If you need assistance call the FAA in Oklahoma City, Oklahoma at (405) 680-3131. They will be glad to help you by answering questions and explaining FAA policy and requirements.

INSURANCE

Insure your airplane from the moment you sign on the dotted line. No one can afford to take risks.

There are two types of insurance: Liability protects you in instances of claims resulting from your operation of the airplane (i.e., bodily injury or property damage). In our society, rest assured that if someone is injured or killed as a result of your flying, you will be sued. Hull insurance protects your investment from the elements of nature, fire, theft, vandalism, or other loss.

Avoid insurance policies burdened with exclusions. Exclusions are language formulated to avoid payoff in the event of a loss. An exclusion may require that all installed equipment be functioning properly during flight. For example:

An accident occurs in the form of a forced landing due to a catastrophic engine failure. During the postcrash investigation the insurance company discovers the ADF wasn't working properly. Although the ADF had nothing to do with the incident, the insurance company sites the exclusion and refuses to pay for the loss.

UNITED STATES OF AMERICA

DEPARTMENT OF TRANSPORTATION — FEDERAL AVIATION ADMINISTRATION

AIRCRAFT BILL OF SALE INFORMATION

PREPARATION: Prepare this form in duplicate. Except for signatures, all data should be typewritten or printed. *Signatures must be in ink.* The name of the purchaser must be identical to the name of the applicant shown on the application for aircraft registration

When a trade name is shown as the purchaser or seller, the name of the individual owner or co-owners must be shown along with the trade name.

If the aircraft was not purchased from the last registered owner, conveyances must be submitted completing the chain of ownership from the last registered owner, through all intervening owners, to the applicant.

REGISTRATION AND RECORDING FEES: The fee for issuing a certificate of aircraft registration is $5.00. An additional fee of $5.00 is required when a conditional sales contract is submitted in lieu of bill of sale as evidence of ownership along with the application for aircraft registration ($5.00 for the issuance of the certificate, and $5.00 for recording the lien evidenced by the contract). The fee for recording a conveyance is $5.00 for each aircraft listed thereon. (There is no fee for issuing a certificate of aircraft registration to a governmental unit or for recording a bill of sale that accompanies an application for aircraft registration and the proper registration fee.)

MAILING INSTRUCTIONS:

If this form is used, please mail the original or copy which has been signed in ink to the FAA Aircraft Registry, P.O. Box 25504, Oklahoma City, Oklahoma 73125.

Fig. 12-8A. Instructions for completing AC Form 8050-2.

Another exclusion example, and all too often seen, says no payment will be made if any FARs have been violated. With the FARs as complicated as they are, it is unlikely many losses occur without at least a slight violation.

Avoid policies that have parts replacement limitations, or other specific rules, setting maximum predetermined values for replacement airframe parts. Called component parts schedule, these policies limit the amount paid for replacement parts. In the case of a classic airplane you could find the amount paid by the insurance carrier to be far less than actual cash value of the loss.

Understand that if you own a two-place airplane and purchase a $1,000,000 passenger liability policy with $100,000 per seat limits, you have only purchased a $100,000 policy. You carry only one other person in a two-placer. Select combined single limit coverage and you will have no per seat limits and understand your total coverage from the very start.

Always read the policy carefully and understand your coverage. Ask questions and demand answers. Insurance, like any other purchased product, must please the purchaser.

A check of any of the various aviation publications will produce telephone numbers for several aviation underwriters. Check with more than one company,

UNITED STATES OF AMERICA

DEPARTMENT OF TRANSPORTATION FEDERAL AVIATION ADMINISTRATION

AIRCRAFT BILL OF SALE

FOR AND IN CONSIDERATION OF $ **THE UNDERSIGNED OWNER(S) OF THE FULL LEGAL AND BENEFICIAL TITLE OF THE AIRCRAFT DESCRIBED AS FOLLOWS:**

UNITED STATES REGISTRATION NUMBER **N**
AIRCRAFT MANUFACTURER & MODEL
AIRCRAFT SERIAL No.

DOES THIS   DAY OF   19

HEREBY SELL, GRANT, TRANSFER AND

DELIVER ALL RIGHTS, TITLE, AND INTERESTS

IN AND TO SUCH AIRCRAFT UNTO:

Do Not Write In This Block
FOR FAA USE ONLY

PURCHASER

NAME AND ADDRESS

(IF INDIVIDUAL(S), GIVE LAST NAME, FIRST NAME, AND MIDDLE INITIAL.)

DEALER CERTIFICATE NUMBER

AND TO   EXECUTORS, ADMINISTRATORS, AND ASSIGNS TO HAVE AND TO HOLD SINGULARLY THE SAID AIRCRAFT FOREVER, AND WARRANTS THE TITLE THEREOF.

IN TESTIMONY WHEREOF   HAVE SET   HAND AND SEAL THIS   DAY OF   19

SELLER

NAME (S) OF SELLER (TYPED OR PRINTED)	SIGNATURE (S) (IN INK) (IF EXECUTED FOR CO-OWNERSHIP, ALL MUST SIGN.)	TITLE (TYPED OR PRINTED)

ACKNOWLEDGMENT   (NOT REQUIRED FOR PURPOSES OF FAA RECORDING: HOWEVER, MAY BE REQUIRED BY LOCAL LAW FOR VALIDITY OF THE INSTRUMENT.)

ORIGINAL: TO FAA

AC FORM 8050-2 (8-85) (0052-00-629-0002)

Fig. 12-8B. AC Form 8050-2 Aircraft Bill of Sale.

UNITED STATES OF AMERICA-DEPARTMENT OF TRANSPORTATION

FEDERAL AVIATION ADMINISTRATION-MIKE MONRONEY AERONAUTICAL CENTER

AIRCRAFT REGISTRATION INFORMATION

PREPARATION: Prepare this form in triplicate. Except for signatures, all data should be typewritten or printed. Signatures must be in ink. The name of the applicant should be identical to the name of the purchaser shown on the applicant's evidence of ownership.

EVIDENCE OF OWNERSHIP: The applicant for registration of an aircraft must submit evidence of ownership that meets the requirements prescribed in Part 47 of the Federal Aviation Regulations. AC Form 8050-2, Aircraft Bill of Sale, or its equivalent may be used as evidence of ownership. If the applicant did not purchase the aircraft from the last registered owner, the applicant must submit conveyances completing the chain of ownership from the registered owner to the applicant.

The purchaser under a CONTRACT OF CONDITIONAL SALE is considered the owner for the purpose of registration and the contract of conditional sale must be submitted as evidence of ownership.

A corporation which does not meet citizenship requirements must submit a certified copy of its certificate of incorporation.

REGISTRATION AND RECORDING FEES: The fee for issuing a certificate of aircraft registration is $5; therefore, a $5 fee should accompany this application. An additional $5 recording fee is required when a conditional sales contract is submitted as evidence of ownership. There is no recording fee for a bill of sale submitted with the application.

MAILING INSTRUCTIONS: Please send the WHITE original and GREEN copy of this application to the Federal Aviation Administration Aircraft Registry, Mike Monroney Aeronautical Center, P.O. Box 25504, Oklahoma City, Oklahoma 73125. Retain the pink copy after the original application, fee, and evidence of ownership have been mailed or delivered to the Registry. When carried in the aircraft with an appropriate current airworthiness certificate or a special flight permit, this pink copy is temporary authority to operate the aircraft.

CHANGE OF ADDRESS: An aircraft owner must notify the FAA Aircraft Registry of any change in permanent address. This form may be used to submit a new address.

AC Form 8050-1 (3/90) (0052-00-628-9006) Supersedes Previous Edition

Fig. 12-9A. Instructions for completing AC Form 8050-1.

UNITED STATES OF AMERICA DEPARTMENT OF TRANSPORTATION
FEDERAL AVIATION ADMINISTRATION-MIKE MONRONEY AERONAUTICAL CENTER
AIRCRAFT REGISTRATION APPLICATION

CERT. ISSUE DATE

UNITED STATES
REGISTRATION NUMBER **N**

AIRCRAFT MANUFACTURER & MODEL

AIRCRAFT SERIAL No.

FOR FAA USE ONLY

TYPE OF REGISTRATION (Check one box)

☐ 1. Individual ☐ 2. Partnership ☐ 3. Corporation ☐ 4. Co-owner ☐ 5. Gov't. ☐ 8. Non-Citizen Corporation

NAME OF APPLICANT (Person(s) shown on evidence of ownership. If individual, give last name, first name, and middle initial.)

TELEPHONE NUMBER: (   )

ADDRESS (Permanent mailing address for first applicant listed.)

Number and street: _____

Rural Route: _____   P.O. Box: _____

CITY	STATE	ZIP CODE

☐ **CHECK HERE IF YOU ARE ONLY REPORTING A CHANGE OF ADDRESS**
ATTENTION! Read the following statement before signing this application.
This portion MUST be completed.

A false or dishonest answer to any question in this application may be grounds for punishment by fine and / or imprisonment (U.S. Code, Title 18, Sec. 1001).

CERTIFICATION

I/WE CERTIFY:

(1) That the above aircraft is owned by the undersigned applicant, who is a citizen (including corporations) of the United States.

(For voting trust, give name of trustee: _____), or:

CHECK ONE AS APPROPRIATE:

a. ☐ A resident alien, with alien registration (Form 1-151 or Form 1-551) No. _____

b. ☐ A non-citizen corporation organized and doing business under the laws of (state) _____
and said aircraft is based and primarily used in the United States. Records or flight hours are available for inspection at _____

(2) That the aircraft is not registered under the laws of any foreign country; and

(3) That legal evidence of ownership is attached or has been filed with the Federal Aviation Administration.

NOTE: If executed for co-ownership all applicants must sign. Use reverse side if necessary.

TYPE OR PRINT NAME BELOW SIGNATURE

	SIGNATURE	TITLE	DATE
EACH PART OF THIS APPLICATION MUST BE SIGNED IN INK.	SIGNATURE	TITLE	DATE
	SIGNATURE	TITLE	DATE
	SIGNATURE	TITLE	DATE

NOTE   Pending receipt of the Certificate of Aircraft Registration, the aircraft may be operated for a period not in excess of 90 days, during which time the PINK copy of this application must be carried in the aircraft.

AC Form 8050-1 (3/90) (0052-00-628-9006) Supersedes Previous Edition

Fig. 12-9B. AC Form 8050-1 Aircraft Registration Application.

THIS FORM SERVES TWO PURPOSES
PART I acknowledges the recording of a security conveyance covering the collateral shown.
PART II is a suggested form of release which may be used to release the collateral from the terms of the conveyance.

PART I – CONVEYANCE RECORDATION NOTICE

NAME (last name first) OF DEBTOR

NAME and ADDRESS OF SECURED PARTY/ASSIGNEE

NAME OF SECURED PARTY'S ASSIGNOR (if assigned)

Do Not Write In This Block
FOR FAA USE ONLY

FAA REGISTRA-TION NUMBER	AIRCRAFT SERIAL NUMBER	AIRCRAFT MFR. (BUILDER) and MODEL
ENGINE MFR. and MODEL		ENGINE SERIAL NUMBER(S)
PROPELLER MFR. and MODEL		PROPELLER SERIAL NUMBER(S)

THE SECURITY CONVEYANCE DATED _____ COVERING THE ABOVE COLLATERAL WAS RECORDED BY THE FAA AIRCRAFT REGISTRY ON _____ AS CONVEYANCE NUMBER _____.

FAA CONVEYANCE EXAMINER

PART II – RELEASE – (This suggested release form may be executed by the secured party and returned to the FAA Aircraft Registry when terms of the conveyance have been satisfied. See below for additional information.)

THE UNDERSIGNED HEREBY CERTIFIES AND ACKNOWLEDGES THAT HE IS THE TRUE AND LAWFUL HOLDER OF THE NOTE OR OTHER EVIDENCE OF INDEBTEDNESS SECURED BY THE CONVEYANCE REFERRED TO HEREIN ON THE ABOVE-DESCRIBED COLLATERAL AND THAT THE SAME COLLATERAL IS HEREBY RELEASED FROM THE TERMS OF THE CONVEYANCE. ANY TITLE RETAINED IN THE COLLATERAL BY THE CONVEYANCE IS HEREBY SOLD, GRANTED, TRANSFERRED, AND ASSIGNED TO THE PARTY WHO EXECUTED THE CONVEYANCE, OR TO THE ASSIGNEE OF SAID PARTY IF THE CONVEYANCE SHALL HAVE BEEN ASSIGNED: PROVIDED, THAT NO EXPRESS WARRANTY IS GIVEN NOR IMPLIED BY REASON OF EXECUTION OR DELIVERY OF THIS RELEASE.

This form is only intended to be a suggested form of release, which meets the recording requirements of the Federal Aviation Act of 1958, and the regulations issued thereunder. In addition to these requirements, the form used by the security holder should be drafted in accordance with pertinent provisions of local statutes and other applicable federal statutes. This form may be reproduced. There is no fee for recording a release. Send to FAA Aircraft Registry, P.O. Box 25504, Oklahoma City, Oklahoma 73125.

ACKNOWLEDGEMENT (If Required By Applicable Local Law):

DATE OF RELEASE: ....

....
(Name of security holder)

SIGNATURE (in ink) ....

TITLE ....

(A person signing for a corporation must be a corporate officer or hold a managerial position and must show his title. A person signing for another should see Parts 47 and 49 of the Federal Aviation Regulations (14 CFR).

Fig. 12-10. AC Form 8050-41 for acknowledging and releasing a lien. Other forms are acceptable, as this particular form is only a suggestion made by the FAA.

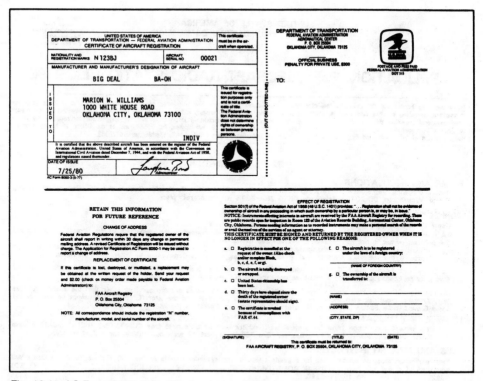

Fig. 12-11. AC Form 8050-3 Certificate of Aircraft Registration.

as services, coverage, and rates do differ. Also, the AOPA and the EAA each have companies they recommend; check with them.

Check your personal health and life insurance policies and assure coverage while flying a small airplane. It is common to find exclusions in personal policies that will leave you completely uncovered in the event of injury or death while flying a small airplane.

BRINGING IT HOME

In most cases the new owner will fly the airplane home to where it will be based. However, sometimes it might be delivered by the past owner, friend, or a dealer. Whatever the case is, be sure the pilot is qualified to handle the airplane, legally and technically.

Legally. Be sure the pilot is properly rated and current for the particular airplane, possessing a current medical, and covered by your insurance.

Technically. Make certain that he can actually handle the airplane in a safe and proper manner.

APPLICATION FOR AIRCRAFT RADIO STATION LICENSE

Public reporting burden for this collection of information is estimated to average twenty minutes per response, including the time for reviewing instructions, searching existing data sources, gathering and maintaining the data needed, and completing and reviewing the collection of information. Send comments regarding this burden estimate or any other aspect of this collection of information, including suggestions for reducing the burden to Federal Communications Commission, Information Resources Branch, Room 416, Washington, DC 20554, and to the Office of Management and Budget, Office of Information and Regulatory Affairs, Paperwork Reduction Project (3060-0040), Washington, DC 20503.

GENERAL INFORMATION

RULES AND REGULATIONS

Before preparing this application, refer to FCC Rules, Part 87, "Aviation Services". Contact the U.S. Government Printing Office, Washington, DC 20402, telephone (202) 783-3238 for the correct price.

CORRECT FORM

Use FCC 404 to apply for:

● A new station license when the station aboard an aircraft is first licensed or the ownership of the aircraft is changed and the previous owner is not to continue as the licensee of the station.

● A modified station license when the licensee remains the same, but the operation is to be different from that provided in the license. If the licensee's name or mailing address changes, notify the Commission by letter, see FCC Rules, Part 87.

To renew your license use FCC 405-B which is normally sent to each licensee at the address of record approximately 60 days prior to license expiration. If you have not received FCC 405-B, you may use FCC 404.

Do not use FCC 404 when applying for transmitters or radio frequencies in radio services other than the aviation services (e.g., Amateur, Industrial) even though these facilities may be placed aboard the aircraft. FCC 404 cannot be used to file for a Ground Radio Station License or Restricted Radiotelephone Operator's Permit.

NUMBER OF APPLICATIONS

Submit a separate application form for each aircraft and for each portable radio (see COMPLETING THE APPLICATION, Item 14), unless the application is for a fleet license. See FCC Rules, Part 87 for those eligible for a fleet license.

FEES AND MAILING INSTRUCTIONS

Each application must be accompanied by a single check or money order payable to the FCC for the Total Fee Due. Mail your application and fee to: FEDERAL COMMUNICATIONS COMMISSION, AVIATION AIRCRAFT SERVICE, P. O. BOX 358280, PITTSBURGH, PA 15251-5280.

FEE EXEMPTIONS: No fee is required for governmental entities. Fee exempt applications should be mailed to: FEDERAL COMMUNICATIONS COMMISSION, 1270 FAIRFIELD ROAD, GETTYSBURG, PA 17325-7245.

COMPLETING THE APPLICATION

ITEM 1. Enter the legal name of the person or entity applying for the license. If you are an individual doing business in your own name, enter your full individual name, (last name, first name, and middle initial).

EXAMPLE: Smith, John A.

If you are an individual doing business under a firm or trade name (sole proprietorship), enter both your name and the firm or trade name.

EXAMPLE: Doe, John H. DBA Doe Construction Co.

Do not apply in the name of more than one individual, except on behalf of a legally recognized partnership. If the applicant is a partnership, list the name of the partner whose address appears in items 2 through 6. List the other partners in item 15. If you are a member of a partnership doing business under a firm or company name, insert the full name of each partner having an interest in the business and the firm or company trade name.

EXAMPLE: Doe, John H. & Doe, Richard A. DBA

Doe Construction Company

If you are filing as a corporation, insert the exact name of the corporation as it appears in the Articles of Incorporation. If you are an unincorporated association, insert the name of the association as it appears in the Articles of Association or By-Laws. If you are a governmental entity, insert the name of the Government entity having jurisdiction of the station.

EXAMPLE: State of California   City of Houston, TX
County of Fairfax, VA

ITEMS 2-6. Enter a permanent mailing address in the United States to which the authorization and any future correspondence related to your station is to be mailed.

ITEM 7. The FAA registration number must be entered on applications submitted for a new station license except those for which FAA registration is not required or those for a fleet or portable license. If exempt from FAA registration, provide an explanation in item 15. When a fleet or portable license is involved, a control number will be assigned by the Commission. When applying for modification or renewal of an existing aircraft radio station license, the FAA registration number or the control number appearing on the license must be entered in item 7.

GOVERNMENTAL ENTITIES ARE EXEMPT FROM FEE REQUIREMENTS AND SHOULD SKIP ITEMS 8 THROUGH 10 OF THE APPLICATION

FCC 404 INSTRUCTIONS
SEPTEMBER 1991

(CONTINUED ON REVERSE)

Fig. 12-12A. Information and instructions for FCC Form 404 Application for Aircraft Radio Station License. Currently there is a $35 filing fee.

COMPLETING THE APPLICATION (CONTINUED)

ITEM 8. Refer to the Private Radio Services Fee Filing Guide for the appropriate Fee Type Code to enter for this application.

ITEM 9. Enter the number of aircraft to be licensed as the Fee Multiple. Normally, the Fee Multiple will be "1", unless the application is for a fleet license, in which case you must show the number of aircraft in the fleet for a new station license, or the number to be added if application is for a modification.

ITEM 10. Refer to the Private Radio Services Fee Filing Guide to determine the fee amount associated with the Fee Type Code in item 8. Multiply the fee amount by the Fee Multiple in item 9, enter the result in item 10, Fee Due. Your check or money order should be for this amount. We will not accept multiple checks.

ITEM 11. Check only one block for the appropriate type of applicant.

ITEM 12. Check the appropriate block for the purpose of filing this application, if for a modification, briefly explain proposed modifications.

ITEM 13. Indicate if application is for a fleet license, if "YES", show the total number of aircraft for a new fleet license, or show the number of aircraft being added or deleted for a modification.

ITEM 14. Check the desired frequencies based on the following information:

PRIVATE AIRCRAFT: These frequencies include those normally available for air traffic control, aeronautical advisory, aeronautical multicom, ground traffic control, and navigation. Refer to Part 87 of the Rules for the specific frequencies available. Private aircraft frequencies are avail- able to any aircraft except those weighing more than 12,500 pounds which are used in carrying passengers or cargo for hire. Do not apply for private aircraft frequencies if the aircraft falls within the latter category.

AIR CARRIER: Refer to Part 87 of the Rules for specific frequencies available.

DO NOT CHECK BOTH PRIVATE AIRCRAFT AND AIR CARRIER IN ITEM 14A.

FLIGHT TEST HF OR VHF OR BOTH: Submit a statement showing that the applicant is a manufacturer of aircraft or major aircraft components. Any request for VHF flight test frequencies must be accompanied by AFTRCC Coordination.

PORTABLE: Submit a statement that it is necessary for the applicant to move the transmitting equipment aboard various U.S. registered aircraft. NOTE: No license is required for a portable radio used only as a back-up on an aircraft which has a station license.

OTHER: Specify any other frequencies you require that are not regularly available for use in accordance with the provisions of Part 87 of the Rules. Each request for "Other" frequencies must be accompanied by a statement showing the need for assignment, including reference to any governmental contracts which may be involved and a description of the proposed use. The emission, power, points of communication, and area of operation should also be included in the statement. In certain cases, AFTRCC Coordination is required.

Application must bear an original signature. Failure to sign the application may result in dismissal of the application and forfeiture of any fees paid.

FCC 404 INSTRUCTIONS
SEPTEMBER 1991

 DETACH HERE

- -

UNITED STATES OF AMERICA
FEDERAL COMMUNICATIONS COMMISSION

Approved by OMB
3060-0040
Expires 7/31/94
See instructions for
public burden estimate.

TEMPORARY AIRCRAFT RADIO STATION
OPERATING AUTHORITY

Use this form if you want temporary operating authority while your regular application, FCC 404, is being processed by the FCC. This authority authorizes the use of transmitters operating on the appropriate frequencies listed in Part 87 of the Commission's Rules.

DO NOT use this form if you already have a valid aircraft station license.
DO NOT use this form when renewing your aircraft license.
DO NOT use this form if you are applying for a fleet license.
DO NOT use this form if you do not have an FAA Registration Number.

ALL APPLICANTS MUST CERTIFY:

1. I am not a representative of a foreign government.
2. I have applied for an Aircraft Radio Station License by mailing a completed FCC Form 404 to the FCC.
3. I have not been denied a license or had my license revoked by the FCC.
4. I am not the subject of any adverse legal action concerning the operation of a radio station license.
5. I ensure that the Aircraft Radio Station will be operated only by individuals properly licensed or otherwise permitted by the Commission's Rules.

WILLFUL FALSE STATEMENTS MADE ON THIS FORM ARE PUNISHABLE BY FINE AND/OR IMPRISONMENT (U.S. CODE, TITLE 18, SECTION 1001), AND/OR REVOCATION OF ANY STATION LICENSE OR CONSTRUCTION PERMIT (U.S. CODE, TITLE 47, SECTION 312(A)(1)), AND/OR FORFEITURE (U.S. CODE, TITLE 47, SECTION 503).

Name of Applicant (Print or Type)	Signature of Applicant
FAA Registration Number (Use as Temporary Call Sign)	Date FCC 404 Mailed

Your authority to operate your Aircraft Radio Station is subject to all applicable laws, treaties and regulations and is subject to the right of control of the Government of the United States. This authority is valid for 90 days from the date FCC 404 is mailed to the FCC.

> **YOU MUST POST THIS TEMPORARY OPERATING AUTHORITY ON BOARD YOUR AIRCRAFT**

FCC 404-A
September 1991

Fig. 12-12B. Further instructions and the Temporary Aircraft Radio Station Operating Authority stub, which will be used while the FCC processes your application.

FOR
FCC
USE
ONLY

UNITED STATES OF AMERICA
FEDERAL COMMUNICATIONS COMMISSION

APPLICATION FOR AIRCRAFT RADIO STATION LICENSE

1. APPLICANT NAME

2. MAILING ADDRESS (Line 1)

3. MAILING ADDRESS (Line 2)

4. CITY

5. STATE

6. ZIP CODE

7. FAA REGISTRATION OR FCC CONTROL NUMBER
(If FAA registration is not required
for your aircraft, explain in item 15) N_____

8. FEE TYPE CODE

9. FEE MULTIPLE

10. FEE DUE

$

FOR FCC USE ONLY

11. TYPE OF APPLICANT

☐ I–Individual

☐ D–Individual with Business Name

☐ P–Partnership

☐ C–Corporation

☐ A–Association

☐ G–Governmental Entity

12. PURPOSE OF APPLICATION

☐ New Station   ☐ Renewal

☐ Modification (Specify) _____

_____

13. IS APPLICATION FOR A FLEET LICENSE?   ☐ YES   ☐ NO

A. If modifying a fleet license, give the number of aircraft to be added. _____
B. If applying for a new or modified fleet license, give the total number of aircraft. _____

14. FREQUENCIES REQUESTED (Check appropriate box(es) in 14A and/or 14B, see Instructions)

A. CHECK ONLY ONE

☐ A–Private Aircraft

☐ C–Air Carrier

B. ADDITIONAL INFORMATION IS REQUIRED IF YOU CHECK HERE

☐ T–Flight Test HF

☐ V–Flight Test VHF

☐ P–Portable (Showing required)

☐ O–Other (Specify) _____

15. ANSWER SPACE FOR ADDITIONAL INFORMATION

CERTIFICATION
1. Applicant waives all claims for the use of any specific frequency regardless of prior use by license or otherwise.
2. Applicant will have unlimited access to the radio equipment and will control access to exclude unauthorized persons.
3. Neither applicant nor any member thereof is a foreign government or representative thereof.
4. Applicant certifies that all statements made in this application and attachments are true, complete, correct and made in good faith.
5. Applicant certifies that the signature that appears on this application is that of a person with the proper authority to act on behalf of the party represented.

WILLFUL FALSE STATEMENTS MADE ON THIS FORM ARE PUNISHABLE BY FINE AND/OR IMPRISONMENT (U.S. CODE, TITLE 18, SECTION 1001), AND/OR REVOCATION OF ANY STATION LICENSE OR CONSTRUCTION PERMIT (U.S. CODE, TITLE 47, SECTION 312(A)(1)), AND/OR FORFEITURE (U.S. CODE, TITLE 47, SECTION 503).

➔ **SIGNATURE**   **DATE**

FAILURE TO SIGN THIS APPLICATION MAY RESULT IN DISMISSAL OF THE APPLICATION AND FORFEITURE OF ANY FEES PAID.

FCC 404
September 1991

Fig. 12-12C. FCC Form 404 Application for Aircraft Radio Station License.

SPECIAL FLIGHT PERMITS

In some instances an airplane may not be legal to fly because of damage, an outdated annual inspection, or not able to meet applicable airworthiness requirements. It could, however, be safe for flight. In the case of classic planes this might include marginal fabric covering, damage to the metal skin, a poor engine, or malfunctioning instruments.

If your plane is such a case, contact the FAA office nearest where the aircraft is located. They can arrange a Special Flight Permit, generally called a ferry permit. The special flight permit is issued to allow the aircraft to be flown to a base where repairs, alterations, or maintenance can be performed. It is issued for one-time use. An FAA inspector may personally inspect the aircraft, or require it to be inspected by a licensed mechanic, to determine its safety for the intended flight. This inspection must be recorded in the logbook.

Before flying an aircraft on a ferry permit, check with your insurance company to assure that you and your investment will be covered in the event of a loss. For further information about special flight permits, contact your nearest FAA installation.

13

FARs
you need to know

THE GOVERNING authority of aviation are Federal Aviation Regulations (FARs). Owners and operators of airplanes must be familiar with those that pertain to their operations.

FARS FOR CLASSICS

A number of FARs directly affect owners of classic airplanes. These have to do with approved design and maintenance. Although not complicated to understand, FARs often leave considerable leeway for interpretation. The interpretation will be done by the FAA, generally from a Flight Standards District Office (FSDO).

Unfortunately, there are some inconsistency problems within the bureaucracy of the FAA and, as a result, you might find that what one office says might go against what is said by another office. My recommendation is to get to know the local office and work with them. It is far easier to work with the FAA than against them.

In general, I have found FAA inspectors to be cooperative and knowledgeable to work with. However, with today's fiscal problems, most are overworked. Additionally, some tend to look at the low end of general aviation (anything less than high-dollar business operations) as a nuisance.

HISTORY OF THE FARS

In the early days of flying the rules for aviation were called Civil Air Regulations (CARs) and were issued by the Civil Aeronautics Administration (CAA). When working with classic airplanes you will no doubt come across references to the CAA and CARs.

In 1959 the Civil Aeronautics Administration name was changed to the Federal Aviation Agency and the Civil Air Regulations renamed Federal Aviation Regulations. In 1967 agency was changed to administration, hence the Federal Aviation

Administration. The FAA is now a part of the U.S. Department of Transportation (DOT).

As with all government regulations, those dealing with aircraft manufacture, modification, maintenance, and pilots are being rewritten and redefined constantly. Of course these changes are intended to improve aviation safety.

The FARs are broken into "parts" applicable to specific subject matter.

FARs

PART 21: CERTIFICATION PROCEDURE FOR PRODUCTS AND PARTS

SUBPART A–General

FAR 21.1 Applicability.

(a) This part prescribes—

(1) Procedural requirements for the issue of type certificates and changes to those certificates; the issue of production certificates; the issue of airworthiness certificates; and the issue of export airworthiness approvals;

(2) Rules governing the holders of any certificate specified in paragraph (a)(1) of this section; and

(3) Procedural requirements for the approval of certain materials, parts, processes, and appliances.

(b) For the purposes of this Part, the word "product" means an aircraft, aircraft engine, or propeller. In addition, for the purposes of Subpart L only, it includes components and parts of aircraft, of aircraft engines, and of propellers; also parts, materials, and appliances, approved under the Technical Standard Order system.

SUBPART B–Type Certificates

FAR 21.11 Applicability.

This subpart prescribes—

(a) Procedural requirements for the issue of type certificates for aircraft, aircraft engines, and propellers; and

(b) Rules governing the holders of those certificates.

FAR 21.31 Type Design

The type design consists of—

(a) The drawings and specifications, and a listing of those drawings and specifications, necessary to define the configuration and the design features of the product shown to comply with the requirements of that part of this subchapter applicable to the product;

(b) Information on dimensions, materials, and processes necessary to define the structural strength of the product;

(c) The Airworthiness Limitations section of the Instructions for Continued Airworthiness as required by Parts 23, 25, 27, 29, 31, 33 and 35 of this chapter; and as specified in the applicable airworthiness criteria for special classes of aircraft defined in 21.17(b); and

(d) Any other data necessary to allow, by comparison, the determination of the airworthiness, noise characteristics, fuel venting, and exhaust emissions (where applicable) of later products of the same type.

FAR 21.41 Type certificate.

Each type certificate is considered to include the type design, the operating limitations, the certificate data sheet, the applicable regulations of this subchapter with which the Administrator records compliance, and any other conditions or limitations prescribed for the product in this subchapter.

SUBPART D–Changes to Type Certificates

FAR 21.91 Applicability.

This subpart prescribes procedural requirements for the approval of changes to type certificates.

FAR 21.93 Classification of changes in type design.

(a) In addition to changes in type design specified in paragraph (b) of this section, changes in type design are classified as minor and major. A "minor change" is one that has no appreciable effect on the weight, balance, structural strength, reliability, operational characteristics, or other characteristics affecting the airworthiness of the product. All other changes are "major changes" (except as provided in paragraph (b) of this section).

FAR 21.97 Approval of major changes in type design.

(a) In the case of a major change in the type design, the applicant must submit substantiating data and necessary descriptive data for inclusion in the type design.

(b) Approval of a major change in the type design of an aircraft engine is limited to the specific engine configuration upon which the change is made unless the applicant identifies in the necessary descriptive data for inclusion in the type design the other configurations of the same engine type for which approval is requested and shows the change is compatible with the other configurations.

SUBPART E–Supplemental Type Certificates

FAR 21.111 Applicability.

This subpart prescribes procedural requirements for the issue of supplemental type certificates.

FAR 21.113 Requirements of supplemental type certificate.

Any person who alters a product by introducing a major change in type design, not great enough to require a new application for a type certificate under 21.19, shall apply to the Administrator for a supplemental type certificate, except the holder of a type certificate for the product may apply for amendment of the original type certificate. The application must be made in a form and manner prescribed by the administrator.

FAR 21.115 Applicable requirements.

(a) Each applicant for a supplemental type certificate must show that the altered product meets applicable airworthiness requirements as specified in paragraphs (a) and (b) of FAR 21.101 and, in the case of an acoustical change described in FAR 21.93(b), show compliance with the applicable noise requirements of FAR 36.7 and FAR 36.9 of this chapter and, in the case of emissions change described in 21.93(c), show compliance with the applicable fuel venting and exhaust emissions requirements of part 34.

(b) Each applicant for a supplemental type certificate must meet FAR 21.33 and FAR 21.53 with respect to each change in the type design.

FAR 21.117 Issue of supplemental type certificates.

(a) An applicant is entitled to a supplemental type certificate if he meets the requirements of FAR 21.113 and FAR 21.115.

(b) A supplemental type certificate consists of—

(1) The approval by the Administrator of a change in the type design of the product; and

(2) The type certificate previously issued for the product.

FAR 21.119 Privileges

The holder of a supplemental type certificate may—

(a) In the case of aircraft, obtain airworthiness certificates;

(b) In the case of other products, obtain approval for installation on certificated aircraft; and

(c) Obtain a production certificate for the change in the type design that was approved by that supplement type certificate.

SUBPART H–Airworthiness Certificates

FAR 21.171 Applicability.

This subpart prescribes procedural requirements for the issue of airworthiness certificates.

FAR 21.173 Eligibility.

Any registered owner of a U.S. registered aircraft (or the agent of the owner) may apply for an airworthiness certificate for that aircraft. An application for an airworthiness certificate must be made in a form and manner acceptable to the Administrator, and may be submitted to any FAA office.

FAR 21.175 Airworthiness certificates: classification.

(a) Standard airworthiness certificates are airworthiness certificates issued for aircraft type certified in the normal, utility, acrobatic, commuter, or transport category and for manned free balloons, and for aircraft designated by the Administrator as special classes of aircraft.

(b) Special airworthiness certificates are restricted, limited and provisional airworthiness certificates, special flight permits, and experimental certificates.

SUBPART K–Approval of Materials, Parts, Process, and Appliances

FAR 21.301 Applicability.

This subpart prescribes procedural requirements for the approval of certain materials, parts, processes, and appliances.

FAR 21.303 Replacement and modification parts.

(a) Except as provided in paragraph (b) of this section, no person may produce a modification or replacement part for sale for installation on a type certificated product unless it is produced pursuant to a Parts Manufacturer Approval issued under this subpart.

(b) This section does not apply to the following:

(1) Parts produced under a type or production certificate.

(2) Parts produced by an owner or operator for maintaining or altering his own product.

(3) Parts produced under an FAA Technical Standard Order.

(4) Standard parts (such as bolts and nuts) conforming to established industry or U.S. specifications.

PART 23: AIRWORTHINESS STANDARDS NORMAL, UTILITY, AND ACROBATIC CATEGORY AIRPLANES

SUBPART A–General

FAR 23.1 Applicability.

(a) This Part prescribes airworthiness standards for the issue of type certificates, and changes to those certificates, for airplanes in the normal, utility, acrobatic, and commuter categories.

(b) Each person who applies under Part 21 for such a certificate or change must show compliance with the applicable requirements of this part.

PART 43: MAINTENANCE, PREVENTIVE MAINTENANCE, REBUILDING, AND ALTERATION

FAR 43.1 Applicability.

(a) Except as provided in paragraph (b) of this section, this part prescribes rules governing the maintenance, preventive maintenance, rebuilding, and alteration of any—

(1) Aircraft having a U.S. airworthiness certificate;

(2) Foreign-registered civil aircraft used in common carriage or carriage of main under the provisions of Part 121, 127, or 135 of this chapter; and

(3) Airframe, aircraft engines, propellers, appliances, and component parts of such aircraft.

(b) This part does not apply to an aircraft for which an experimental airworthiness certificate has been issued, unless a different kind of airworthiness certificate had previously been issued for that aircraft.

FAR 43.3 Persons authorized to perform maintenance, preventive maintenance, rebuilding, and alterations.

(a) Except as provided in this section and 43.17, no person may maintain, rebuild, alter, or perform preventive maintenance on an aircraft, airframe, aircraft engine, propeller, appliance, or component part to which this part applies. Those items, the performance of which is a major alteration, a major repair, or preventive maintenance are listed in Appendix A.

(b) The holder of a mechanic certificate may perform maintenance, preventive maintenance, and alterations as provided in Part 65 of this chapter.

(c) The holder of a repairman certificate may perform maintenance and preventive maintenance as provided in Part 65 of this chapter.

(d) A person working under the supervision of a holder of a mechanic or repairman certificate may perform maintenance, preventive maintenance, and alterations that his supervisor is authorized to perform, if the supervisor personally observes the work being done to the extent necessary to ensure that it is being done properly and if the supervisor is readily available, in person, for consultation. However, this paragraph does not authorize the performance of any inspection required by Part 91 or Part 125 of this chapter or any inspection performed after a major repair or alteration.

(e) The holder of a repair station certificate may perform maintenance, preventive maintenance, and alterations as provided in Part 145 of this chapter.

(f) The holder of an air carrier operating certificate or an operating certificate issued under Part 121, 127, or 135, may perform maintenance, preventive maintenance, and alterations as provided in Part 121, 127, or 135.

(g) The holder of a pilot certificate issued under Part 61 may perform preventive maintenance on any aircraft owned or operated by that pilot which is not used under Part 121, 127, 129, or 135.

(h) Note: applicable only to Part 135 operations, ed.

(i) A manufacturer may—

(1) Rebuild or alter any aircraft, aircraft engine, propeller, or appliance manufactured by him under a type or production certificate;

(2) Rebuild or alter any appliance or part of aircraft, aircraft engines, propellers, or appliances manufactured by him under a Technical Standard Order Authorization, an FAA-Parts Manufacturer Approval, or Product and Process Specification issued by the Administrator; and

(3) Perform any inspection required by Part 91 or Part 125 of this chapter on aircraft it manufacturers, while currently operating under a production certificate or under a currently approved production inspection system for such aircraft.

FAR 43.5 Approval for return to service after maintenance, preventive maintenance, rebuilding, or alteration.

No person may approve for return to service any aircraft, airframe, aircraft engine, propeller, or appliance, that has undergone maintenance, preventive maintenance, rebuilding, or alteration unless—

(a) The maintenance record entry required by 43.9 or 43.11, as appropriate, has been made;

(b) The repair or alteration form authorized by or furnished by the Administrator has been executed in a manner prescribed by the Administrator; and

(c) If a repair or an alteration results in any change in the aircraft operating limitations or flight data contained in the approved aircraft flight manual, those operating limitations or flight data are appropriately revised and set forth as prescribed in FAR 91.9 of this chapter.

FAR 43.7 Persons authorized to approve aircraft, airframes, aircraft engines, propellers, appliances, or component parts for return to service after maintenance, preventive maintenance, rebuilding, or alteration.

(a) Except as provided in this section and 43.17, no person, other than the Administrator, may approve an aircraft, airframe, aircraft engine, propeller, appliance, or component part for return to service after it has undergone maintenance, preventive maintenance, rebuilding, or alteration.

(b) The holder of a mechanics certificate or inspection authorization may approve an aircraft, airframe, aircraft engine, propeller, appliance or component part for return to service as provided in Part 65 of this chapter.

(c) The holder of a repair station certificate may approve an aircraft, airframe, aircraft engine, propeller, appliance, or component part for return to service as provided in Part 145 of this chapter.

(d) A manufacturer may approve for return to service any aircraft, airframe, aircraft engine, propeller, appliance, or component part which that manufacturer has worked on under FAR 43.3(h). However, except for minor alterations, the work must have been done in accordance with technical data approved by the Administrator.

(e) The holder of an air carrier operating certificate or an operating certificate issued under Part 121, 127, or 135, may approve an aircraft, airframe, aircraft engine, propeller, appliance, or component part for return to service as provided in Part 121, 127, or 135 of this chapter, as applicable.

(f) A person holding at least a private pilot certificate may approve an aircraft for return to service after performing preventive maintenance under the provisions of 43.3(g).

PART 43: Appendix B Recording of Major Repairs and Major Alterations.

(a) Except as provided in paragraphs (b), (c), and (d) of this appendix, each person performing a major repair or major alteration shall—

(1) Execute FAA Form 337 at least in duplicate;

(2) Give a signed copy of that form to the aircraft owner; and

(3) Forward a copy of that form to the local FAA District Office within 48 hours after the aircraft, airframe, aircraft engine, propeller, or appliance is approved for return to service.

(b) For major repairs made in accordance with a manual or specification acceptable to the Administrator, a certificated repair station may, in place of the requirements of paragraph (a)—

(1) Use the customer's work order upon which the repair is recorded;

(2) Give the aircraft owner a signed copy of the work order and retain a duplicate copy for at least two years from the date of approval for return to service of the aircraft, airframe, aircraft engine, propeller, or appliance;

(3) Give the aircraft owner a maintenance release signed by an authorized representative of the repair station and incorporating the following information:

(i) Identity of the aircraft, airframe, aircraft engine, propeller, or appliance.

(ii) If an aircraft, the make, model, serial number, nationality and registration marks, and location of the repaired area.

(iii) If an aircraft, airframe, aircraft engine, propeller, or appliance, give the manufacturer's name, name of the part, model, and serial numbers (if any); and

(4) Include the following or a similarly worded statement—"The aircraft, airframe, aircraft engine, propeller, or appliance identified above was repaired and inspected in accordance with current Regulations of the Federal Aviation Agency and is approved for return to service.

Pertinent details of the repair are on file at this repair station under

Order No. _____

Date_____

Signed_____
(For signature of authorized representative)

_____
(Repair Station Name)   (Certificate No.)

_____
(Address)

(c) For a major repair or major alteration made by a person authorized in FAR 43.17, the person who performs the major repair or major alteration and the person authorized by FAR 43.17 to approve that work shall execute FAA Form 337 at least in duplicate. A completed copy of that form shall be—

(1) Given to the aircraft owner; and

(2) Forwarded to the Federal Aviation Administration Aircraft Registration Branch, P.O. Box 25082, Oklahoma City, OK 73125, within 48 hours after the work is inspected.

SUBPART E: Maintenance, Preventive Maintenance, and Alterations

FAR 91.401 Applicability.

(a) This subpart prescribes rules governing the maintenance, preventive maintenance, and alterations of U.S. registered civil aircraft operating within or without the United States.

(b) Sections 91.405, 91.409, 91.411, 91.417, and 91.419 of this subpart do not apply to aircraft maintained in accordance with a continuous airworthiness maintenance program as provided in Part 121, 127, 129, or 135.411(a)(2) of this chapter.

FAR 91.403 General.

(a) The owner or operator of an aircraft is primarily responsible for maintaining that aircraft in an airworthy condition, including compliance with Part 39 of this chapter.

(b) No person may perform maintenance, preventive maintenance, or alterations on an aircraft other than as prescribed in this subpart and other applicable regulations, including Part 43 of this chapter.

(c) No person may operate an aircraft for which a manufacturer's maintenance manual or instructions for continued airworthiness has been issued that contains an airworthiness limitations section unless the mandatory replacement times, inspection intervals, and related procedures specified in that section or alternative inspection intervals and related procedures set forth in an operations specification approved by the Administrator under part 121, 127, or 135 of this chapter or in accordance with an inspection program approved under 91.409(e) have been complied with.

FAR 91.405 Maintenance required.

Each owner or operator of an aircraft—

(a) Shall have that aircraft inspected as prescribed in Subpart E of this part and shall between required inspections, except as provided in paragraph (c) of this section, have discrepancies repaired as prescribed in part 43 of this chapter;

(b) Shall ensure that maintenance personnel make appropriate entries in the aircraft and maintenance records indicating the aircraft has been approved for return to service.

(c) Shall have any inoperative instrument or item of equipment, permitted to be inoperative by 91.213(d)(2) of this part, repaired, replaced, removed, or inspected at the next required inspection; and

(d) When listed discrepancies include inoperative instruments or equipment, shall ensure that a placard has been installed as required by 43.11 of this chapter.

FAR 91.7 Civil aircraft airworthiness

(a) No person may operate a civil aircraft unless it is in an airworthy condition.

(b) The pilot in command of a civil aircraft is responsible for determining whether that aircraft is in condition for safe flight. He shall discontinue the flight when unairworthy mechanical, electrical, or structural conditions occur.

WHAT THE FARS MEAN

The FARs are often not completely clear in their meaning, therefore a few comments are offered the reader to clarify some very important points.

Part 21

In general, FAR Part 21 specifies the procedural requirements for issuance of the type certificate, changes via the Supplemental Type Certificate, and maintenance of airworthiness.

After reviewing all data accumulated during the development and testing of an aircraft, and assuring same is in compliance with all regulations, the FAA grants a type certificate for the design. From that time on, each aircraft manufactured by the type certificate holder in compliance with the type design on file, will be eligible for an airworthiness certificate.

FAR 21 also requires that an aircraft be repaired using the same type materials as the original or materials at least equal to the original. This could include bolts, nuts, screws, tubing, aluminum sheet, tires, plywood, instruments, control cables, pulleys, etc. Additionally, workmanship and repair methods must be acceptable to the FAA.

When a modification is made to an airplane, such as installing a different make/model engine, landing gear, high capacity fuel tank, wing tips, fabric recover, etc., that is not stated in the type design, the airworthiness certificate is automatically canceled. This is because that particular aircraft no longer conforms to the type design on file. Remember, the type design is the basis for the granting a type certificate and the airworthiness certificate.

Before an aircraft airworthiness certificate can be renewed a record of the change must be made and approved by the FAA. Generally this is by means of an STC (supplemental type certificate) or FAA field approval (sometimes referred to as Form 337).

When purchasing parts assure you are in compliance with FAR 21.303, which requires parts for use on type certificated aircraft be produced under the quality control of a Parts Manufacturers Approval (PMA). An exception to this is parts manufactured from raw stock and approved on a Form 337 for a specific airplane.

Part 23

FAR Part 23 sets the minimum structural standards and flight characteristic requirements for normal, utility, and aerobatic category aircraft. This FAR is closely related to FAR 21 and Airworthiness Certification.

Part 43

FAR Part 43 covers maintenance (preventive, rebuilding, and alteration) of aircraft having U.S. airworthiness certification. It states, emphatically, who is allowed to work on an airplane. Documentation requirements are stated, as are return to service requirements. Also included in Part 43, and seen in another chapter of this book, is a section on preventive maintenance.

FAR Part 43 details field approval in instances where a modification from the original design does not reduce the airworthiness of the aircraft. Take note, however, that a field approval (by use of FAA Form 337) is for one specific airplane only and does not mean that a similar approval will be granted again in the future (an example of FAA inconsistency).

Part 91

FAR Part 91 fixes ultimate responsibility for maintaining an aircraft in an airworthy condition. To be specific, FAR 91.7 sums it up in (a) by saying, "No person may operate a civil aircraft unless it is in an airworthy condition." The pilot is responsible, not the FBO, mechanic, line boy, dealer, or anyone else!

A few questions to keep you awake at night while your airplane is being repaired: Will the work be done in the prescribed manner? Will proper parts be utilized? Will all work be recorded as required?

14

Maintenance

AS SEEN in the last chapter, FAR 91.403(a): "The owner or operator of an aircraft is primarily responsible for maintaining that aircraft in an airworthy condition . . . ." and FAR 91.7(a): "No person may operate a civil aircraft unless it is in an airworthy condition." Maintenance is the vehicle by which airplanes are kept in airworthy condition.

At the top of the maintenance list is the annual inspection of each small airplane in the civil fleet. The inspection is designed to find all discrepancies in an airplane in order that necessary repairs be made to ensure continued airworthiness.

ANNUAL INSPECTIONS

Annual inspections are forever with airplane ownership. To understand how comprehensive an annual inspection is, review the following recommended inspection instructions. Although for a Taylorcraft BC-12D (courtesy of UNIVAIR), it is quite typical of inspections required for all the airplanes covered in this book.

ENGINE OPERATION:

Run engine to minimum 120 degrees oil temperature—check full throttle static rpm (consult specifications for propeller used).
Check magnetos 75 rpm drop at 1800 rpm.
Check carburetor heat 100 rpm drop at full throttle.
Check ignition switch for operation.
Check idle rpm 550–600 rpm with carburetor heat off.
Oil pressure 10–35 lbs., 30 good.

Engine mounts and attachments:

Check engine mount for damage and cracks at gussets or in corners.
Inspect protective finish on mount; sand and touch up bare areas.
Inspect rubber shock mounts for rubber deterioration and tension.

Engine mount bolts should be tightened to 60–80 inch lbs.
Check mount bolts for safety.

Cowling and baffles:

Clean and inspect engine cowling for dents and cracks at hinges and reinforcement.

Check for tension adjustment on cowl door at fasteners.

Tension prevents vibration and cowl door at fasteners.

Check baffles for cracks and leather installation to prevent chafing.

Magnetos, wiring, and shielding (if installed):

Check magneto for secure attachment.

Check breaker point housing for excessive oil.

Check points for gap pitting. For correct gap.

Check plug wiring connections at magneto and insulation for deterioration and chafing.

Check for grommets at baffles and firewall.

Oil drain and safety plug:

Drain oil and check for metal particles.

Remove, clean and check oil screen for metal particles, drain plug and inlet oil temperature housing.

Reinstall oil drain plug.

Change oil filter if installed and check flexible lines for deterioration.

Spark plug service:

Remove plugs, abrasive blast and clean.

Plugs with badly burned electrodes should be replaced.

Reset gap to .016 on C26 plugs, consult manufacturer's charts for others.

Reinstall using thread lubricant and new gaskets to prevent leakage and seizing. Torque to 300 to 360 inch lbs.

Carburetor and heater:

Check carburetor for mounting security.

Inspect carburetor bowl for cracks, particularly at inlet.

Drain carburetor float chamber and check inlet finger screen carefully.

Operate throttle in cockpit to be sure that throttle arm hits stops in open and closed positions without binding or sticking.

Check operation of mixture control (if installed) for binding or sticking and full rich position.

Inspect carburetor air box for security and cracks-heater valve for full travel.

Check rubber intake hose connections for deterioration and clamp security.

Check intake system for leaks and cracks.

Clean air filter in kerosene and saturate with #10 oil and allow to drain before installation.

Fuel lines and strainer:

Check fuel lines for leaks and hose deterioration.

Check hose supports for security and chafing. Drain and clean fuel strainer and re-safety.

Check for stains around fuel system indicating leaks.

Check all connections for tightness.

Exhaust stack:

Check stack flanges for security, cracks and leaks.

Remove all heater shrouds and inspect for corrosion, cracks and leaks that might transfer gas to the cockpit, particularly through the cabin heater system.

Check tail pipe and stacks for security at all clamps and joints.

Check cabin heater box and control valve for operation.

Check cabin and carburetor heat flexible tubing for security and general condition.

Engine controls and firewall:

Check firewall for open holes and gas leaks from engine compartment. (If open holes, use zinc chromate putty or some other recommended commercial brand.)

Check all controls for grommets and sealing putty.

Propeller:

Remove spinner and check for cracks or dents in spinner and back plates.

Check propeller for separated laminations, cracks, loose metal tipping and protective finish. Blade track within $\frac{1}{16}$".

Wood propeller hub bolts are to torque from 140 to 150 inch lbs.

Metal propeller hub bolts are to torque from 350 to 375 inch lbs.

Cockpit and baggage area:

Seats: Check general condition.

Check condition of safety belts, Airworthiness Directives on seat belts—if frayed, replace.

Check baggage area canvas—if deteriorated, or ripped, replace.

Windshield:

Check weatherstripping for security in channels and for leaks.

Check plastic windshield and side windows for cracks, crazing, distortion and discoloration.

Powerplant instruments:

Check powerplant instruments for mounting security.

Check connections and plugs.

Check placards and limitation markings.

Tachometer: red line—2300 rpm

Oil pressure: red line 10 psi and 35 psi.

Oil temperature: red line—220 degrees F, green arc—120 to 220 degrees F, yellow arc—40 to 120 degrees F.

Flight instruments:

Check flight instruments for mounting security.

Check connections and plugs.

Check placards and limitation markings.

Airspeed: red line—140 mph landplane (129 mph seaplane)

Door latch and hinges:

Check door hinge and rivets for looseness.

Check door latch plunger for complete extension to prevent doors opening while taxiing.

Check door for proper fit or damage resulting from air leaks.

Engine controls:

Check mixture control for panel placard and operation smoothness.

Check carburetor heat for panel placard and smoothness of operation.

Check throttle for smooth operation and operation of friction lock.

Check primer for operation and leaks behind the panel.

Check cabin heat for panel placard and full travel of heater butterfly valve.

Check ignition switch for panel and terminal security.

Check for placard—off, left, right and both.

Rudder pedals and linkage:

Check rudder pedal assemble for play and travel freedom.
Lubricate hinges and torque tube bearings and check for safety.
Check rudder pedal return springs for attachment.

Cables and pulleys:

Check all cables for broken strands.
Remove butt fairings and check top deck aileron pulleys for wear and security.
Check aileron pulleys at both ends of panel. Remove floorboards and check pulleys.

Flight control operation:

Check aileron, rudder and elevator controls from cockpit for smooth operation.
Check wheel for neutral position with control surfaces streamlines.

Trim tab controls:

Check stabilizer trim control for smooth operation.
Check indicator against stabilizer for proper position.

Fuel selector valve:

Check fuel valve for smooth operation.
Check placard for on and off positions.
Check valve for leaks.

Landing gear:

Shock cord—for broken strands and elongation.
Hoist aircraft (by engine mount at firewall) and check gear bushings, vee bushings are replaceable if worn.
Check for skin wrinkles indicative of inside damage.

Axles and wheels:

Remove wheels, wash, check and relubricate bearings.
Check brake shoes for wear and drums for scoring.
Install wheel and axle nut only tight enough to remove end play.

Tires and fairings:

Check tires for 20 lbs. of air pressure.
Replace tires that have cord showing.
Check gear fairings for security and chafing.

Wing fittings:

With wing root fairings removed, inspect wing fittings with a flashlight and magnifying glass for minute cracks in the ears.

Check bolts to be sure there are no threads in bearing, and bolts are properly safetied.

Check wing fitting holes for elongation by having someone pull up and down on wing tips.

Landing gear fittings:

Remove both landing gear fairings and inspect all fittings with flashlight and magnifying glass for signs of cracks or hole elongation.

Fuselage structure:

Through inspection openings and through the baggage compartment cover, check the condition of all tubing for rust, damage and protective coating.

Check all wood stringers for damage and security.

Debris accumulation:

Check the bottom of the fuselage and fabric under floorboards for bolts, nuts and other objects that might jam controls or pulleys.

Check the rear of fuselage for open drain grommets. If considerable dirt or oil exists on the fuselage bottom use a non-caustic soap and wash out the dirt to prevent fabric rot.

Control cables and pulleys:

Check for broken control cable strands by sliding a cloth over the cable in vicinity of fairleads.

Check upper and lower elevator turnbuckles for safety and maximum of three threads showing outside of barrel.

Check stabilizer control for slippage. Increase tension by tightening nut on idler pulley.

Fairings:

Check all fairings for cracks and missing screws.

Wings and ailerons:

Check left and right wing fabric for holes, cracks or checks in the finish and open drain grommets at each rib bay trailing edge. Fabric usually deteriorates on the upper surface of the wing or along the trailing edge.

Install inspection grommets at drag wire fitting to inspect drag wires for tension and wing ribs and compression members for damage.

Struts—lift:

Check right and left wing strut fittings for elongation by having someone lift up and down on the wing.

Check bolts for fitting attachment to the spar.

Check struts for dents or cracks, also sight down strut trailing edge to ascertain that struts are straight.

Check strut end forks and fork lock nut.

Wing bolts:

Check strut attachment bolts to be sure there are no threads in bearing, that nuts are not bottoming on unthreaded part of bolt and bolts are properly safetied.

Ailerons:

Check both ailerons for wrinkles which are possible sign of structural damage.

Check each rib bay for an open drain grommet.

Check condition of fabric and finish, refinishing any dope cracks, checks or ringworm.

Aileron hinges:

Check aileron hinge legs for security at rear spar and false spar.

Check hinge pins for wear and safety. Worn or loose pins must be replaced.

Aileron controls:

Remove inspection covers and check the two cables in each wing for interference and chafing.

Check the two pulleys in each wing for condition, wear and safety.

Lubricate pulley bearings.

Check travel, 23 degrees up, 23 degrees down.

Check the four aileron horn bolts, threads in bearing and safety.

Check the six turnbuckles in the center top of fuselage for safety and not more than three threads showing outside the barrel.

To locate broken strands at fairleads or pulleys, slide a cloth over the cable. All cables with broken strands are to be replaced.

Wing root fairings:

Check left and right fairings for tension.
Check all metal screws for security and the fairings for cracks.

Stabilizer:

Check stabilizer fabric condition and drain grommets for restrictions.
If the fabric strength is suspected a Seybooth tester may be used to accurately test the strength.
Lift up and down on the stabilizer checking for excessive play.

Fin:

Inspect vertical fin for fabric condition and finish.
Check for wrinkles, dents and signs of internal damage.

Rudder:

Inspect the fabric cover on the rudder for fabric and dope condition.
Check bottom of rudder for an open drain grommet.
Check rudder for alignment and possible internal damage usually indicated by a wrinkle in the fabric.
Inspect rudder hinge pins for wear and safety.
Check hinge bushings for play. These bushings are pressed in and should be replaced when worn.
Check rudder travel, 26 degrees left, 26 degrees right.

Elevators:

Check fabric condition and finish on the elevators. Check for open drain grommets along the elevator trailing edge.
Sight one elevator against the other for alignment.
Check hinge pins and bushing for wear and replace any worn pins or bushings.
Check elevator cable horns for safety, worn bolts and clearance in travel.
Check elevator travel, 27 degrees up, 25 degrees down.

External bracing:

Check empennage rigging wires for corrosion and cracks or nicks that might result in failure.
Check fittings for alignment with the wire and check bolts for safety.
Rigging wires should be taut with little hand deflection.
Check each wire to be sure there are no loose fork lock nuts.

Rudder and elevator:

Check rudder and elevator horns for worn bolts and safety with no threads in bearing.

Check horns for alignment with the cable and freedom of travel.

Top and bottom cable turnbuckles for safety and a maximum of three threads showing outside the barrel.

Sight the cables through the fuselage for interference and chafing.

FAA requirements:

Check all Airworthiness Directives (ADs) for applicability and compliance.

Check for presence of Airworthiness Certificate.

Check for presence of Certificate of Registration.

Check for operations limitation/flight manual.

Above items are required in cockpit when aircraft is currently licensed.

MAINTENANCE YOU CAN DO

The FARs (Federal Aviation Regulations) specify that preventive maintenance may be performed by pilots/owners on airplanes not utilized in commercial service. Preventive maintenance is simple or minor preservation operations and the replacement of small standard parts not involving complex assembly operations, in accordance with regulations.

ENCOURAGEMENT BY THE FAA

The FAA encourages pilots and owners to carefully maintain their airplanes and recognizes that preventive maintenance provides the pilot or owner a better understanding of his airplane, added safety, saves money, and offers a great sense of accomplishment. Advisory Circular 150/5190-2A states, in part:

"Restrictions on Self-Service: Any unreasonable restriction imposed on the owners and operators of aircraft regarding the servicing of their own aircraft and equipment may be considered as a violation of agency policy. The owner of an aircraft should be permitted to fuel, wash, repair, paint, and otherwise take care of his own aircraft, provided there is no attempts to perform such services for others. Restrictions which have the effect of diverting activity of this type to a commercial enterprise amount to an exclusive right contrary to law."

PREVENTIVE MAINTENANCE ITEMS

The FARs list 28 preventive maintenance items in Appendix A of part 43.13. This means that only those operations listed are considered preventive maintenance.

(1) Removal, installation and repair of landing gear tires. When changing/repairing a tire on an airplane, the plane is jacked up, much like a car.

However, particular care must be taken, as improper jacking can damage the airframe. Check your owners manual for the proper jacking procedure. The actual tire change is quite straightforward. The wheel is removed, the tire deflated, and the bead broken. After the bead is broken on both sides of the wheel, the nuts on the through bolts can be removed, and the wheel split. Installation is just the opposite. If you are installing a tube, you must be careful not to pinch it between the wheel halves. (See Fig. 14-1.)

(2) Replacing elastic shock-absorber cords on landing gear. This particular job is difficult at best, due to the tensions required and the tools involved. Talk to your mechanic before you attempt it. You may find that this job is more trouble than it's worth to you. It can very easily result in personal injury and/or damage to your airplane. I'll leave to your determination which is worse. A product designed to help is the Bungee-Master. For information contact: G&S Manufacturing at (816) 246-4629.

(3) Servicing landing-gear struts by adding oil, air or both. This maintenance procedure is simple, and requires a minimum of tools. The plane must be on jacks. Open strut filler hole carefully, releasing air/oil pressure, then refill with hydraulic oil. Close the filler hole and inflate with air pressure, if required.

(4) Servicing landing-gear wheel bearings, such as cleaning and greasing. If you are familiar with servicing the bearings on your auto, then this job will present no particular challenge. The wheels are removed as when you change a tire, and the bearings are pulled out. At this point the old grease is cleaned out by use of a solvent. The bearings and their mating surfaces are inspected for damage, then the bearings are repacked with the appropriate grease. Put the bearings back into position, and place the wheel on the axle. Tighten the wheel nut only as is necessary to eliminate any side play. Safety the nut by use of a cotton pin placed through the castellated nut.

(5) Replacing defective safety wiring or cotter pins. Nuts and bolts are items that must be safety wired. The reason for safetying is to prevent them from becoming loose during flight.

Nuts: Any nuts and bolts that do not move will have nuts locked into place by use of a plastic insert that prevents the nut from moving on the bolt. If the bolt/nut combination can move, then the bolt must be drilled and a castellated nut used. A cotter pin will be used as a safety.

Bolts: Drilled head bolts are most often seen fastening the propeller to the flange on the engine. A safety wire of steel, brass, or stainless steel will be run and twisted through each of these bolts. The wire will run from one bolt to the next. The object of the safety wire is to prevent the bolt from turning. The wires are neatly twisted, and must pull on the bolt in the direction of tightening.

(6) Lubrication not requiring disassembly other than removal of nonstructural items such as cover plates, cowlings and fairings. First check the chart of lubrication requirements for your airplane. Specific types and mounts of grease will be given. In addition, the desired frequency of lubrication will be shown. Do not over-lubricate.

(7) Making simple fabric patches not requiring rib stitching or the removal of structural parts or control surfaces. Due to the wide variety of fabrics and finishes

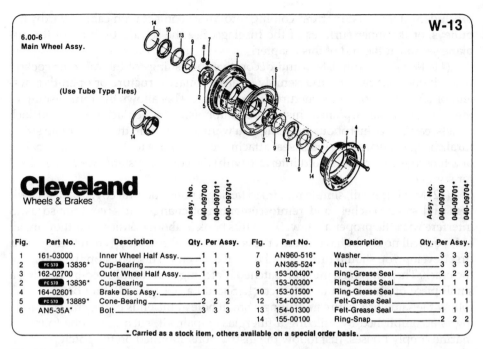

W-13

6.00-6
Main Wheel Assy.

(Use Tube Type Tires)

Cleveland
Wheels & Brakes

Fig.	Part No.	Description	Qty. Per Assy. Assy. No. 040-09700	040-09701*	040-09704*	Fig.	Part No.	Description	Qty. Per Assy. Assy. No. 040-09700	040-09701*	040-09704*
1	161-03000	Inner Wheel Half Assy.	1	1	1	7	AN960-516*	Washer	3	3	3
2	PC 570 13836*	Cup-Bearing	1	1	1	8	AN365-524*	Nut	3	3	3
3	162-02700	Outer Wheel Half Assy.	1	1	1	9	153-00400*	Ring-Grease Seal	2	2	2
2	PC 570 13836*	Cup-Bearing	1	1	1		153-00300*	Ring-Grease Seal	1	1	1
4	164-02601	Brake Disc Assy.	1	1	1	10	153-01500*	Ring-Grease Seal	1	1	1
5	PC 570 13889*	Cone-Bearing	2	2	2	12	154-00300*	Felt-Grease Seal	1	1	1
6	AN5-35A*	Bolt	3	3	3	13	154-01300	Felt-Grease Seal	1	1	1
						14	155-00100	Ring-Snap	2	2	2

* Carried as a stock item, others available on a special order basis.

Fig. 14-1. The airplane wheel splits apart for tire changing. Care must be taken during reassembly to prevent the tube from being crushed between the halves. UNIVAIR

found on airplanes today, I suggest you refer to your airframe log first to determine exactly what process was used in the covering of your airframe. After making this determination, check with the manufacturer for the proper procedure for patching.

(8) Replenishing hydraulic fluid in the hydraulic reservoir. If you have ever filled the brake reservoir of your car with brake fluid, then you are qualified for this job. Just be sure to not overfill, and keep the fluids off of the aircraft finish.

(9) Refinishing decorative coatings of the fuselage, wing, and tail-group surfaces (excluding balanced control surfaces), fairings, cowlings, landing gear, cabin or cockpit interior when removal or disassembly of any primary structure or operating system is not required. This allows you to make touch-ups to your airplane. Before you attempt a touch-up, ascertain what type paint you are touching up. You may have enamel, lacquer, acrylic lacquer, or polyurethane. Type must be matched, as well as color, or the job will not be successful, and could even do more damage than you are trying to fix. The manufacturer of the paint product will supply directions. See Appendix B for suppliers.

(10) Applying preservative or protective material to components when no disassembly of any primary structure or operating system is involved and when such coating is not prohibited or is not contrary to good practices. Normally this will be more important to seaplane operators; however, anyone near the coast should be interested. The job is merely the application of grease or other proper coating to

preclude water/moisture from coming into direct contact with cables, hardware, pulleys, or the inner surfaces of the fuselage. See the self destruction of the airplane section at the end of this chapter.

(11) Repairing upholstery and decorative furnishings of the cabin or cockpit when it does not require disassembly of any primary structure or operating system or affect the primary structure of the aircraft. This allows the refurbishing of the interior of the airplane. This includes upholstering, replacing side and kick panels, carpets, or just about anything you want to do within the limits of no structural changes, such as the seats, seat attachments, changes to the instrument panel, or alterations to (or that would interfere with) the control system. See Appendix B for suppliers.

(12) Making small, simple repairs to fairings, nonstructural cover plates, cowlings and small patches, and reinforcements not changing the contour so as to interfere with the proper airflow. Since this book is about classics, and they are all old, you will no doubt have stress cracks in the metal cowling. When these cracks first develop you should drill a small hole at each end. This will stop the spread of the crack. Then the crack must be patched. Patching is accomplished by riveting a small piece of aluminum over the crack. Should a fiberglass fairing be involved, follow the same procedure in drilling a small hole at the ends of the cracks. Patching is accomplished by utilizing a fiberglass repair kit, such as can be found in marine supply houses. Just follow the instructions supplied on the patch product.

(13) Replacing side windows where that work does not interfere with the structure or any operating system such as controls and electrical equipment. Replacement windows are made of an acrylic material. This material can be purchased in bulk from plastic supply houses, or pre-cut windows can be purchased from a number of suppliers (just look in *Trade-A-Plane*). Installation is simply removal and replacement. Be sure to seal the new window in place with a recommended aircraft sealer. If in doubt, one of the flexible silicone glues will do a good job (Fig. 14-2).

Tip: Never work with plastic windows during cold weather, as the plastic will be very stiff and break/crack easily.

(14) Replacing safety belts. This is a very simple job. Just remove the old belts and install the new belts. However, there are two areas of caution: Be sure the new belts have TSO-C-22 on all parts and that new belts are installed in their original configuration.

(15) Replacing seats or seat parts with replacement parts approved for the aircraft, not involving disassembly of any primary structure or operating system. For this to be done properly you may use only direct replacement approved seats. No welding or riveting is allowed.

(16) Troubleshooting and repairing broken landing light wiring circuits. For any home electrician equipped with a VOM (volt ohm meter), this should be quite easy. First check the bulb, then check to see if there is voltage at the lamp. After that, check at the circuit breaker panel for voltage. Some of the more common places for problems are the connect points at the wing roots and the connect points at the breaker panel. Crimp-on connectors can be used to replace broken original connectors.

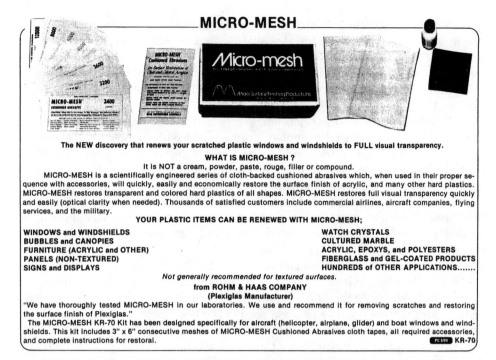

MICRO-MESH

The NEW discovery that renews your scratched plastic windows and windshields to FULL visual transparency.

WHAT IS MICRO-MESH ?

It is NOT a cream, powder, paste, rouge, filler or compound.

MICRO-MESH is a scientifically engineered series of cloth-backed cushioned abrasives which, when used in their proper sequence with accessories, will quickly, easily and economically restore the surface finish of acrylic, and many other hard plastics. MICRO-MESH restores transparent and colored hard plastics of all shapes. MICRO-MESH restores full visual transparency quickly and easily (optical clarity when needed). Thousands of satisfied customers include commercial airlines, aircraft companies, flying services, and the military.

YOUR PLASTIC ITEMS CAN BE RENEWED WITH MICRO-MESH;

WINDOWS and WINDSHIELDS	WATCH CRYSTALS
BUBBLES and CANOPIES	CULTURED MARBLE
FURNITURE (ACRYLIC and OTHER)	ACRYLIC, EPOXYS, and POLYESTERS
PANELS (NON-TEXTURED)	FIBERGLASS and GEL-COATED PRODUCTS
SIGNS and DISPLAYS	HUNDREDS of OTHER APPLICATIONS.......

Not generally recommended for textured surfaces.

**from ROHM & HAAS COMPANY
(Plexiglas Manufacturer)**

"We have thoroughly tested MICRO-MESH in our laboratories. We use and recommend it for removing scratches and restoring the surface finish of Plexiglas."

The MICRO-MESH KR-70 Kit has been designed specifically for aircraft (helicopter, airplane, glider) and boat windows and windshields. This kit includes 3" x 6" consecutive meshes of MICRO-MESH Cushioned Abrasives cloth tapes, all required accessories, and complete instructions for restoral. `PC 699` **KR-70**

Fig. 14-2. Micro-Mesh is produced by Rohm & Haas, makers of Plexiglass. Its use can often repair an otherwise unusable windshield or window. UNIVAIR

(17) Replacing bulbs, reflectors, and lenses of position and landing lights. The only place you could have a problem with this maintenance item would be in utilizing the wrong bulb. Be sure the proper bulbs are utilized.

(18) Replacing wheels and skis where no weight and balance computation is required. The best recommendation I can give here is to follow the instructions that came with your skis. Just be sure that the cable is connected that holds the front of the ski up.

(19) Replacing any cowling not requiring removal of the propeller or disconnection of flight controls. Many cowlings are split into two pieces, and come off quite easily for engine inspection and servicing. Just be careful about tightening the retaining screws. They will only go in and out a limited number of times before the hole becomes enlarged.

(20) Replacing or cleaning spark plugs and setting of spark plug gap clearance. Before attempting this job solo, I recommend that you have your mechanic do it once with you. However, if you are a competent auto mechanic, you'll have little trouble with this procedure. Remove the plugs in order, and keep them that way. You're going to inspect them for wear and deposits, and you will want to know what cylinder they came out of. If the same plugs are going back in, put the bottom plugs in the top, and the top in the bottom. This plug rotation will extend plug life. A special tool is recommended for the adjustment of aviation spark plugs. These are available from most aircraft tools suppliers. Be sure to torque plugs as

per specs when installing them. It's a good idea to use an anti-seize compound on the threads. This will ease their removal at a later date. For an excellent package of information about spark plugs, write to any of the manufacturers. You'll be rewarded with usage charts, how-to instructions, and a color chart to compare your plugs. This will assist you with the identification of potential problems (Figs. 14-3 and 14-4).

(21) Replacing any hose connection except hydraulic connections. Most of the hoses that you are allowed to replace are involved with the instrument system. These are either push-on friction fit, or push-on clamp fit. The clamps are either squeeze or screw type. Both may be seen on automobiles. When replacing hoses be sure to use approved parts. Order by part number.

(22) Replacing prefabricated fuel lines. This is simply the replacing of flexible fuel lines of like part number. One word of caution: Don't overtighten these lines, as their seal is developed by a tapered thread, not tightness.

(23) Cleaning fuel and oil strainers.

Fuel: Turn off the fuel to the strainer bowl, then drain the bowl using the quick drain. Cut the safety wire and slide the clip out of the way. This should allow you to pull the bowl off. At this point the strainer screen should drop out. Clean it with solvent and replace it with a new gasket. Put the bowl back into place and fasten the clip. Install new safety wire.

Oil: Your airplane may use an oil screen or an automotive-type canister oil filter. Referring to your engine manual, remove the oil screen and check it for metal flakes, a sure sign of problems. Clean the screen in a solvent, and reinstall same. A spin-on filter is removed and installed much the same as in a car. For inspectional reasons the filter will be cut open and inspected for metal particles.

(24) Replacing batteries and checking fluid level and specific gravity. Just as for boats and autos, terminals must remain clean, electrolyte levels must be kept up, and the battery box must be checked for corrosion.

(25) Applicable to gliders only.

GENERAL SPARK PLUG CROSS REFERENCE

AUBURN PLUGS	CHAMPION PLUGS 14 mm	AUBURN PLUGS	CHAMPION PLUGS 18mm Massive Electrode (Short Reach)
SA-43	REJ38	A-88	M41E, M42E
A-44	J43	S-88	EM42E
SR-47P	REL37W	HS-88	HM41E
18 mm Fine Wire (Long Reach)		SR-88	REM40E
181	REB36W, REB36P	HSR-88	RHM40E
281	RHB36P	SR-87	REM38E
291	RHB36W	HSR-87	RHM38E
283	RHB32P	SR-86	REM38E
293	RHB32W	HSR-86	RHM-38E
286	—	18 mm Massive Electrode (Long Reach)	
18 mm Fine Wire (Short Reach)		171	REB37E, REB37N
SR-83P	REM38P	271	RHB37N, RHB37E, RHB38E
HSR-83P	RHM38P	172	REB87N
SR-93	REM38W	273	RHB32N, RHB32E, RHB33E
HSR-93	RHM38W	175	REB29N
		275	RHB29N, RHB29E

Fig. 14-3. General spark plug cross-reference chart for AC and Champion plugs. UNIVAIR

AUBURN SPARK PLUGS

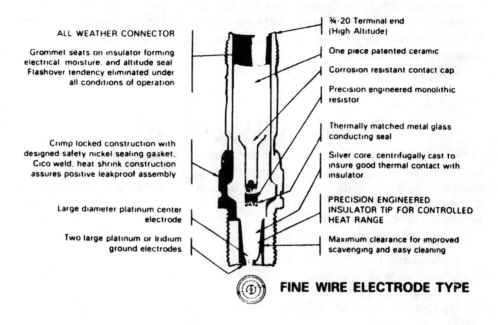

ALL WEATHER CONNECTOR

Grommet seats on insulator forming electrical, moisture, and altitude seal Flashover tendency eliminated under all conditions of operation

Crimp locked construction with designed safety nickel sealing gasket, Cico weld, heat shrink construction assures positive leakproof assembly

Large diameter platinum center electrode

Two large platinum or iridium ground electrodes

¾-20 Terminal end (High Altitude)

One piece patented ceramic

Corrosion resistant contact cap

Precision engineered monolithic resistor

Thermally matched metal glass conducting seal

Silver core, centrifugally cast to insure good thermal contact with insulator

PRECISION ENGINEERED INSULATOR TIP FOR CONTROLLED HEAT RANGE

Maximum clearance for improved scavenging and easy cleaning

FINE WIRE ELECTRODE TYPE

INSIDE A SPARK PLUG

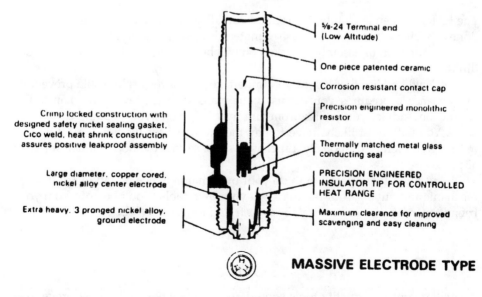

Crimp locked construction with designed safety nickel sealing gasket, Cico weld, heat shrink construction assures positive leakproof assembly

Large diameter, copper cored, nickel alloy center electrode

Extra heavy, 3 pronged nickel alloy, ground electrode

⅝-24 Terminal end (Low Altitude)

One piece patented ceramic

Corrosion resistant contact cap

Precision engineered monolithic resistor

Thermally matched metal glass conducting seal

PRECISION ENGINEERED INSULATOR TIP FOR CONTROLLED HEAT RANGE

Maximum clearance for improved scavenging and easy cleaning

MASSIVE ELECTRODE TYPE

Fig. 14-4. An explanation of the fine wire electrode and massive electrode spark plugs. UNIVAIR

(26) Applicable to balloons only.

(27) Replacement or adjustment of nonstructural standard fasteners incidental to operations. This is the tightening or replacement of screws (etc.) that hold fairings and cowlings in place. Some airplane owners replace all the old hardware with stainless steel. If you wish to do this, please consult your mechanic first, he no doubt will have some advice.

(28) Applicable to balloons only.

LOGBOOK REQUIREMENTS

Entries must be made in the appropriate logbook whenever preventive maintenance is done. The aircraft cannot legally fly without the logbook entry, which must include a description of work, the date completed, the name of the person doing the work, and approval for return to service (signature and certificate number) by the pilot approving the work.

A logbook entry must include:

(1) description of all work performed

(2) date the work was completed

(3) name of the person doing the work

(4) approval for return to service with signature & certificate number (pilot approving the work).

ADVICE

The FARs, as seen in chapter 13, require that all preventive maintenance work be done in such a manner, and by use of materials of such quality, that the airframe, engine, propeller, or assembly worked on will be at least equal to its original condition.

I strongly advise that before you undertake any of these allowable preventive maintenance procedures you discuss your plans with a licensed mechanic. The instructions/advice you receive from him may help you avoid making costly mistakes. You will, most likely, have to pay the mechanic for his time, but it will be money well spent. Additionally, purchase a set of service or shop manuals for your airplane.

In addition to preparation to do your own maintenance by talking with your mechanic and buying your manuals, get your own tools. Don't borrow from your friend the mechanic, or he won't be your friend long.

TOOLS

A small quantity of quality tools should allow the owner to do most preventive maintenance operations on his airplane (Figs. 14-5 and 14-6):

Multipurpose Swiss army knife

⅜" ratchet drive with a flex head as an option

2, 4, 6" drive extensions

Sockets from ⅜" to ¾" in ¹⁄₁₆" increments

6" crescent wrench

10" monkey wrench

6 or 12-point closed (box) wrenches from ⅜" to ¾"

Set of open-end wrenches from ⅜" to ¾"

Pair of channel lock pliers (medium size)

Phillips screwdriver set in the three common sizes

Flathead screwdriver set short (2") to long (8") sizes

Plastic electrician's tape

Container of assorted approved nuts and bolts

Spare set of spark plugs

10x magnifying glass

Inspection mirror

A bag or box is handy to keep tools in order and protected

SELF DESTRUCTION OF THE AIRPLANE

Corrosion is the single most powerful destroyer of airplanes in the world. In practice, corrosion is the returning to earth of refined metals. To draw a parallel, wood rots and returns to nature. Given enough time and lack of care, an airplane will do the same.

HOW CORROSION HAPPENS

All metals used in the construction of airplanes are subject to corrosion. Contaminants carried in the air are the prime causes of corrosion. Salt laden coastal air is an example and air pollution has become a powerful contributor. The polluted air carries acids, alkalies, and salts. All these items are electrolytes, allowing the transfer of ions from one location to another. When ions exchange places at points of contact of dissimilar metals, corrosion occurs.

In a metal airplane you will find dissimilar metals in constant and unavoidable contact. Remember, the plane's structure consists of several different aluminum alloys and alloys are made by mixing different metals with pure aluminum. Copper and zinc are the most commonly used alloying metals.

SURFACE PITTING

The most common form of corrosion is surface pitting. If left uncontrolled, the pits will deepen and broaden until an unacceptable amount of metal has been eaten away. An unacceptable amount is the quantity eaten away for a part to lose its structural integrity. Sometimes a white powder will be seen on the surface at the point of pitting.

AN – GUIDE

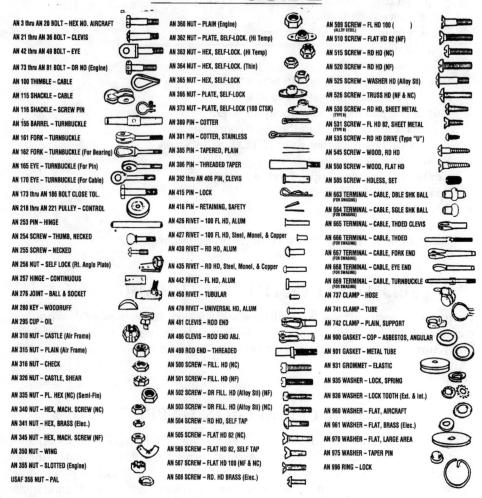

AN 3 thru AN 20 BOLT – HEX NO. AIRCRAFT
AN 21 thru AN 36 BOLT – CLEVIS
AN 42 thru AN 49 BOLT – EYE
AN 73 thru AN 81 BOLT – DR NO (Engine)
AN 100 THIMBLE – CABLE
AN 115 SHACKLE – CABLE
AN 116 SHACKLE – SCREW PIN
AN 155 BARREL – TURNBUCKLE
AN 161 FORK – TURNBUCKLE
AN 162 FORK – TURNBUCKLE (For Bearing)
AN 165 EYE – TURNBUCKLE (For Pin)
AN 170 EYE – TURNBUCKLE (For Cable)
AN 173 thru AN 186 BOLT CLOSE TOL.
AN 218 thru AN 221 PULLEY – CONTROL
AN 253 PIN – HINGE
AN 254 SCREW – THUMB, NECKED
AN 255 SCREW – NECKED
AN 256 NUT – SELF LOCK (Rt. Angle Plate)
AN 257 HINGE – CONTINUOUS
AN 276 JOINT – BALL & SOCKET
AN 280 KEY – WOODRUFF
AN 295 CUP – OIL
AN 310 NUT – CASTLE (Air Frame)
AN 315 NUT – PLAIN (Air Frame)
AN 316 NUT – CHECK
AN 320 NUT – CASTLE, SHEAR
AN 335 NUT – PL. HEX (NC) (Semi-Fin)
AN 340 NUT – HEX, MACH. SCREW (NC)
AN 341 NUT – HEX, BRASS (Elec.)
AN 345 NUT – HEX, MACH. SCREW (NF)
AN 350 NUT – WING
AN 355 NUT – SLOTTED (Engine)
USAF 356 NUT – PAL

AN 360 NUT – PLAIN (Engine)
AN 362 NUT – PLATE, SELF-LOCK. (Hi Temp)
AN 363 NUT – HEX, SELF-LOCK. (Hi Temp)
AN 364 NUT – HEX, SELF-LOCK. (Thin)
AN 365 NUT – HEX, SELF-LOCK
AN 366 NUT – PLATE, SELF-LOCK
AN 373 NUT – PLATE, SELF-LOCK (100 CTSK)
AN 380 PIN – COTTER
AN 381 PIN – COTTER, STAINLESS
AN 385 PIN – TAPERED, PLAIN
AN 386 PIN – THREADED TAPER
AN 392 thru AN 406 PIN, CLEVIS
AN 415 PIN – LOCK
AN 416 PIN – RETAINING, SAFETY
AN 426 RIVET – 100 FL HD, ALUM
AN 427 RIVET – 100 FL HD, Steel, Monel, & Copper
AN 430 RIVET – RD HD, ALUM
AN 435 RIVET – RD HD, Steel, Monel, & Copper
AN 442 RIVET – FL HD, ALUM
AN 450 RIVET – TUBULAR
AN 470 RIVET – UNIVERSAL HD, ALUM
AN 481 CLEVIS – ROD END
AN 486 CLEVIS – ROD END ABJ.
AN 490 ROD END – THREADED
AN 500 SCREW – FILL. HD (NC)
AN 501 SCREW – FILL. HD (NF)
AN 502 SCREW – DR FILL. HD (Alloy Stl) (NF)
AN 503 SCREW – DR FILL. HD (Alloy Stl) (NC)
AN 504 SCREW – RD HD, SELF TAP
AN 505 SCREW – FLAT HD 82 (NC)
AN 506 SCREW – FLAT HD 82, SELF TAP
AN 507 SCREW – FLAT HD 100 (NF & NC)
AN 508 SCREW – RD. HD BRASS (Elec.)

AN 509 SCREW – FL HD 100 (   )
(ALLOY STEEL)
AN 510 SCREW – FLAT HD 82 (NF)
AN 515 SCREW – RD HD (NC)
AN 520 SCREW – RD HD (NF)
AN 525 SCREW – WASHER HD (Alloy Stl)
AN 526 SCREW – TRUSS HD (NF & NC)
AN 530 SCREW – RD HD, SHEET METAL
(TYPE B)
AN 531 SCREW – FL HD 82, SHEET METAL
(TYPE B)
AN 535 SCREW – RD HD DRIVE (Type "U")
AN 545 SCREW – WOOD, RD HD
AN 550 SCREW – WOOD, FLAT HD
AN 585 SCREW – HDLESS, SET
AN 663 TERMINAL – CABLE, DBLE SHK BALL
(FOR SWAGING)
AN 664 TERMINAL – CABLE, SGLE SHK BALL
(FOR SWAGING)
AN 665 TERMINAL – CABLE, THDED CLEVIS
AN 666 TERMINAL – CABLE, THDED
(FOR SWAGING)
AN 667 TERMINAL – CABLE, FORK END
(FOR SWAGING)
AN 668 TERMINAL – CABLE, EYE END
(FOR SWAGING)
AN 669 TERMINAL – CABLE, TURNBUCKLE
(FOR SWAGING)
AN 737 CLAMP – HOSE
AN 741 CLAMP – TUBE
AN 742 CLAMP – PLAIN, SUPPORT
AN 900 GASKET – COP – ASBESTOS, ANGULAR
AN 901 GASKET – METAL TUBE
AN 931 GROMMET – ELASTIC
AN 935 WASHER – LOCK, SPRING
AN 936 WASHER – LOCK TOOTH (Ext. & Int.)
AN 960 WASHER – FLAT, AIRCRAFT
AN 961 WASHER – FLAT, BRASS (Elec.)
AN 970 WASHER – FLAT, LARGE AREA
AN 975 WASHER – TAPER PIN
AN 996 RING – LOCK

Fig. 14-5. AN Hardware Guide. UNIVAIR

Alloys 2024, the most common copper/aluminum alloy used in aircraft construction, is typified by pitting type corrosion. The skins of most metal airplanes are 2024 alloy.

INTERGRANULAR CORROSION

The most devastating form of corrosion is intergranular. It is most common to the 7000 series of alloys (those containing zinc). Structures made of these alloys are the weight and load bearing parts of the airplane: spars, stringers, etc.

DECIMAL EQUIVALENTS
OF WIRE, LETTER AND FRACTIONAL SIZE DRILLS

DRILL SIZE NO.	DECIMAL	DRILL SIZE NO.	DECIMAL	DRILL SIZE NO.	DECIMAL
80	.0135	29	.1360	21/64	.3281
79	.0145	28	.1405	Q	.3320
1/64	.0156	9/64	.1406	R	.3390
78	.0160	27	.1440	11/32	.3437
77	.0180	26	.1470	S	.3480
76	.0200	25	.1495	T	.3580
75	.0210	24	.1520	23/64	.3594
74	.0225	23	.1540	U	.3680
73	.0240	5/32	.1562	3/8	.3750
72	.0250	22	.1570	V	.3770
71	.0260	21	.1590	W	.3860
70	.0280	20	.1610	25/64	.3906
69	.0292	19	.1660	X	.3970
68	.0310	18	.1695	Y	.4040
1/32	.0313	11/64	.1719	13/32	.4062
67	.0320	17	.1730	Z	.4130
66	.0330	16	.1770	27/64	.4219
65	.0350	15	.1800	7/16	.4375
64	.0360	14	.1820	29/64	.4531
63	.0370	13	.1850	15/32	.4687
62	.0380	3/16	.1875	31/64	.4843
61	.0390	12	.1890	1/2	.5000
60	.0400	11	.1910	33/64	.5156
59	.0410	10	.1935	17/32	.5313
58	.0420	9	.1960	35/64	.5469
57	.0430	8	.1990	9/16	.5625
56	.0465	7	.2010	37/64	.5781
3/64	.0469	13/64	.2031	19/32	.5937
55	.0520	6	.2040	39/64	.6094
54	.0550	5	.2055	5/8	.6250
53	.0595	4	.2090	41/64	.6406
1/16	.0625	3	.2130	21/32	.6562
52	.0635	7/32	.2187	43/64	.6719
51	.0670	2	.2210	11/16	.6875
50	.0700	1	.2280	45/64	.7031
49	.0730	A	.2340	23/32	.7187
48	.0760	15/64	.2344	47/64	.7344
5/64	.0781	B	.2380	3/4	.7500
47	.0785	C	.2420	49/64	.7656
46	.0810	D	.2460	25/32	.7812
45	.0820	E 1/4	.2500	51/64	.7969
44	.0860	F	.2570	13/16	.8125
43	.0890	G	.2610	53/64	.8281
42	.0935	17/64	.2656	27/32	.8437
3/32	.0937	H	.2660	55/64	.8594
41	.0960	I	.2720	7/8	.8750
40	.0980	J	.2770	57/64	.8906
39	.0995	K	.2811	29/32	.9062
38	.1015	9/32	.2812	59/64	.9219
37	.1040	L	.2900	15/16	.9375
36	.1065	M	.2900	61/64	.9531
7/64	.1093	19/64	.2968	31/32	.9687
35	.1100	N	.3020	63/64	.9844
34	.1110	5/16	.3125	1	1.0000
33	.1130	O	.3160		
32	.1180	P	.3230		
31	.1200				
1/8	.1250				
30	.1285				

UNIVAIR

Fig. 14-6. Quick reference decimal equivalent chart.

Intergranular corrosion is so serious that when discovered, the part must be replaced.

FILIFORM CORROSION

Filiform corrosion is usually found under the surface of paints. Its presence is indicated by fine worm-like lines rising from under the paint. It can form on any surface, however, anywhere on the airplane.

One of the most important means for preventing filiform corrosion is the proper surface preparation of the airplane before painting.

FRETTING CORROSION

When parts move against each other, friction will wear them down. For example: two parts held together by rivets begin to move slightly. The rubbing (friction) produces a smokey-gray powder that acts as a grinding grit. This grit will continue cutting into metal until nothing is left.

Generally, fretting corrosion involves rivets. The method of controlling this problem is to tighten the surface's contact, specifically, by replacing the rivets.

FERROUS RUST

Just as corrosion can destroy a metal airplane, rust can do just as bad a job on the iron-containing parts of a tube and fabric airplane. Additionally, don't forget that many parts on an all-metal plane are ferrous in nature. For example: hinges, landing gear, engine mounts, wing struts, etc.

On a tube and fabric airplane the most devastating form of corrosion is the rust that destroys the tubular framing itself. This threat applies to all tubular structures, including engine mounts and wing struts (also found on all metal planes).

Surface rusting can progress to the point that the inside meets the outside, however, the part will usually fail before this point. Engine mounts and the rear parts (low to the ground) of taildraggers are very prone to surface rusting.

PREVENTION

An ounce of prevention will save pounds (literally) of correction. Preventing corrosion is fairly simple.

First and foremost: Keep the airplane clean and dry. The cleaner the aircraft, the less likely corrosion is to occur. This means not just washing, but a thorough cleaning inside and out of airframe.

Water carries many of the chemicals necessary for corrosion and provides the electrolyte necessary for corrosive action to take place. This is why airplanes spending their lives in dry desert climates are far less likely to exhibit corrosion problems. No water - no corrosion. Therefore it is necessary to assure that no trapped water remains in the airplane. This means checking drains in the fuselage, wings, etc.

Effective products are available to displace water from surfaces and leave a protective film to prevent further contamination. Such products must be able to get in around laps and rivets to prevent corrosion starts.

A very popular product for this application is LPS-3, available from many automotive supply stores, which displaces water and forms a coating that will prevent further water contamination. The coating is not permanent, and must be renewed from time to time. For more information about LPS-3 contact LPS Laboratories at (800) 241-8334.

XP-400A ACM-Protector is also an excellent product for the prevention of rust and corrosion. Properly applied it can protect metals for up to two years. Severe outdoor conditions will, of course, reduce this time. For additional information contact United States Rust Control Corp. at (305) 634-6564.

Both products are superb for use on landing gear, wheels, internal structures (wings, fuselage, belly, etc.), cables, hinges on doors and control surfaces, and other areas requiring protection.

Second: Surface protection is primary in the prevention of corrosion. Protection can be in the form of specially made metal sheeting for skins such as Alclad. Alclad is typically 2024 alloy material with an applied surface of .0002-inch-thick pure aluminum (pure aluminum is quite corrosion resistant). Ferrous parts are often plated for the same purposes.

Chemical treatments are also effective. Alodyned surface protection is excellent, and is generally used during painting preparations. The remaining treatment is surface coatings such as paint or wax.

Internal treatment, such as oil filling of tubular structures is very effective, providing the integrity of the seal remains intact. Tubular structures include the airframe, engine mounts, struts, landing gear, etc.

VERY SERIOUS PROBLEM

The following information, based upon an AD and Service Bulletins involving Piper airplanes, shows the seriousness of metal corrosion and rusting. Common sense tells us that it certainly does find application to far more than the mentioned Piper products. Service Bulletin no. 528B (courtesy of UNIVAIR) is partially reproduced for informational purposes:

Subject: Inspection of Wing Lift Strut Assembly

(1) Revised compliance requirements for factory treated and non-factory treated (re-corrosion impedance) lift struts—see Compliance time, below; and,

(2) Revised identification of field-treated lift struts (i.e., struts having had corrosion impedance measures applied in the field per Piper Service Bulletin No. 528A)—see instruction No. 4.

Models affected: All airplanes incorporating steel lift struts on PA-18 Super Cub Serial No. 18-1 through 18-7609035 and PA-25 Pawnee Serial No. 25-1 to 25-7656009.

COMPLIANCE TIME:

(1) Aircraft with NON-FACTORY TREATED lift struts having five (5) years or more time in service: At the next 100 hour inspection or annual inspection, whichever occurs first, and at least every annual inspection thereafter until corrosion impedance measures are applied.

(2) Aircraft with FACTORY TREATED (identified per Instruction No. 4, below) lift struts, with less than five (5) years service time: Inspection is required when lift struts reach five (5) years time in service, to be repeated at each subsequent five (5) year interval thereafter.

(3) Aircraft with lift struts having had corrosion impedance measures applied IN THE FIELD in compliance with Piper Service Bulletin No. 528 dated October 28, 1976 or No. 528A dated August 16, 1977: Inspection is required at each five (5) year interval (since corrosion-impedance measures accomplished). See NOTE, Instruction No. 4 concerning revised identification of field-treated struts.

Purpose: We are advised by the FAA that a campaign to require specific formal inspections of the wing lift strut assemblies on the above referenced aircraft is being finalized. The intended objective of this program is to detect internal lift strut tube corrosion, most likely to occur in the lower lift strut extremity. Since lift struts are closed tubular structures, internal corrosion in most cases may not be readily apparent until corrosion has advanced completely through the tube wall. This Service Release provides an inspection procedure to detect evidence of wing lift strut tube internal corrosion.

INSTRUCTIONS:

(1) Accomplish inspection per attached Inspection Procedure.

(2) Lift strut tubes indicating presence of internal corrosion may either be repaired per FAA Advisory Circular 43.13-1A, pp 81 (Repair of Wing and Tail Brace Struts by an FAA approved repair facility) or replaced; NOTE: see Material Required Section relative to lift strut replacements.

(3) Aircraft whose records indicate that lift struts have been switched from one side of the aircraft to the other or which indicate that struts have been interchanged from another aircraft (i.e., inverted from original installation) should have lift struts inspected on both top and bottom surfaces—per attached inspection procedure.

(4) Lift Strut assemblies which have been factory treated with corrosion preventive measures by the factory are identified by the installation of a Cherrylock rivet installed at the upper (wing attachment) end.

Note: Lift struts that have had corrosion impedance measures applied in the field (per S.B. 528 or 528A) and have had the NAS1738B4-4 Cherrylock rivet installed on the strut (to signify treated strut) must have the Cherrylock rivet removed and a sheet metal screw installed (see instruction procedure for further details).

(5) Alternative preservative materials: In addition to the preservatives "Valoil" and "Lionoil" specified in Service Bulletin No. 528, it is permissible to use the following alternate preservatives—Paralketone, linseed oil or any alternate preservatives that satisfy the requirements of Federal Specification TT-S-176D.

MATERIAL REQUIRED:

(1) PA-18, PA-22 and PA-25 Series Aircraft: Refer to applicable model parts catalog for part identification information. Replacement lift struts may be obtained at owner/operator's discretion, as required, in the normal manner.

Note: Due to limited wing lift strut requirements over the past years, factory stock may, at times, not be able to immediately provide replacement lift struts per this service release. Should this occur, alternate methods of compliance with this service release are denoted in No. 2, below.

(2) All other models: Replacement lift struts no longer maintained in factory inventory: Consider (1) repair—per above instructions, (2) fabrication—factory will supply fabrication drawings at no charge on request, or (3) obtain from non-affiliated local aircraft parts supply source.

Availability of parts: See above.

Effective date: This service release is effective upon receipt.

Summary: This service release is submitted to assist above referenced aircraft owner/operators in conducting a positive, universally feasible wing lift strut (corrosion) inspection procedure.

INSPECTION PROCEDURE:

(1) Securely tape a sheet of ¼-inch grid graph paper to the lower 11 inches of the bottom surface on all wing lift struts.

(2) Using a Maule Fabric Tester (Fig. 14-7) and holding tool normal to strut contour, apply pressure at a scale reading of 80 in each of the grid blocks.

(3) Remove the paper and inspect the lift struts tubes. A perceptible dent will appear if internal corrosion is present. If any dents are found, be certain the dents are in the metal by carefully removing the paint.

(a) Lift strut tubes indicating the presence of any perceptible dent in the metal must either be repaired per FAA Advisory Circular 43.13-1A by an approved FAA repair facility or replaced with new lift strut assembly before further flight.

(b) If no dents appear in the metal, the lift strut may be considered airworthy.

Note: Further internal corrosion may be impeded per the following procedure:

(a) Remove left strut from aircraft.

(b) Inject one quart of Valoil, Lionoil Multi-Purpose L-1, Linseed Oil, Paralketone or any alternate preservative conforming to Federal Specification TT-S-176D, into the bolt hole at the top of the strut.

(c) Plug the bolt holes and slosh oil until interior of the strut is thoroughly coated.

(d) Drain oil from strut (through bolt holes) and install MS51861-44 sheet metal screw, as shown, for future identification.

(e) Reinstall strut to aircraft and rig.

(4) Record lift strut inspection in aircraft logbook.

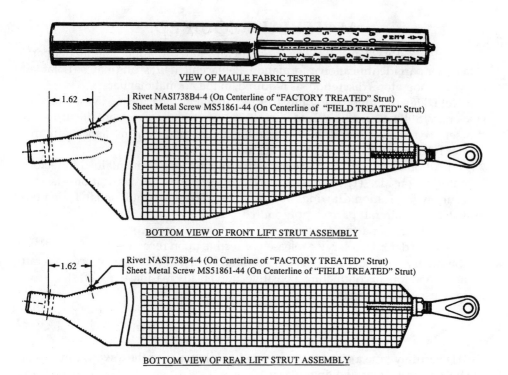

VIEW OF MAULE FABRIC TESTER

←1.62→ Rivet NASI738B4-4 (On Centerline of "FACTORY TREATED" Strut)
Sheet Metal Screw MS51861-44 (On Centerline of "FIELD TREATED" Strut)

BOTTOM VIEW OF FRONT LIFT STRUT ASSEMBLY

←1.62→ Rivet NASI738B4-4 (On Centerline of "FACTORY TREATED" Strut)
Sheet Metal Screw MS51861-44 (On Centerline of "FIELD TREATED" Strut)

BOTTOM VIEW OF REAR LIFT STRUT ASSEMBLY

Fig. 14-7. The Maule Fabric Tester and ¼" graph paper used in testing for corrosion damage of the wing lift struts. UNIVAIR

15

Re-covering your
fabric airplane

FABRIC WORK is very expensive today; however, most of the expense is in labor. Re-covery of tube-and-fabric airplanes is an art form, and the only way to learn is under the direct supervision of a master. Although many good points are brought out in this chapter about re-covering, it is by no means an exhaustive instruction manual. However, with this information, and good supervision, anyone can re-cover an airplane.

DIRTY WORK

The following general instructions for the removal of old fabric coverings and the precover airframe preparations are based upon the Stits Poly-Fiber Covering and Painting Manual, by permission of the author, Ray Stits:

Fabric should be removed from the airframe carefully to avoid damaging the structure.

Any screws in wing ribs are removed after spinning a small sharpened tube around the screws or using a razor blade to cut and peel off the finishing tape. Blind rivets through the ribs are removed by carefully drilling in the center to undercut the head with one drill size smaller than the rivet. If a steel mandrel interferes with center drilling it may be recessed with a small drift punch.

Original wire clips should be removed carefully to avoid bending or damage since they will be reused unless replacements can be found. Continuous wire barbs originally designed for the Taylorcraft metal ribs and installed on thin Piper ribs under an STC should be removed very carefully by folding the correct end back to reduce the barb cross section. Any force will split and damage the rib, requiring expensive repair or replacement.

Any oversize rivet holes, screw holes or thin rib caps split during the removal of wire barbs should be tagged immediately for easy location and repair by methods acceptable to FAA before re-covery.

After removing all mechanical fasteners the fabric is removed from the wing by carefully cutting just forward of the trailing edge, top and bottom, and peeling the fabric forward and around the wing leading edge. Trying to cut through at the trailing and leading edge with a razor blade or other sharp object will usually result in a deep groove on the metal or plywood surface.

Fabric attached to the wings with lacing cord should be removed by peeling the fabric forward from the trailing edge and cutting the laces progressively, rather than trying to fail the rib lace by jerking the fabric, resulting in broken or bent rib caps.

When removing fabric from a plywood wing leading edge, or other plywood surface, care should be taken not to peel sections of plywood skin with the fabric. If the fabric will not peel easily when folded back 180 degrees it may be soaked with Poly-Fiber reducer to soften the coating bond. If the solvent cannot penetrate through the outside of a solvent resistant finish coat, Poly-Fiber reducer may be applied with a brush along the bond interface to progressively penetrate under the fabric.

Fabric is carefully removed from the fuselage and controls in the same manner as the wings. Avoid damage by not cutting structures under the fabric with a sharp knife or bending/breaking the fabric forming members by trying to rip the fabric off. It is advisable to remove the fabric in large sections, and set it aside for future reference to help establish locations for inspection access holes, drain grommets, and reinforcing tapes.

Old fabric covering is not always a reliable guide to position new inspection access holes. A photo or a sketch should be made of the structures to record those areas which will require and inspection access hole for later maintenance or inspection.

Cellulose-coated fabric removed from an airplane should be considered an extreme fire hazard and not be stored near a flame source or in a residence.

Before installing fabric on the airplane or component, a thorough inspection should be made to assure the structure is ready for covering. Theoretically it will be many years before the fabric is removed as polyester filaments do not deteriorate in any environment in which aircraft, including AG aircraft, are operated. They deteriorate only when exposed to direct UV radiation. When our (Stits) coating system is used as directed, all UV radiation is blocked.

Old one-component varnish on wood structures that will not be in contact with the fabric should be re-coated with EV-400 Epoxy Varnish. One-component varnishes, commonly referred to as spar varnish are easily lifted and destroyed when in contact with solvents used in aircraft coatings. The term spar varnish refers to a quality recommended for annual application on sailboat spars or masts, not aircraft spars.

Moisture-curing one-component so-called urethane varnishes are also very sensitive to solvents and will wrinkle and lift. Solvent sensitivity tests may be made with Poly-Fiber reducer on a rag, allowing 15 minutes soak time.

Old wood surfaces which will be in contact with the fabric should be dry sanded to remove the majority of the residue of one-component varnishes, wood sealers, or cellulose dope coatings, then sealed with two brush coats of epoxy varnish.

All metal and plywood surfaces which will be covered with fabric are pre-coated with two brush coats of Poly-Brush reduced with equal parts Poly-Fiber Reducer.

Do not coat wood with a metal primer because it does not have the needed flexibility and hides any cracks and decay.

Wood components which will be covered with fabric should never be coated with any solvent soluble lacquer sealers which will absorb and retain solvents from coatings like a sponge and cause bubbles to form or cement seams to slip after the fabric is installed.

Ferrous metal components on which fabric will be cemented or in contact, such as fuselage longerons, tail surface tubes, window and door frames, etc., which are bare or were previously coated with any one component metal primer should be recoated with EP-420 Epoxy Primer. Special attention should be given bottom longeron areas where water may be trapped and cause corrosion. Any one-component metal primer will be softened and penetrated and alkyd types will be wrinkled when in contact with solvents used in aircraft fabric coatings. The damaged primer is not noticed under the fabric until the corrosion stain migrates through the fabric finish surface four or five years later. EP-420 Epoxy Primer will not lift or damage one-component metal primers, therefore there is no purpose in removing old, sound primers before applying epoxy primers.

An asphaltic or rubber base coating should be applied by brush to the structure adjacent and below the battery box for additional protection from the sulfuric acid electrolyte. Control cables routed through the battery box area should be coated with paralketone.

A close inspection should be made of all hardware, clevis pins, jam nuts, screws, rivets, etc., to assure their security and airworthiness. Drag and anti-drag wires should be protected from chafing at the cross point.

All sharp edges which will be in contact with the fabric covering should be taped to smooth the edges and avoid cutting or chafing through the fabric. There are no specifications for the quality or strength of an anti-chafe tape, however I warn against the use of a paper masking tape for this purpose. Paper tape retains moisture and is subject to bacteria degradation. The resin adhesives on paper masking tape, as well as many economical duct tapes, will migrate with age or heat and show as a dark spot through light-colored finishes. Dye on duct tape may be released by fabric coatings and migrate. We recommend natural white cotton cloth adhesive tape similar in appearance to surgical adhesive tape for anti-chafe purposes.

All wrinkles, dents, repairs, and patches on aluminum fairings which form shapes or contours, such as wing leading edges and turtle decks, will show through the fabric covering when the fabric is bonded directly to the aluminum surface. Rough fabric contouring surfaces may be smoothed and any rivet and screw head protrusions reduced by installing polyester flannel cloth weighing approximately 2.7 oz. per square yard. Flannel available is available at most domestic fabric stores. White is preferred, however the color is not important as long as it is a non-bleeding dye. The flannel is cemented around the perimeter of the leading edge or turtle deck with Poly-Tak, being careful not to saturate and fill the outside fibers of the flannel. Sufficient adhesive to secure the flannel in position is all that is required.

The use of a flannel cushion on the leading edge eliminates the option of using an overlap cement seam span-wise on the wing. The fabric must wrap around the wing with an overlap cement seam at the trailing edge as a blanket, or an envelope may be used. Flannel cloth provides an escape route for the coating solvent vapors and reduces the possibilities of pinholes through the finish. Flannel cloth may be used on any structure where the bond of the fabric directly to the primary structure is not required as part of the fabric covering procedure. Generally this limits the use of a flannel cushion to convex surfaces such as leading edges and turtle decks and large aluminum fairings at fuselage corners.

Before a component is covered with fabric it must be inspected and the re-covery authorized by an FAA representative, certified repair station, or a mechanic authorized by the FAA to conduct the inspection.

Ed. note: Reference in the foregoing was made to numerous Stits products. Similar products, from other manufacturers may be utilized in a like fashion.

RE-COVERY SYSTEMS

Originally, all the classics were covered in either cotton or linen. These fabrics do not hold up as well as the new synthetics, but require the same labor to install.

There are several standard covering systems available in today's market. All are advertised in *Trade-A-Plane* and other publications.

Each system described here is complete; complete, meaning that the installer will use only the items called for in the installation/instruction manual provided by the manufacturer and follow the prescribed methods. The complete system carries an STC for the re-covery of an airframe issued by the FAA, and is based upon each re-covery job being performed exactly as called for by the manufacturer. If you do not comply, the STC is not valid, and neither is your Airworthiness Certificate.

The typical system includes the synthetic fabric polyester—Dacron or Fiberglass—glues, tapes, and coatings.

STITS POLY-FIBER

The Stits system (Fig. 15-1) is based upon a polyester fabric that can be attached to the airframe by stitching, as in the case of the original cover, or may be glued by use of Poly-Tak, a high strength fabric cement. The latter method is a real time-saver.

After the fabric is in place, it is heat shrunk by use of a hot iron. This is the only tightening that will occur, as the Stits system coatings are non-tightening.

The coatings provide protection from the sun's ultraviolet rays, which are quite destructive to fabrics. The final coats are for color and finish. For more information contact:

Stits Poly-Fiber Aircraft Coatings
Box 3084
Riverside, CA 92519
(714) 684-4280

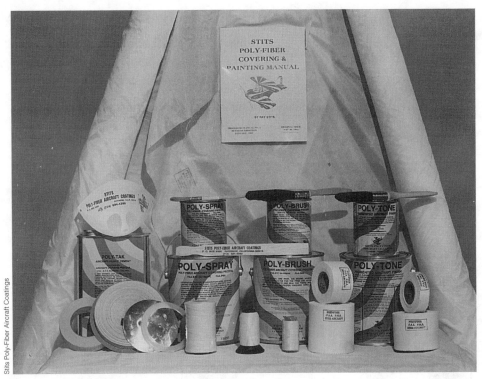

Fig. 15-1. Stits covering products necessary for a re-cover.

CECONITE

Basically the Ceconite system is similar to Stits; however, the coatings differ. The coatings, butyrate and nitrate, used in the Ceconite system are tightening dopes. This, in addition to the thermal shrinking done after attachment of the fabric. Contact:

Ceconite Co.
3815 Medford St.
Los Angeles, CA 90063
(213) 724-7244

AIR-TECH COATINGS

Air-Tech provides a complete system for re-covery including the fabric, glues, coatings, etc. Its system makes use of various Ceconite or Stits polyester/Dacron fabrics. They may be contacted at:

Air-Tech Coatings, Inc.
2300 Redmond Rd.
Jacksonville, AR 72076
(800) 325-1650
(501) 985-1484

RAZORBACK FIBERGLASS

The Razorback method of re-covering differs from the first two by use of a different fabric. Fiberglass is utilized and is considered permanent; so much so that there is no requirement for fabric punch testing at annual inspection time if your plane has been covered with Razorback system.

As with the other synthetic systems, seams and attachments are glued, rather than sewed. Initial coatings are made by spraying of butyrate dopes, which cause tightening of the fabric. Other coatings of silver (for protection from ultraviolet rays) and finish coloring are made with nontightening materials (Fig. 15-2). Contact:

Razorback Fabrics, Inc.
Manila, AR 72442
(501) 561-4447

Fig. 15-2. This decal is required by the STC to appear on the tail surface of any aircraft covered with Razorback. It indicates there is no requirement for annual fabric testing.

Razorback Fabrics

CECONITE 7600

Perhaps this is the most interesting system that is currently available for re-covering airplanes. It's the Eonnex system, developed some years ago by Bill Lott. The system is now produced by Ceconite, under the name of Ceconite 7600, and is distributed by Blue River Aircraft Supply.

The basic application of the fabric is similar to Stits and Ceconite (Figs. 15-3, 4, 5); however, the coatings are completely different.

Unlike the smelly and flammable coating products utilized in the other systems, the 7600 coatings are water-based and interact with a pretreatment in the fabric. If you are doing a re-covery project at home, I am sure the lack of smell will please the wife, family, and neighbors; they will enjoy the improved atmosphere. Your home-owners insurance company will no doubt approve of the nonflammable materials used. Only the finish coat will produce toxic/flammable fumes.

Other positive points for the 7600 system include the ease of application, as the coatings are applied by use of brushes and/or pads. Additionally, there is the lack of temperature/humidity difficulties encountered with the other systems. 7600 may be applied at all temperatures above freezing (Figs. 15-6, 7, 8, 9).

For additional information contact:

Blue River Aircraft Supply
Box 460
223 North Clay
Harvard, NE 68944
(402) 772-3651

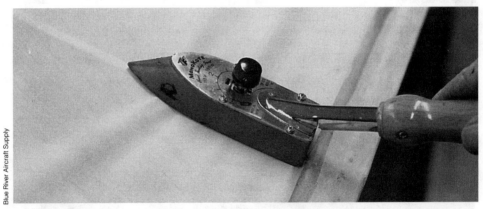

Fig. 15-3. After the fabric has been installed on the airframe it must be heat-shrunk for proper fit. Here the close quarter iron is used to start the tightening process. Tighten over the ribs first to prevent small wrinkles from showing up later in the process.

ACCEPTED PRACTICES

FAA publication 43.13 is the bible for aircraft maintenance and repair. I recommend that anyone who owns, or thinks about owning, an airplane purchase a copy. Among the extensive contents of 43.13 is an entire chapter on airframe fabric covering. Included in this information is instructions for the stitching and attachment of fabric coverings. This reading is mandatory for all who plan to re-cover their aircraft.

Fig. 15-4. In this photo, reinforcing tape is being placed over the ribs prior to rib stitching. Notice the rib stitch spacing is marked and the holes are punched before centering the tape.

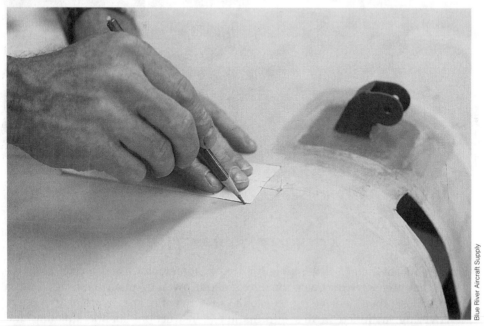

Fig. 15-5. Using a guide made from sandpaper, mark the width of the surface tape prior to applying the cement. This will prevent excess cement from being applied outside the tape area and aids in keeping the tape absolutely straight during application.

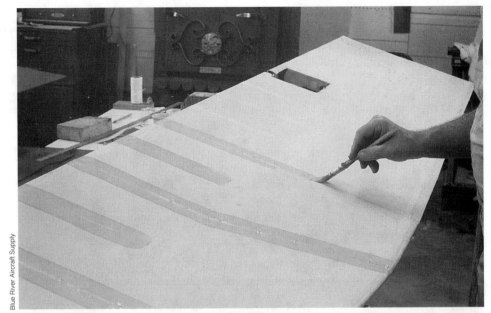

Fig. 15-6. Apply the surface tape cement only within the areas marked (as in Fig. 15-5). This will keep the job neat.

Fig. 15-7. Dampening the fabric just prior to applying the filler coating. The dampening is done with water. There are no flammable or noxious fumes from this process.

Fig. 15-8. A paint pad is used to apply the filler coat, which fills the weave and provides UV (ultra-violet) protection.

Fig. 15-9. This nicely equipped shop is typical of many used for airplane construction and restoration. Note the wood stove used to provide heat on cold winter nights, something that would normally be very dangerous, except in the case of the Ceconite 7600 process which produces no explosive fumes.

TOOLS AND EQUIPMENT

9" pinking shears.
9" straight shears.
Assorted 3" to 6" needles.
Long needles, 12" to 18" with curved tips.
Many T-headed pins.
Razor blade knife.
Brushes 1" to 4" (no nylon bristles).
Paint stir sticks.
Paint filter cones.
Assorted clean tin cans.
Several clean/new paint buckets.
Paper/cloth towels.
Pair of sawhorses (line top with carpets).
Tape measure.

16

Refinishing
metal airplanes

Paint applied to the exterior surfaces of alclad aluminum aircraft is not required to qualify for a type certificate or to maintain the airworthiness certificate. The protection provided to the aluminum alloy by the aluminum cladding on the surface is considered adequate to qualify for the initial airworthiness certificate. Cladding is the bonding of a thin overcoat of pure aluminum to the sheet alloy material utilized on an airplane. This cladding resists atmospheric corrosion.

In most cases, leaving the aircraft bare and occasionally washing it to remove airborne particles deposited on the surfaces of unpainted aluminum surfaces will offer adequate corrosion control. This policy seems to work for many airline and military aircraft.

About the only economical justification for painting an aircraft exterior surface is to protect the alloy skins that have lost their aluminum cladding, possibly as a result of age, or by abuse (scrubbing or sanding with extremely abrasive materials will remove the cladding). Painting is also recommended if the aircraft will be stored in a corrosive climate for a long period of time. A corrosive climate refers to salt air, or areas of the country that have heavy industrial pollution.

Pride of ownership no doubt has quite some effect on the appearance of airplanes, and surely results in many of the brightly painted aircraft seen today.

SUMMARY OF AIRCRAFT FINISHES

Based upon research and product testing by major suppliers of paints for aircraft use it has been determined that epoxy primers and urethane finishes will give the best results.

A properly applied quality urethane finish should retain its gloss for up to eight years in severe conditions. These conditions are typified by strong sunlight or severe air pollution.

Automobile type acrylic polyurethane enamels will last about three years before they begin to deteriorate.

Epoxy finishes and synthetic enamels will both begin to lose their gloss and start to chalk in about eighteen months under the same severe conditions as stated previously. Epoxy finishes provide far better chemical and solvent resistance than synthetic enamel finishes.

Acrylic lacquer rates about the same as synthetic enamel, with no solvent resistance. Catalyzed acrylic enamel provides fair solvent and chemical resistance and rates between epoxy and urethane enamels.

Keep the airplane locked in the hangar and all these finishes will still look good in ten or more years. The true test is exposure and operation.

AIRCRAFT PAINTING COSTS

As with covering a tube-and-fabric airplane, it's estimated that 85 to 90 percent of the cost of stripping and repainting an airplane is labor.

The best quality materials should be used and their application procedures followed closely. All come with complete detailed application instructions. Don't settle for an inferior product just to save a few dollars. The labor expended will be the same whether applying a high quality product or a poor one, but the higher quality materials will result in a better, longer lasting job.

SPRAYING EQUIPMENT

Most syphoned type spray guns rated by their manufacturer as all-purpose are suitable for spraying lacquers, synthetic enamels, and primers are recommended for the application of aircraft finishes. There are three well-known companies that manufacture spraying equipment: DeVilbiss, Binks, and Sharpe. Further information on spray guns may be obtained from local distributors or by writing to:

DeVilbiss Company
Toledo, OH 43692

Binks Manufacturing Company
9201 W. Belmont Ave.
Franklin Park, IL 60131

Sharpe Manufacturing Company
1224 Wall St.
Los Angeles, CA 90015

SPRAY OPERATIONS

Follow the instructions that come with the spray gun. Whether a spray gun is purchased new or used, the manufacturer can provide details for the operation, adjustments, dismantling, and cleaning.

Often in reading application instructions you'll see the terms single coat or double coat. A spray single coat is applied by overlapping each consecutive pass 50 percent of the fan width. A double coat is applied by repeating the coating application in the same direction or at 90 degrees to the first coat (cross coat) before the first coat has flashed off (dried dust free).

REFINISHING THE AIRPLANE

There are numerous finish systems available on the market and most of the manufacturers, or their distributors, advertise in *Trade-A-Plane* and are glad to send you literature about their products.

I have utilized Stits materials in the following instructions, showing the basics of refinishing a metal airplane. Similar results should be attained by following the instructions that apply to any of the current manufacturers' products.

Two notes of caution: First, read and follow the manufacturer's instructions that are given on the products you choose. Second, never mix products from different suppliers, as they may fail to function as planned.

STRIPPING THE AIRFRAME

Mask any area that could be damaged by paint stripper with polypropylene or cloth masking tape and polypropylene plastic sheet or equivalent material.

Be very careful around windows and windshields. The methylene chloride component found in paint strippers will damage polymethyl methacrylate, a transparent polymer better known by its Rohm and Haas trade name of *Plexiglass*.

Stripper is easily applied with a brush. After the old paint has softened, rinse the area with cold water to remove the residue. The use of a high pressure washer is recommended.

Note: Be sure to wear rubber gloves, face, and eye protection whenever stripping.

After the initial stripping has been completed you will find areas of old paint that are still solidly in place. These may be removed with "soft" tools such as plastic scrapers, Scotch Brite pads, or the like.

Don't use hard tools for paint stripping, as they will damage the cladding. Additionally, *never* use steel wool. It will leave microscopic particles that will later cause corrosion. Aluminum wool is an adequate replacement for steel wool.

A new product for paint removal is Paint Buster. Its literature states the product contains no methylene chloride, caustics, acids, or lyes and will not burn or blister the skin. For information about this product contact:

Redam Corp.
321 Ross Ave.
Hamilton, OH 45013

CORROSION

Corrosion discovered during the stripping procedure should be cleaned with Aluma-Dyne E-2311 Phosphoric Acid Etch and Brightener.

The remainder of the aircraft (areas where no corrosion was found) is given a complete scrubbing with Scotch Brite pads and 310 Alkaline Cleaner. The scrubbing action cleans the surface and leaves it slightly rough, providing teeth good adhesion of the primer coating. An acid etch (can aid in primer bonding) of the entire craft is optional at this point.

Within eight hours, the freshly scrubbed surfaces must be treated with Aluma-Dyne E-2300 Chromic Etch Conversion Coating. Application is made with a brush or sponge. Be sure to protect your hands, face, and eyes from these chemicals.

A complete water rinse is again made to remove the conversion coating materials. Left behind will be a thin oxide film on the aluminum surface.

PRIMING

Wipe all surfaces down with clean towels wetted with C-2200 Metl-Sol cleaner. Do not use shop rags that come from a supplier, as they may be contaminated, even though clean. Contamination could leave a residue that would spoil the finish job.

The EP-420 Epoxy Primer is applied, first with a wet tack coat, then two medium coats at 30-minute intervals. For best results, the primer should be applied within 24 hours of the conversion coating.

SMALL REPAIRS

After priming, you can take care of any body work that is necessary, such as filling in small dents on the leading edges of the wings. Utilizing Micro-Putty, fill in and sand dents. After sanding, apply primer over the repaired area.

FINISH

For best results the finish coat should be applied within 48 hours of priming. If more time than that has elapsed, the primed surfaces will require a complete sanding. If sanding is not done, the primer will not provide good adhesion for the finish coat.

Fingerprints or oily spots must be removed with C-2210 Paint Surface Cleaner. Go over the entire airplane with a good quality tack rag.

Follow all directions supplied for mixing and reducing the Aluma-Thane enamel. The first coat should be a wet tack coat, followed by two heavier coats at 15-to-20 minute intervals. Allow sufficient time between applications to prevent runs and sags.

INTERIOR SURFACES

The interior surfaces in airplanes are generally painted only for cosmetic reasons. Because these surfaces are not exposed to the elements of nature, their prefinish preparation is quite simple.

Cleaning is done with C-2200 Metl-Sol followed by priming. The color coating can be the same as the exterior, or an inexpensive automotive lacquer spray may be utilized. Remember, these are cosmetic coatings only and are not going to suffer from the ravages of the elements.

REFINISHING OLD PAINT

If you have a plane that has sound acrylic lacquer, epoxy paint, or synthetic enamel, you may be able to apply a new finish over it. Sound means no peeling, chipping, cracking, etc.

Clean the painted surface with 310 Alkaline Cleaner and sand it smooth. Be sure that all oils, waxes, and silicones are removed from the old finish. After these preparations have been made you can coat it with Aero-Thane Enamel.

FINISHING TIPS

(1) Do not use wax-coated paper cups for measuring, transferring, or storing the various liquids. Solvents in the coatings may dissolve the wax and contaminate the material in the cup.

(2) Do not intermix coatings, reducers, cleaners, or solvents from one brand to another. Although similar in nature, they may not mix well, causing a poor paint job.

(3) Do not force urethane finishes to dry with heat, or even sunlight for that matter. The heat will cause blistering.

(4) Unless the urethane has been given at least 12 hours of cure, do not put it outside in dampness. The result could be a flat finish.

(5) Excessive humidity can cause the urethane finish to blush, and dry with no gloss.

(6) Apply your coats of urethane within 30 minutes of one another, not several days apart. Fresh solvents from new paint applied to partially cured urethane can lift the paint, resulting in a real mess.

(7) Should you touch your face or hair, you will transmit body oils to whatever else you touch. Keep your oily fingers off the airplane during the painting proc-ess. If you suspect you may have touched something, wipe that area with solvent.

(8) Pay attention to the pot life of your two-part paints.

(9) Use a proper respirator when spraying. The fumes are not good for you, can make you ill immediately, and may have cumulative effects after long periods of exposure.

POLISHING AN AIRPLANE

The following appeared in the Luscombe Association newsletter, and is reprinted here with their permission:

For all those who are considering polishing a metal airplane, I have some advice: Don't! But since I know you will not listen to me about that, I hope you will listen to me about how to polish it.

The first step is to remove all the paint. This will take several gallons of good paint remover and lots of time. Do not use any kind of metal scraper, steel wool, or sandpaper on the metal skin. This will leave marks impossible to polish out. Use only a scraper made of some material such as micarda. Micarda is a material similar to the material used in the pulleys for controls on the Luscombe.

After the paint is removed, you will see that the skin has a rather dull, milky look to it. This look is caused by the metal surface being etched before it was painted. This etching was necessary to make the paint adhere properly to the skin. At this point you need a good electric buffer of some kind. Any automotive type buffer will work, but the best one to use is the one sold by the Swift Association. This machine leaves no swirl marks such as you get from the rotating disc type. It is called the #5 Cyclo Polisher. Write Box 644, Athens, TN 37303 for more information.

You will also need some sort of polishing compound to use with the polisher. The best thing to use seems to be a hand rubbing compound of the type intended to be used on automotive paints. I like Dupont #606S. This is a good fast-cutting compound that will not cut too fast and will leave a good fine polish job. You might also want to use a dusting of corn starch to help remove the last of the film left by the polishing compound. (The #606S is cheaper by the gallon.)

Now that you have polished the aircraft, you will notice that there is some black powder scattered around by the polishing. It is on the aircraft as well as the person who does the polishing. Wash both the aircraft and the polisher with good soap to remove the black powder. Dry the aircraft thoroughly with soft cloths. Old diapers, T-shirts, or towels work well.

It is time now to put the finishing touches on the polish job. I like Met-All polish. It is a bit finer polish than 606S and it will be all you need to keep the shine up. The more you polish, the better the shine will get. You must keep polishing since any kind of moisture is now your enemy. It is nice to live in a hot, dry climate, or at least to keep the aircraft in a dry warm hangar. You can follow the polishing with any good automotive wax.

After you complete polishing, you will notice that some panels will not shine as well as others. The drawn panels, such as the cowl nose piece, window panels, lower cowl, cowl top panel and others are made of a different alloy than the rest of the skins. The alloy for these parts cannot be of the same hard type alloys since they must be soft enough to be drawn and formed. These soft alloys were never given the final coating of pure aluminum that the other skins were. This final coat is the one that shines so well. So be prepared to see a rather dark film look to these panels. Also, if you polish the other panels too vigorously you will polish this film away and these panels will also look dark and not shine as well. Once this film is gone, it is gone forever, so be careful as you polish.

To the best of my knowledge there is nothing you can do to keep the shine except polish. There is no miracle polish to keep the shine forever. Nor will any type of clear lacquer, varnish, or plastic coating work—only good honest elbow grease. Hope this information helps you.

Richard Lawrence
Lincoln Park, MI

17

Alternatives to true classics

NOT EVERYONE wants an old airplane. For one reason or another, you might want a new airplane built by the old methods. Of course there are some advantages to this thinking, the first being less immediate maintenance. There are also disadvantages, such as the high initial cost of the plane.

CHRISTEN

Good ideas are hard to kill, as Christen Industries showed when they introduced their Husky (Fig. 17-1) in 1987. The plane closely resembles the Piper PA-18 Super Cub and it is meant to fill in the gap left when Piper stopped building the Cub.

There are not a large number of used Husky airplanes currently on the used market, due to newness and low production numbers. However, a Husky could be considered as an alternative to purchasing an aging Super Cub.

On March 19, 1991, Aviat, Inc. purchased the rights to produce the Husky A-1. The 1992 base price was over $65,000.

Engine
    Make: Lycoming
    Model: O-360-C1G
    Horsepower: 180
    TBO: 2000 hours
Speeds
    Maximum: 145 mph
    Cruise: 140 mph
    Stall: 42 mph
Fuel capacity: 52 gallons
Rate of climb: 1500 fpm
Transitions

Fig. 17-1. Aviate Huskey.

Aviate, Inc.

Takeoff over 50 ft obs: NA
Ground run: 200 feet
Landing over 50 ft obs: NA
Ground roll: 350 feet
Weights
Gross: 1800 pounds
Empty: 1190 pounds
Seats: Two tandem
Dimensions
Length: 22 feet 7 inches
Height: 6 feet 7 inches
Span: 35 feet 6 inches

WAG-AERO KITS

If the idea of a classic airplane appeals to you, but you don't care to fly an airplane
that is approaching 50 years of age and do not wish to spend your child's college
fund on a new plane, there is an alternative—build an airplane based upon the
classics.

Building an airplane is lots of work; however, the rewards are plenty, and
there are certain side benefits. You have the pride of your work and a plane that is
custom built for and by you. You can legally maintain it, including giving the
annual inspections, and make any changes or repairs to it.

The plane you build can be an authentic replica or improved to suit your individual needs or taste. In any case you will have a brand new, rigged correctly,
trimmed right, and perfect to fly airplane.

Wag-Aero says you, as a builder, can now reproduce the most nostalgic, reliable, and economical plane of all time—a classic design of proven performance
and serviceability. The kits have been engineered by Wag-Aero to allow the cus-

tomer the least amount of effort in locating the necessary items to build an airplane, and at the same time providing a considerable savings from individual purchase price. Materials are conveniently divided into distinct kits, allowing separate purchases as the project is completed, and purchases of only needed items at a reasonable cost. The material kits and engineered drawings are a culmination of past experience, along with a genuine interest among aircraft enthusiasts for the classic design of airplanes.

To aid your project, you have at your disposal many sheets of detailed drawings, plus isometrics, full-sized patterns, and references to part numbers; individual material kits which allow ease of purchasing and considerable savings; many preassembled parts, allowing speedy completion and minimum tool investment. Availability of parts is vast. All of these advantages put together a unique program to aid you in constructing the airplane of your dreams.

SPORT TRAINER

The Sport Trainer is a replica of the Piper J3 that will take off in 375 feet and land in less, is extremely maneuverable in the air, and can be built with a wide range of engines to suit your desires and budget.

It is a fun airplane—interesting to build and fun to fly (Fig. 17-2). You can feel the pleasure and accomplishment of not only building, but owning the finest two-place utility aircraft.

Engine
    Make: Continental
    Model: C-85

Fig. 17-2. The Wag-Aero Sport Trainer.

hp: 85
Seats: 2 tandem
Speed
    Max: 102 mph
    Cruise: 94 mph
    Stall: 39 mph
Fuel capacity: 12 gal
Rate of climb: 490 fpm
Weights
    Gross: 1400 lbs
    Empty: 720 lbs

WAG-AERO SPORTSMAN 2+2

The Sportsman 2+2 (Figs. 17-3 and 17-5) is a replica of the Piper PA-14 Family Cruiser. It retains the docile maneuverability and short field capabilities of the Sport Trainer (Fig. 17-6). Wide-stance landing gear and slow-speed characteristics make it an ideal trainer for you or your family.

The Sportsman utilizes large tires for off-airport operation, and has instrument panel layout to accommodate full IFR radio and gyro group.

Engine
    Make: Lycoming
    Model: O-290D2
    hp: 135
Seats: 4
Speed
    Max: 129 mph

Fig. 17-3. The Wag-Aero Sportsman 2+2.

Cruise: 124 mph
Stall: 38 mph
Fuel capacity: 39 gal
Rate of climb: 800 fpm
Weights
    Gross: 2200 lbs
    Empty: 1080 lbs
Dimensions:
    Length: 23 ft 4 in
    Height: 6 ft 7 in
    Span: 35 ft 9 in

THE WAG-A-BOND

The Wag-A-Bond (Fig. 17-4) is a replica of the Piper PA-15/17 Vagabond and seats two side-by-side. The plane can be modified to your needs.

Engine
    hp: 65 to 100
Seats: 2 side-by-side
Speed
    Max: 105 mph
    Cruise: 95 mph
    Stall: 45 mph
Fuel capacity: 12 gal
Rate of climb 625 fpm
Weights

Wag-Aero

Fig. 17-4. The Wag-A-Bond.

Fig. 17-5. The basic superstructure of the Sport Trainer. Notice the similarity to the Piper J3.

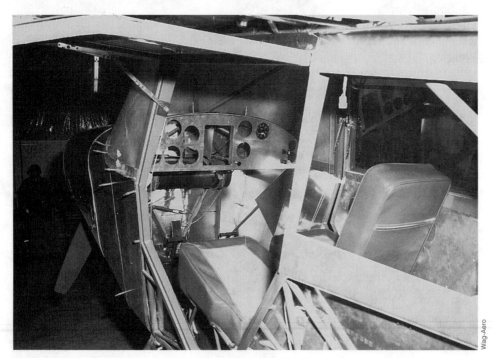

Fig. 17-6. Cockpit of a partially completed Sportsman 2+2.

Gross: 1250 lbs
Empty: 640 lbs
Dimensions:
Length: 18 ft 6 in
Height: 6 ft
Span: 29 ft 4 in

For further information about Wag-Aero airplanes, contact:

Wag-Aero, Inc.
P.O. Box 181
1216 North Road
Lyons, WI 53148
(800) 766-1216

THE KITFOX

No kit airplane has made the building of an airplane more pleasurable and easy than SkyStar's KITFOX (Fig. 17-7), formally produced by Denny Aircraft Company. This small two-seater can be built in nearly any garage, towed (with foldable wings) to the airport for use, and kept back in the family garage.

The plane can be ordered as a complete kit with everything needed to build it. No parts scrounging is necessary and all the welding is done for you.

Fig. 17-7. KITFOX, one of the most popular kit built airplanes ever made.

Engine
   Make: Rotax
   Model: 912
   hp: 80
Seats: 2 side-by-side
Speed
   Max: 125 mph
   Cruise: 105 mph
   Stall: 28 mph
Rate of Climb: 1700 fpm
Transitions
   Takeoff roll: 100 feet
   Landing roll: 150 feet
Weights
   Gross: 1050 lbs
   Empty: 440 lbs
Dimensions:
   Length: 17 ft 8 in
   Span: 32 ft

For further information about the KITFOX contact:

SkyStar Aircraft Company
100 N. Kings Rd.
Nampa, ID 83687
(208) 466-1711

Appendix A

Type clubs

WHENEVER people have a common interest to bond them together, some form of social organization is usually developed. Such is the case with type clubs and classic airplanes. The typical airplane type club is formed with the idea in mind to get as many owners of a particular make/model of airplane together, either physically or by newsletter.

Most classic clubs have at least one fly-in each year. These fly-ins usually result in much handshaking, making new friends, seeing old ones, and, of course, the chance to see other planes of similar manufacture to your own. Often there are exchanges, either formal or otherwise, of technical know-how and how-to information. Sometimes there is even a small flea market, giving the attendee a chance to purchase a hard-to-find part or other nicety. A few of the larger organizations have several geographical divisions, with local activities directed at specific regions.

Newsletters are a mainstay of the typical club. Bringing social information and technical know-how to the members, these information sheets are possibly the best reason for membership in a classic club. The newsletters range from one-page information sheets to a bimonthly booklet that includes information and pictures about recent club events, service information, safety notices, and even classified ads.

Additionally, some clubs maintain excellent technical libraries that include original blueprints, maintenance manuals, operations manuals, and even Federal Aviation Regulations. Several clubs have a photographic history and scrapbook that circulates among the members.

All in all, I feel that you as a classic owner should belong to the club that supports your particular aircraft. I also feel that if you are not an owner, but are arm-chairing, you should belong to clubs that interest you. There is, in most cases, no better method for obtaining information about these fine airplanes. After all, none of these airplanes is still manufactured today, and most of the companies that did manufacture them are only distant memories.

AERONCA

International Aeronca Association

The International Aeronca Association, often referred to as the Aeronca Lover's Club, is ten years old. It was started by Buzz Wagner, a well-known expert on Aeroncas who annually holds forums at Oshkosh. The club has a quarterly newsletter for the exchange of information pertaining to maintenance and general Aeronca news. Total membership is approximately 300. Annual dues are $20 yearly. For further information contact:

International Aeronca Association
Box 3
401 1st St. E
Clark, SD 57225
(605) 532-3862

Aeronca Aviators Club

The Aeronca Aviators Club was started about ten years ago and provides information and assistance in research for parts, service, maintenance, and restorations. The club issues a 20-page newsletter approximately four times yearly and is very proud of its question-and-answer column. A newsletter subscription is $16 for four issues. For further information contact:

Aeronca Aviators Club
511 Terrace Lake Rd.
Columbus, IN 47201
(812) 342-6878

Aeronca Sedan Club

The Aeronca Sedan Club is more than fifteen years old and has about 130 members. Through a newsletter members exchange Sedan-related information including STCs, where to get parts, and classified ads. Four newsletters are sent out yearly and the subscription rate is $5 per four issues. For further information about the club contact:

Aeronca Sedan Club
115 Wendy Ct.
Union City, CA 94587
(510) 487-3070

Bellanca-Champion Club

The Bellanca-Champion Club supports the owners of 1954–1964 Champions. This includes some of the airplanes covered in this book. A quarterly newsletter contains news, loads of technical information, and word of social gatherings. Membership is $32 annually. For further information contact:

Bellanca-Champion Club
P.O. Box 708
Brookfield, WI 53008
(414) 784-4544

CESSNA

Cessna Owner Organizations

The Cessna Owner Organizations publishes a monthly full color magazine, the *Cessna Owner Magazine*, for its members. The magazine includes news, safety, AD, service difficulty reports, classified ads, and product reviews. Want ads are included in each issue.

C.O.O. supports all models of Cessna airplanes including those covered in this book. They offer a toll-free information hot line for help in locating service and/or parts. Annual dues are $36. For further information contact:

Cessna Owner Organizations
P.O. Box 337
Iola, WI 54945
(800) 331-0038

International Cessna 170 Club

The International Cessna 170 Club was formed to keep the 170s flying as inexpensively and easily as possible by furnishing information about service, parts, and flying techniques to its members. The club publishes a quarterly magazine, *170 News*, containing photos, news items, want ads, articles, and letters. Additionally, it publishes a monthly newsletter, *Flypaper*, which also includes want ads.

The club has an annual convention in the summer which is advertised as a week of family fun with a little education thrown in. There are also regional get-togethers. The dues are $25 per year. For further information contact:

International Cessna 170 Club
P.O. Box 1667
Lebanon, MO 65536
(417) 532-4847

The International Cessna 120/140 Association

The International Cessna 120/140 Association saw its beginnings in 1976 and now claims 1500 to 1600 members. The association hosts a national convention each year and prints a very nice monthly newsletter. Dues are $15 annually. For further information contact:

International Cessna 120/140 Association
Box 830092
Richardson, TX 75083
(817) 497-4757

ERCOUPE

Ercoupe Owners Club

The Ercoupe Owners Club is made up of persons interested in the history, restoration, and flying of the Ercoupe, and Ercoupe-type airplanes. This includes the Ercoupe, Forney, Alon, and Mooney models.

The club newsletter is the *Coupe Capers* and is published monthly as a nice combination of general information for the Ercoupe owner, including fly-ins, technical help, letters to the editor, classified ads, and parts for sale. Of particular interest is the stressed importance of safety and accident prevention that abounds in the newsletter. Information about past crashes is given in hopes of preventing similar occurrences.

The club has 11 regions in the U.S. and two in Canada. Each region has social and flying events and a few produce their own newsletters of primary interest to members residing in that particular geographical area.

The E.O.C. sponsors a national fly-in on an annual basis. The annual dues to the club are $20.00 U.S. and Canada ($32 for first class and foreign). For further information contact:

Ercoupe Owners Club
3557 Roxboro Road
Box 15388
Durham, NC 27704
(919) 471-9492

LUSCOMBE

The Luscombe Association

The Luscombe Association states NO WOOD—NO NAILS—NO GLUE on their emblem, attesting to their love for the all-metal Luscombe airplanes. The association supports the 8 series and the 11 series Sedans.

They say in their membership literature, "The Luscombe Association is composed of people who are interested in the Luscombe Corporation, aircraft, and the history and accomplishments of Luscombe aircraft."

The association publishes a monthly newsletter, The *Luscombe Association News*, that includes want ads, maintenance and modification information, repair techniques and ideas, flying stories, historical articles. It also maintains a collection of paperwork for Luscombe modifications and helps members locate aircraft or parts. The dues for the association are $15.00 yearly. For further information, contact:

Luscombe Association
6438 W. Millbrook
Remus, MI 49340
(517) 561-2393

Continental Luscombe Association

The Continental Luscombe Association, Inc., has over 500 members and publishes a bimonthly newsletter which includes technical and social information for members' use. The stated purpose of the association is to be a clearinghouse of Luscombe information.

When asked about the types of airplanes they support, they replied, "Luscombes, there aren't any other types to discuss."

Association membership is $10 annually. For further information about the Continental Luscombe Association, contact:

Continental Luscombe Association, Inc.
5736 Esmar Rd.
Ceres, CA 95307
(209) 537-9934

PIPER

Cub club

The Cub Club states its purpose as making available to anyone interested in the long wing Pipers: J-3, J-4, L-4, J-5, PA-11, PA-12, PA-14, and/or PA-18 an organization whose purpose is to: Preserve and promote the restoration, maintenance and use of Cubs.

The club produces a newsletter every other month, The *Cub Club Newsletter*, containing Cub history, maintenance, rare and unusual Cubs, member stories, sources for parts, and want ads.

The club has over 2800 members (about 2000 owner members). Dues for the Cub club are $10.00 per year, U.S. and Canada (U.S. funds), $15.00 per year foreign. For further information, write to:

Cub Club
6438 W. Millbrook
Remus, MI 49340
(517) 561-2393

Piper Owner Society

The Piper Owner Society publishes a monthly full color magazine, *Pipers Magazine*, which includes news, safety, AD, service difficulty reports, classified ads, and product reviews. Want ads are included in each issue.

P.O.S. supports all models of Piper airplanes including those covered in this book. They offer a toll-free information hot line for help in locating service and/or parts. Annual dues are $36. For further information contact:

Piper Owner Society
P.O. Box 337
Iola, WI 54945
(800) 331-0038

Short Wing Piper Club

The Short Wing Piper Club is for persons whose interests are the PA-15, PA-16, PA-17, PA-20, PA-22, and the PA-22 (108). It is a large club with several geographical regions, each hosting get-togethers and events. *Short Wing Piper News* is their bimonthly magazine, and is probably the most extensive and largest of all the various club newsletters.

Included in each edition of SWPN are articles and photographs about social events, safety, mechanical difficulties, parts availability, display and classified ads, general aviation info, etc. Classified ads by members are free.

The SWPC has a very extensive library that is available to members. Included in this library are publications involving regulations, Piper Service Bulletins, Lycoming info, parts catalogs, documents showing aircraft specifications, books on Piper aircraft and other information of a more general aviation nature.

Membership for the SWPC is $30 yearly in US and Canada ($40 foreign). For further information, contact:

Short Wing Piper Club
Editor: Bob Mills
220 Main
Halstead, KS 67056
(316) 835-2235

Super Cub Pilot's Association

The Super Cub Pilot's Association is a group of 1300 members. It publishes the SCPA Newsletter with question and answers, technical information about mods, ADs, and STCs and lists want ads. Dues are $25 in US and $35 in Canada and $40 overseas. For information contact:

Super Cub Pilot's Association
P.O. Box 9823
Yakima, WA 98909
(509) 248-9491

STINSON

The Southwest Stinson Club

The Southwest Stinson Club sponsors an annual fly-in, publishes a newsletter which includes classifieds, social, and technical information important to Stinson owners and pilots. Membership is $16 yearly. For further information contact:

Southwest Stinson Club
10411 Alta Mesa Rd.
Galt, CA 95632
(510) 228-4176

TAYLORCRAFT

Taylorcraft Owners Club

The Taylorcraft Owners Club puts out a quarterly newsletter that has everything from club news and happenings to items for sale in it. Very interesting bits of aviation history are included, in particular, copies of old flyers and information sheets that show a bygone era.

Each year the club sponsors a fly-in at Barber Airport in Alliance, Ohio. This is the airport that Al Barber once owned and which he used to flight test new Taylorcraft airplanes. The airport now belongs to Forrest Barber, Al's son. Forrest, like his father, was a test pilot for Taylorcraft.

With a membership of about 700, dues are a modest $10 per year. For further information, contact the Taylorcraft Owners Club at:

Taylorcraft Owners Club
12809 Greenbower Rd.
Alliance, OH 44601
(216) 823-9748

OTHER ORGANIZATIONS

In addition to the clubs specializing in a particular aircraft, there are several other organizations with a broader interest range. Each has a monthly magazine and offers other side benefits (research library, insurance, discount purchases, etc.).

The Experimental Aircraft Association

The EAA, as the Experimental Aircraft Association (Fig. A-1) is generally referred to is a group that covers general aviation from antique airplanes through homebuilts. The association produces a fine monthly magazine, *Sport Aviation*, and offers a special division and magazine for antique and classic buffs.

The EAA sponsors the famous Oshkosh Fly-in held in August of each year and has local chapters all over the world. For information contact:

EAA Membership
P.O. Box 3086
Oshkosh, WI 54903
(800) 322-2412

Fig. A-1. The headquarters of the Experimental Aircraft Association, home of the EAA museum and the largest annual air show for small aviation in the world—OSHKOSH.

OTHER ORGANIZATIONS TO CONTACT ARE:

Aircraft Owners and Pilots Association
421 Aviation Way
Frederick, MD 21701
Phone: (301) 695-2000

Seaplane Pilots Association
421 Aviation Way
Frederick, MD 21701
Phone: (301) 695-2000

Appendix B

Manufacturers and suppliers

CLASSIC airplanes, like anything else, need service and repairs from time to time. Also, some might require complete rebuilding. It can be difficult to get the necessary parts and materials to refurbish these older planes, but several large companies specialize in the support of these older airplanes (Fig. B-1).

The companies listed below have been in business many years and are personally known to me. A short description of the level of their support accompanies their address and telephone numbers.

ALEXANDER AEROPLANE

Alexander Aeroplane Company, Inc., has an extensive supply of re-covering and refinishing materials and supplies. The company also sells Aircraft hardware, cable, and fittings, decal logos, cabin interiors, wood, sheet aluminum and tubing, instruments, tools, wheels and brakes, and windshields. It supports the generic needs of classic airplanes. However, it does not sell specific airframe parts. For more information contact:

Alexander Aeroplane Company, Inc.
900 S. Pine Hill Rd.
P.O. Box 909
Griffin, GA 30224
(800) 831-2949

UNIVAIR

UNIVAIR Aircraft Corporation sells the parts, hardware, re-cover materials, and other necessities to keep most classics flying. Additionally, they supply many airframe parts specific to Aeronca, Cessna, Luscombe, Piper, Stinson, and Taylorcraft.

Fig. B-1. Replacement parts for classic airplanes are often made one-at-a-time using great skill and precision.

The company holds the type certificates for Ercoupe, Alon, Mooney M-10, and Stinson 108 airplanes (Fig. B-2). UNIVAIR also is a supplier of parts and materials needed for maintenance on Continental, Franklin, and Lycoming engines. For more information about UNIVAIR contact:

UNIVAIR Aircraft Corporation
2500 Himalaya Road
Aurora, CO 80011
(303) 375-8882

WAG-AERO

Wag-Aero, Inc., is a major supplier of skis, instruments, seat belts, propellers, avionics, replica Piper airplane kits, exhaust systems, aircraft hardware, tires and wheels, molded fiberglass wheel pants, cowlings, and wing tips, tools, engine

Fig. B-2. Only a fully equipped shop with thousands of dollars worth of equipment and skilled technicians can produce complete assemblies, such as this complete wing, for use on classic airplanes.

mounts, fuel tanks, re-cover supplies, and electrical parts. The company supports Aeronca, Cessna, Piper. Contact it at:

Wag-Aero, Inc.
P.O. Box 181
1216 North Road
Lyons, WI 53148
(800) 766-1216

OTHER SUPPLIERS INCLUDE:

Aero Fabricators, Inc. (exhaust systems and engine mounts)
P.O. Box 181
1216 North Rd.
Lyons, WI 53148
(414) 763-3145

Air-Tech Coatings, Inc. (re-cover and paint)
2300 Redmond Rd.
Jacksonville, AR 72076
(800) 325-1650
(501) 985-1484

Airtex Products Inc. (interiors)
259 Lower Morrisville Rd.
Fallsington, PA 19054
(215) 295-4115

American Champion Aircraft Corporation (parts)
P.O. Box 37
32032 Washington Ave., Hwy D
Rochester, WI 53167
Phone (414) 534-6315

Blue River Aircraft Supply (re-cover)
Box 91
223 North Clay
Harvard, NE 68944
(402) 772-3651

Ceconite Co. (re-cover)
3815 Medford St.
Los Angeles, CA 90063
(213) 724-7244

Cessna Aircraft Co. (parts)
Box 1521
Wichita, KS 67201
(316) 685-9111
(316) 941-6118 for service bulletin information
(800) 545-4611

David Clark Co. (headsets)
P.O. Box 15054
Worcester, MA 01615
(508) 751-5800

II Morrow, Inc. (avionics)
P.O. Box 13549
Salem, OR 97309
(800) 535-6726

King Radio Corp. (avionics)
400 N. Rogers Rd.
Olathe, KS 66062
(913) 782-0400

Maule Air, Inc. (manufacturer)
Lake Maule - Rte 5
Moultrie, GA 31768
(912) 985-2045

Narco Avionics (avionics)
270 Commerce Dr.
Ft. Washington, PA 19034
(215) 643-2900

Piper Aircraft (parts)
2926 Piper Dr.
Vero Beach, FL
(407) 567-4361

Radio Systems Technology, Inc. (avionics)
13281-T Grass Valley Ave.
Grass Valley, CA 95945
(916) 272-2203

Razorback Fabrics, Inc. (re-cover)
Manila, AR 72442
(501) 561-4447

Sensenich Corp. (propellers)
Box 4187
Lancaster, PA 17604
(717) 569-0435

Skyport Aircoupe Svcs. (Ercoupe parts)
P.O. Box 355
32032 Washington Ave.
Rochester, WI 53167
(800) 624-5312

Stits Poly-Fiber Aircraft Coatings (re-cover)
Box 3084
Riverside, CA 92519
(714) 684-4280

Taylorcraft Aircraft Company (parts)
P.O. Box 480
820 E. Bald Eagle St.
Lock Haven, PA 17745
(717) 748-8262

Teledyne-Continental (engines)
Box 90
Mobile, AL 36601
(205) 438-3411

Terra Corp. (avionics)
3520 Pan American Freeway, NE
Albuquerque, NM 87107
(505) 884-2321

Textron-Lycoming (engines)
Williamsport, PA 17701
(203) 385-2000 or (717) 323-6181

VAL Avionics, Ltd.
P.O. Box 13025
Salem, OR 97309-1025
(503) 370-9429

As a final recommendation, I suggest the purchase of the Aviation Telephone Directory. This publication provides complete telephone listings for aviation related businesses, airports, FBOs, and a very good yellow pages of products and services. It is available by region (Atlantic and eastern states, southwest and gulf states, Pacific and western states, and mid-continent states). For further information contact:

Aviation Telephone Directory
515 West Lambert Rd. Suite D
Brea, CA 92621
(714) 990-5115

Appendix C

FAA locations

WHENEVER you need a question about general aviation answered you can always turn to the Federal Aviation Administration. The agency has many offices spread around the country with experts to serve the public. In the many years that I have been associated with general aviation I have never been disappointed with the help I received from the FAA. When a problem arises, contact them.

Alabama

FSDO 09
6500 43rd Avenue North
Birmingham, AL 35206
(205) 731-1393

Alaska

FSDO 01
6348 Old Airport Way
Fairbanks, AK 99709
(907) 474-0276

FSDO 03
4510 West Int'l Airport Road, Suite 302
Anchorage, AK 99502-1088
(907) 243-1902

FSDO 05
1910 Alex Holden Way, Suite A
Juneau, AK 99801
(907) 789-0231

Arizona

FSDO
15041 North Airport Drive
Scottsdale, AZ 85260
(602) 640-2561

Arkansas

FSDO 11
1701 Bond Street
Little Rock, AR 72202
(501) 324-5565

California

LAX FSDO
5885 West Imperial Hwy
Los Angeles, CA 90045
(310) 215-2150

FSDO
831 Mitten Rd., Rm 105
Burlingame, CA 94010
(415) 876-2771

FSDO
16501 Sherman Way, Suite 330
Van Nuys, CA 91406
(818) 904-6291

FSDO
1250 Aviation Ave., Suite 295
San Jose, CA 95110-1130
(408) 291-7681

FSDO
8525 Gibbs Drive, Suite 120
San Diego, CA 92123
(619) 557-5281

FSDO
Fresno Air Terminal
4955 East Anderson, Suite 110
Fresno, CA 93727-1521
(209) 487-5306

FSDO
6961 Flight Road
Riverside, CA 92504
(714) 276-6701

FSDO
6650 Belleau Wood Lane
Sacramento, CA 95822
(916) 551-1721

FSDO
P.O. Box 2397
Airport Station
Oakland, CA 94614
(510) 273-7155

FSDO
2815 East Spring Street
Long Beach, CA 90806
(310) 426-7134

Colorado

FSDO
5440 Roslyn St., Suite 201
Denver, CO 80216
(303) 286-5400

Connecticut

FSDO 03
Building 85-214 1st Flr
Bradley International Airport
Windsor Locks, CT 06096
(203) 654-1000

Florida

FSDO
FAA Building
Craig Municipal Airport
855 Saint John's Bluff Road
Jacksonville, FL 32225
(904) 641-7311

FSDO 15
9677 Tradport Dr., Suite 100
Orlando, FL 32827
(407) 648-6840

FSDO 17
286 South West 34th St.
Ft. Lauderdale, FL 33315
(305) 463-4841

FSDO 19
P.O. Box 592015
Miami, FL 33159
(305) 526-2572

Georgia

FSDO 11
1680 Phoenix Pkwy., Second Flr
College Park, GA 30349
(404) 994-5276

Hawaii

FSDO
90 Nakolo Place,
Room 215
Honolulu, HI 96819
(808) 836-0615

Illinois

FSDO 03
Post Office Box H
DuPage County Airport
West Chicago, IL 60185
(708) 377-4500

FSDO 19
Capitol Airport
#3 North Airport Dr.
Springfield, IL 62708
(217) 492-4238

FSDO 31
9950 West Lawrence Ave., Suite 400
Schiller Park, IL 60176
(312) 353-7787

Indiana

FSDO 11
6801 Pierson Drive
Indianapolis, IN 46241
(317) 247-2491

FSDO 17
1843 Commerce Drive
South Bend, IN 46628
(219) 236-8480

Iowa

FSDO 01
3021 Army Post Road
Des Moines, IA 50321
(515) 285-9895

Kansas

FSDO 64
Mid-Continent Airport
1801 Airport Rd., Rm 103
Wichita, KS 67209
(316) 941-1200

Kentucky

FSDO
Kaden Building, 5th Flr
6100 Dutchmans Lane
Louisville, KY 40205-3284
(502) 582-5941

Louisiana

FSDO
Ryan Airport
9191 Plank Rd.
Baton Rouge, LA 70811
(504) 356-5701

Maine

FSDO 05
2 Al McKay Ave.
Portland, ME 04102
(207) 780-3263

Maryland

FSDO 07
P.O. Box 8747
BWI Airport, MD 21240
(410) 787-0040

Massachusetts

FSDO 01
Civil Air Terminal Bldg., 2nd Flr.
Hanscom Field
Bedford, MA 01730
(617) 274-7130

Michigan

FSDO 09
Kent County International Airport
P.O. Box 888879
Grand Rapids, MI 49588-8879
(616) 456-2427

FSDO 23
Willow Run Airport (east side)
8800 Beck Road
Belleville, MI 48111
(313) 487-7222

Minnesota

FSDO 15
6020 28th Ave. South, Rm 201
Minneapolis, MN 55450
(612) 725-4211

Mississippi

FSDO 07
120 North Hangar Drive, Suite C
Jackson Municipal Airport
Jackson, MS 39208
(601) 965-4633

Missouri

FSDO 03
FAA Bldg
10801 Pear Tree Ln., Suite 200
St. Ann, MO 63074
(314) 429-1006

FSDO 05
Kansas City International Airport
525 Mexico City Ave.
Kansas City, MO 64153
(816) 243-3800

Montana

FSDO
FAA Building, Room 3
Helena Airport
Helena, MT 59601
(406) 449-5270

Nebraska

FSDO 09
General Aviation Building
Lincoln Municipal Airport
Lincoln, NE 68524
(402) 437-5485

Nevada

FSDO
210 South Rock Blvd.
Reno, NV 89502
(702) 784-5321

FSDO
6020 South Spencer, Suite A7
Las Vegas, NV 89119
(702) 388-6482

New Jersey

FSDO 25
150 Fred Wehran Drive, Room 1
Teterboro Airport
Teterboro, NJ 07608
(201) 288-1745

New Mexico

FSDO
1601 Randolph Road, SE Suite 200N
Albuquerque, NM 87106
(505) 247-0156

New York

FSDO 01
Albany County Airport
Albany, NY 12211
(518) 869-8482

FSDO 11
Administration Building
Suite #235 RTE 110
Republic Airport
Farmingdale, NY 11735
(516) 694-5530

FSDO 15
181 South Franklin Ave, 4th Flr
Valley Stream, NY 11581
(718) 917-1848

FSDO 23
1 Airport Way, Suite 110
Rochester, NY 14624
(716) 263-5880

North Carolina

FSDO 05
8025 North Point Blvd., Suite 250
Winston-Salem, NC 27106
(919) 631-5147

FSDO 06
2000 Aerial Center Pkwy., Suite 120
Morrisville, NC 27263
(919) 840-5510

FSDO 08
FAA Building
5318 Morris Field Drive
Charlotte, NC 28208
(704) 359-8471

North Dakota

FSDO 21
1801 23rd Ave. N.
Fargo, ND 58102
(701) 232-8949

Ohio

CVG FSDO
4242 Airport Road
Lunken Executive Building
Cincinnati, OH 45226
(513) 533-8110

FSDO 07
3939 International Gateway, 2nd Flr.
Port Columbus International Airport
Columbus, OH 43219
(614) 469-7476

FSDO
Federal Facilities Building
Cleveland Hopkins International Airport
Cleveland, OH 44135
(216) 265-1345

Oklahoma

FSDO
1300 South Meridian, Suite 601
Bethany, OK 73108
(405) 231-4196

Oregon

FSDO
Portland/Hillsboro Airport
3355 NE Cornell Road
Hillsboro, OR 97124
(503) 326-2104

Pennsylvania

FSDO 03
Allegheny County Airport
Terminal Bldg., Rm 213
West Mifflin, PA 15122
(412) 462-5507

FSDO 05
3405 Airport Rd. North
Allentown, PA 18103
(215) 264-2888

FSDO 13
400 Airport Dr., Rm 101
New Cumberland, PA 17070
(717) 774-8271

FSDO 17
Scott Plaza 2, 2nd Flr.
Philadelphia, PA 19113
(215) 596-0673

FSDO 19
One Thorn Run Center, Suite 200
1187 Thorn Run Ext.
Corapolis, PA 15108
(412) 644-5406

South Carolina

FSDO 13
103 Trade Zone Dr.
West Columbia, SC 29169
(803) 765-5931

South Dakota

FSDO
Rapid City Regional Airport
Route 2 Box 4750
Rapid City, SD 57701
(605) 393-1359

Tennessee

FSDO 03
2 International Plaza Dr., Suite 700
Nashville, TN 37217
(615) 781-5437

FSDO 04
3385 Airways Blvd., Suite 115
Memphis, TN 38116
(901) 544-3820

Texas

FSDO
7701 North Stemmons Fwy Suite 300
Lock Box 5
Dallas, TX 75247
(214) 767-5850

FSDO
Dallas Ft. Worth Regional Airport
P.O. Box 619020
Dallas Ft. Worth Airport, TX 75261
(214) 574-2150

FSDO
8800 Paul B Koonce Drive
Room 152
Houston, TX 77061-5190
(713) 640-4400

FSDO
Route 3, Box 51
Lubbock, TX 79401
(806) 762-0335

FSDO
10100 Reunion Place, Suite 200
San Antonio, TX 78216
(512) 341-4371

Utah

FSDO
116 North 2400 West
Salt Lake City, UT 84116

(801) 524-4247

Virginia

FSDO 21
Richmond International Airport
Executive Terminal, 2nd Flr.
Sandstone, VA 23150-2594
(804) 222-7494

FSDO 27
GT Building, Suite 112
Box 17325
Dulles International Airport
Washington, D.C. 20041
(703) 557-5360

Washington

FSDO
1601 Lind Ave., SW
Renton, WA 98055-4046
(206) 227-2810

West Virginia

FSDO 09
Yeager Airport
301 Eagle Mountain Road, Room 144
Charleston, WV 25311
(304) 343-4689

Wisconsin

FSDO 13
4915 South Howell Avenue, 4th Flr.
Milwaukee, WI 53207
(414) 747-5531

Appendix D

NTSB accident ranking of small airplanes

ALL AIRPLANE accidents are investigated by the National Transportation Safety Board (NTSB) and FAA. Based upon thousands of investigations, the board has amassed a tremendous amount of numerical data. This information has been reduced to chart form by comparing specific types of aircraft accidents with makes/models of small airplanes.

The placement of an aircraft make/model on NTSB charts is determined by the frequency of accidents compared to other aircraft listed on the same chart; aircraft with poor accident records at the top, aircraft with better records at the bottom.

Note: Some make/models do not appear on a chart due to the limited numbers of records available for analysis and that all data is based upon rate per 100,000 flying hours.

ACCIDENTS CAUSED BY ENGINE FAILURE

Stinson 108	10.65
Ercoupe	9.50
Piper J-3	7.61
Luscombe 8	7.58
Cessna 120/140	6.73
Piper PA-12	6.54
Piper PA-22	5.67
Aeronca 7	4.23
Aeronca 11	4.10
Taylorcraft	3.81
Piper PA-18	3.37
Cessna 170	2.88

ACCIDENTS CAUSED BY
IN-FLIGHT AIRFRAME FAILURE

Ercoupe	0.97
Aeronca 11	0.59
Luscombe 8	0.54
Cessna 170	0.36
Piper PA-22	0.30
Aeronca 7	0.27
Cessna 120/140	0.27
Taylorcraft	0.24
Piper J-3	0.23

ACCIDENTS RESULTING FROM A STALL

Aeronca 7	22.47
Aeronca 11	18.21
Taylorcraft	6.44
Piper J-3	5.88
Luscombe 8	5.78
Piper PA-18	5.49
Cessna 170	4.38
Piper PA-12	3.27
Cessna 120/140	2.51
Stinson 108	2.09
Piper PA-22	1.78
Ercoupe	1.29

ACCIDENTS CAUSED BY HARD LANDINGS

Ercoupe	2.90
Luscombe 8	2.35
Cessna 170	1.89
Cessna 120/140	1.35
Aeronca 7	1.20
Piper J-3	1.04
Piper PA-22	0.69
Taylorcraft	0.48
Piper PA-18	0.43
Piper PA-12	0.23
Stinson 108	0.19

ACCIDENTS RESULTING
FROM A GROUND LOOP

Stinson 108	13.50
Luscombe 8	13.00

Cessna 170	9.91
Cessna 120/140	8.99
Aeronca 11	7.86
Aeronca 7	7.48
Piper PA-12	4.67
Piper PA-18	3.90
Taylorcraft	3.58
Piper PA-22	2.76
Ercoupe	2.74
Piper J-3	2.07

ACCIDENTS CAUSED BY UNDERSHOT LANDINGS

Ercoupe	2.41
Luscombe 8	1.62
Piper PA-12	1.40
Taylorcraft	0.95
Piper PA-22	0.83
Aeronca 11	0.59
Aeronca 7	0.59
Piper J-3	0.57
Stinson 108	0.57
Cessna 120/140	0.53
Piper PA-18	0.43
Cessna 170	0.36

ACCIDENTS RESULTING FROM LANDING OVERSHOOT

Piper PA-22	1.33
Stinson 108	1.33
Aeronca 11	1.17
Luscombe 8	1.08
Cessna 170	0.99
Piper PA-12	0.93
Piper PA-18	0.81
Cessna 120/140	0.71
Ercoupe	0.64
Aeronca 7	0.48
Piper J-3	0.34

Appendix E

Prices of classics

IT IS DIFFICULT to place exact values on any airplane, and classic airplanes are even more difficult than most. The reasons for this difficulty are the differences among the various examples found on the market. Among these variables are:

History of the airplane
Total hours
Engine condition
Fabric/metal skin condition
Corrosion
Interior condition
Avionics
Prior damage
Quality of recent work
Availability of parts
Insurability

And the list could go on; however, these are the more common variables you must consider when purchasing a classic airplane. As an additional point, a classic airplane that has been properly restored and/or modernized will command a premium price while a basket case sitting in some farmer's barn will bring little. What you pay for a classic generally depends on what you want in the airplane; immediate flying or a restoration project.

PRICE GUIDE

The following is a list of various classics by make and model with an average asking price based upon the 1992 market. It is reasonable to assume, based on recent market history, that the prices will increase at a rate of about ten percent annually. The average price shown must be adjusted up/down depending on the above variables. Actual selling prices will vary from asking prices proportionately with the buyer's desire to purchase and the seller's wish to market. Buyer beware!

Make	Model	Average price ($)	Make	Model	Average price ($)
Aeronca				PA-16	15,000
	7AC	11,500		PA-17	11,000
	7BCC	11,900		PA-18/90	18,000
	7CCM	12,500		PA-18/150	18,500 and up
	7DC	11,200		PA-20	16,500
	7EC	11,900		PA-22/125	11,500
	11AC	10,200		PA-22/150	12,500
	11C	10,900		PA-22/Colt	10,900
	(Champion)		Stinson		
	7EC	13,000			
	7FC	12,500		108	14,000
	7ACA	11,200		108-1	14,500
				108-2	15,000
Cessna				108-3	16,000
	120	11,100			
	140	12,200	Taylorcraft		
	140A	14,000		BC12-D	11,000
	170	16,000		19	12,500
	170A	18,000		F-19	14,000
	170B	22,100		F-21	19,000
Ercoupe					
	415C	9,500			
	415D	9,500			
	415E	9,600			
	(Forney)	10,100			
	(Alon)	11,200			
	(Mooney)	14,100			
Luscombe					
	8A	10,000			
	8B	10,000			
	8C	10,200			
	8D	10,300			
	8E	14,000			
	8F	14,500			
Piper					
	J3	16,000			
	J4A	10,500			
	J5	11,000			
	J5C	12,000			
	PA-11	18,000			
	PA-12	17,500			
	PA-14	12,000			
	PA-15	10,100			

Index